LUDWIG VAN BEETHOVEN

Bust of Beethoven by Franz Klein (1812). Beethoven-Haus, Bonn.

LUDWIG VAN BEETHOVEN

The Piano Sonatas

History • Notation • Interpretation

JAN MARISSE HUIZING

Translated by

GERALD R. METTAM

Yale

UNIVERSITY PRESS

New Haven and London

Published with assistance from the Annie Burr Lewis Fund.

Published with assistance from the Mary Cady Tew Memorial Fund.

Originally published in German. Title of the original German edition: *Ludwig van Beethoven: Die Klaviersonaten. Interpretation und Aufführungspraxis* by Jan Marisse Huizing, ED 21349, © 2012 Schott Music, Mainz, Germany.

Set in Janson Text type by Newgen North America, Austin, Texas.
Printed in the United States of America.

Library of Congress Control Number: 2021933966
ISBN 978-0-300-25160-9 (paper : alk. paper)

A catalogue record for this book is available from the British Library.

This paper meets the requirements of ANSI/NISO Z39.48-1992 (Permanence of Paper).

10 9 8 7 6 5 4 3 2 1

For Floris and Han

Contents

Preface

WHILE MANY STUDIES OF Beethoven's piano sonatas, for example those of Schenker, Tovey, Uhde, Rosen,[1] and many others, concentrate specifically on analytical aspects such as form and harmony, this book has its origins in the need to highlight a number of other, no less important themes.

Questions like the correlation of the musical content and form, knowledge of historical performance practice, and the choice of instrument contribute just as significantly to the insight we can gain into Beethoven's piano sonatas.

In addition, for a well-considered interpretation, attention must be paid to the manner in which Beethoven expressed his musical objectives, to his own specific sound-image, his pianism, and the way in which he expressed his intentions in the notation. The significance of Beethoven's handwriting along with knowledge of the various editions, from the original printing[2] through to the current urtext, are equally necessary for the creation of a convincing interpretation.

Of course, this book also investigates the playing of great interpreters, both past and present, whereby a historical overview is presented of the many recordings that have been made of Beethoven's piano sonatas, including filmed recordings on DVD.

Many of these subjects came to the fore during my years as professor of piano and piano methodology at the Amsterdam Conservatory, where it was my privilege to find a kindred spirit in the person of my colleague, the pianist Willem Brons. Over the years it was an inspiring journey of exchanging discoveries and ideas about new language for each individual sonata and formulating his ideas, not only within each separate movement, but also for the work as a whole. In this first chapter, as an overview, his piano sonatas are briefly discussed, with special attention paid to the connection between form and content, as illustrated by a number of characteristic examples from each sonata.

To begin with, his Sonatas Op. 2 were commended by Beethoven's publisher, Artaria, in an advertisement in the *Wiener Zeitung* of March 9, 1796, in which passing reference is also made to the success of the Piano Trios Op. 1.

> Three sonatas for pianoforte by Herr Ludwig van Beethoven. Since this author's previous work, the three piano trios opera 1 of the same, that are already in the hands of the public, have been received with such great approval, one expects likewise from the present work, all the more because, besides the worthiness of the composition, it also has the merit that we can detect in it not only the strength that Herr van Beethoven possesses as a piano player, but also the delicacy with which he treats this instrument.
>
> THOMAS-SAN-GALLI, p. 87

"Strength and delicacy": extremes in Beethoven's piano playing that also come abundantly to the fore in the musical expression of his Sonatas Op. 2: No. 1 in F minor, full of drama; No. 2 in A major, spontaneous and lyrical; and No. 3 in C major, with its humor and sparkling virtuosity.

As in the Piano Trios Op. 1, Beethoven provides these sonatas with a fourth movement, a Minuet or a Scherzo, introduced after the slow movement. Although this was an accepted structure for a symphony or chamber-music works such as string quartets, an expansion like this had not previously been encountered in the piano sonatas of Haydn or Mozart, and must certainly have surprised his contemporaries.

Even more surprising is the dramatic opening of the first sonata. Not only Beethoven's unconventional choice for the key of F minor, but also the striking beginning, where the dynamics develop within the space of only seven measures from *piano* to *fortissimo*.

Thrilling *sforzandi* and full chords in the bass, gaining even more in significance through a rest on the first beat, push the music irresistibly forward.[1]

Sonata Op. 2 No. 1, 1st movement

The pressing tension in this movement is never surrendered as it progresses and culminates in the compelling *sforzati* and *fortissimo* chords of the final measures.

For the second movement, an Adagio in F major, Beethoven used material from a piano quartet he had composed in 1785 in Bonn. The subdued mood of the first theme is maintained in an expressive dialogue between the treble and a single bass note, as if a pair of wind instruments are talking to each other. Thereafter, increasingly rich figurations lend direction to the work until a couple of chords round off the movement in *pianissimo.* The Minuet that follows—again in F minor, like the first movement—carries an undertone of melancholy. This mood then dissipates in the polyphonic lines of the major-key Trio, but returns with the *da capo* of the Minuet. The last movement, a daring, stormy Prestissimo, again in F minor, explores the drama of the first movement with even more intensity. The chords at the beginning are like exclamations. Supported by rolling triplets in the bass, the music drives forward, coming to rest only in a completely new section in A-flat major, where in *sempre piano e dolce* introspection can be found. Then all the drama returns; building from *pianissimo* to an even more vigorous outbreak, the work heads to a dramatic conclusion.

It is remarkable how Beethoven lends form to this sonata by placing an overall dramatic mood center stage in the outer movements. The Adagio and Minuet-Trio are, as it were, encompassed by them.

In the subsequent sonatas, too, the character of a particular movement is a reaction to what has gone before, and it is therefore not surprising that after the fresh and unrestrained opening movement of Op. 2 No. 2, an expressive second movement with the indication Largo appassionato follows in which the quasi-*pizzicati* in the left hand lend direction as "steps" in the melodic progression. In the performance of the movement, too, Beethoven is making demands at the limits of exploration. A sustained, broad, poised performance designated solely by the word "Largo" will not succeed. This specific interpretation must, according to Beethoven's notation, be "appassionato," too—an indication that we will observe many years later in the third movement of his monumental "Hammerklavier" Sonata, Op. 106, marked Adagio sostenuto—Appassionato e con molto sentimento.

In Op. 2 No. 2 the contrast with the second movement is achieved in a dancing and uncomplicated Scherzo, here counteracted by a Minore interlude that, due partly to the many *sforzati*, has an agitated undertone. The last movement—indicated by Beethoven not by a tempo marking but simply as Grazioso—is, like the first movement, light in character. Interrupted by a vivid and forward-pushing *staccato* section in full *fortissimo*, the Grazioso soon returns. In it Beethoven plays a game, if only for a few measures (mm. 148–152), with the material of the opening theme in various ways, and even the notation *mf* occurs. This marking returns in his piano sonatas only once more, very briefly, in the first movement of Op. 101. In the finale of Op. 2 No. 2 it is really a surprise that, after these few measures in *mezzo forte*, the head of the theme appears in m. 153 again, but now, completely unexpectedly, in *forte*. Soon the *staccato* section also returns, the flashing *sforzati* even more assertive than before. Then the moment has been reached at which the circle can be closed. A long descending scale, *staccato* and in *decrescendo*, introduces in m. 173 a last appearance of the theme in another embellishment, after which this sonata dwindles into nothingness.

In comparison with his first sonata, therefore, the opposite process is now taking place, the drama of the central movements being framed by the unrestrained first and fourth movements.

With the virtuoso outer movements of Op. 2 No. 3, written in the "open" key of C major, the contrast arises in the inquisitive rhetoric of an Adagio in E major, the theme of which is continually interrupted by eloquent rests.

But here, too, follows a surprise: in the subsequent E-minor section the musical lines move forward as if in a Bach prelude. Contrasts are also striking in the ensuing Scherzo and Trio. The polyphonically constructed Scherzo in C major alternates with a Trio in A minor that is fast, soft, and even ominous. Even within the Scherzo itself there are dual aspects due to Beethoven's game with light and shade. Compare the beginning with the continuation in m. 17, or with the final measures of the Coda.

Sonata Op. 2 No. 3, 3rd movement, Theme

Sonata Op. 2 No. 3, 3rd movement, m. 17

Sonata Op. 2 No. 3, 3rd movement, Coda

That this work, alone of the three Sonatas Op. 2, has gained a permanent place on the concert platform is certainly due to the copious virtuosity of the outer movements. This is even emphasized in the Coda of the first movement by a short cadenza, as in a concerto—a fortuitous idea of Beethoven's to show off his pianistic abilities to Viennese audiences.

He certainly could be pleased with the success of his Op. 2, and it was therefore not long before yet another sonata could be published, this time not in a set of three, but as an independent opus.

The *Grande Sonate* in E-flat major, Op. 7, which appeared in 1797 and again was published by Artaria, is exceeded in length only by the monumental "Hammerklavier" Sonata, Op. 106, which was composed ten years before Beethoven's death. Perhaps because he dedicated Op. 7 to the seventeen-year-old Countess Babette von Keglević, the sonata soon gained the nickname "Die Verliebte" (The Beloved).

Beethoven, who lived opposite her, dropped in now and then to give her a piano lesson and, apparently regularly in a somewhat presumptuous state of mind, did not pay all that much attention to etiquette. One of Babette's nephews later wrote in a letter to his daughter:

> The Sonata was composed for her when she was still a maiden. It was one of the whims, of which he [Beethoven] had many, that, living as he did *vis-à-vis*, he came in morning gown, slippers and tasseled cap (*Zipfelmütze*) to give her lessons.
>
> THAYER/FORBES, Vol. I, p. 198

In this sonata, the first movement, Allegro molto e con brio, starts energetically with a repeating bass that plunges forward, whereby the melody is spread over the measures like resounding calls by a French horn. In m. 59, a dance-like theme is introduced in the dominant, after which effervescent sixteenth-note passages, wherein a melody lies concealed in the first note of each group, bring the Exposition to a close. The Development, full of surprising modulations, is brief, as if Beethoven is in a hurry to let the French horn call out again in the Recapitulation. The jubilant mood is enhanced in the Coda by a long *crescendo*, after which the *fortissimo* conclusion is supported by lively "timpani rolls" in the bass.

Sonata Op. 7, 1st movement

The subsequent Largo con gran espressione in C major is abundantly rhetorical in character. Just as in the Adagio of Op. 2 No. 3, the rests in the first theme attract attention, and for quite a while the music is even more speech-like than singing. As a contrast, Beethoven inserts a middle section in A-flat major, in which the chorale-like melody is levitated by light *staccati* in the bass. Immediately before the Recapitulation the rhetorical character returns imperatively, *tenute* and *pianissimo*, after which the final chord is reached via contrasting dynamics and varied themes.

All the aroused emotions are cast aside in the lyricism of the subsequent Allegro, the carefree character of which is interrupted only by an ominous, surging Minore in E-flat minor, a movement that seems to anticipate Schubert's Klavierstück No. 1, D. 946, in the same key.

The sonata's last movement, Rondo: Poco allegretto e grazioso, also features a light and carefree beginning. Here the contrast comprises a turbulent *fortissimo* middle section, followed by effervescent thirty-second notes and fierce chords that catch their breath only in a *decrescendo*, making way for the return of the gracious initial theme. In the course of the movement, constructed around the theme with all kinds of variations, Beethoven drastically alters the character of the first theme by a sudden move from E-flat major to E major in m. 155. When, after a few measures, E-flat major regains the initiative, yet another surprise is in store. The turbulent *fortissimo* chords of the middle section have fallen apart. Provided with an *acciaccatura*, and supported by fluently moving thirty-second-note passages that restore tranquility, they devolve into a collection of loose notes—an image of waving goodbye.

Sonata Op. 7, 4th movement

Whereas the sonatas composed up to this point appear to be intended for Beethoven's own performances, it seems as if, with his Sonata in C minor, Op. 10 No. 1, he for the first time takes into account the technical possibilities of the connoisseurs and enthusiasts (*Kenner und Liebhaber*) of his time. It is also his first piano sonata in three movements, the structure with which the Viennese had become familiar through Haydn and Mozart. It is clear that for the opening of Op. 10 No. 1 Beethoven had in mind the first movement of Mozart's Sonata K. 457 in the same key. That Mozart's sonata inspired him may also be due to the C-minor tonality, which is exceptional in Mozart's sonatas but was one of Beethoven's favorite keys, later on so characteristic of dramatic works such as the *Coriolan* Overture and the Fifth Symphony. The full, compact first *forte* chord and the broken C-minor chord, rhythmically profiled and rocketing upward, receive, as in Mozart's sonata, a subdued response.

Mozart, Sonata K. 457, 1st movement

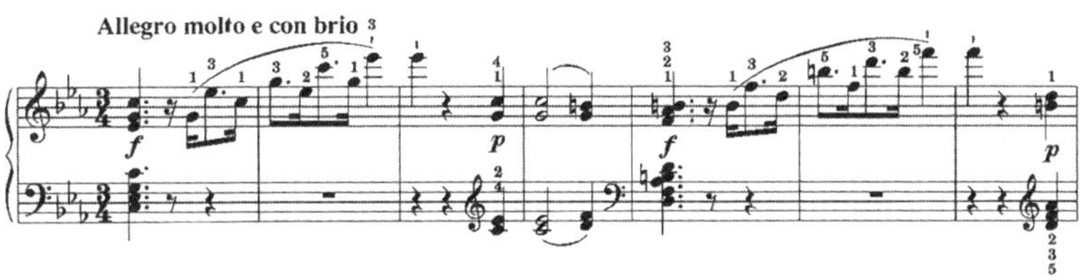

Sonata Op. 10 No. 1, 1st movement

After the fiery conclusion of the first theme with large leaps in *fortissimo* (mm. 28–30), a very *cantabile* transition, beginning at m. 32, could easily have been set for string instruments—a not totally unexpected way of writing, for Beethoven completed his Serenade Op. 8 for String Trio and his String Trios Op. 9 around the same time.

Sonata Op. 10 No. 1, 1st movement

The second theme, entering in m. 56, pushes forward, and the huge leaps that dramatically rounded off the first theme then return even more forcefully. The broken triads of the first theme, now in a shorter motif and even more tense due to the syncopated chords in the bass, are also to be found. That Beethoven homes straight in on his target can be seen in the Development, in which the first theme, as in Mozart's sonata, immediately sets out in C major. When subsequently a new episode diverges in m. 118 that leads to a sequential development in D-flat major (m. 136), he opts for a lengthy path back to the Recapitulation, thereby offering some respite in this highly dramatic movement.

In the Adagio molto that follows, Beethoven demonstrates his ability to make a simple theme sound continually different. In this, the accompaniment plays a decisive role, first as static chords but soon in fast-moving, melodic eighth or sixteenth notes. When at last the voices intertwine, the bass has become totally independent and even has the last word.

It is noticeable that in many movements, in both slow and fast tempi, Beethoven bestows an important role on rests, something he may have borrowed from Haydn, who regularly applies this idea, often with a humorous effect. However, in the last movement of Op. 10 No. 1, Prestissimo, which begins *unisono* in C minor, the rests have a different outcome. They enhance the agitated tension, as if pausing for breath each time. In the second theme in E-flat major, too, rests play a significant role, in this case enhancing the music's optimistic character.

Then, just before the Recapitulation sets in, in a very short Development section, Beethoven plays a game with the first theme, transforming the mood in only a few measures. Here, in a dramatic *fortissimo* outburst, the four-note motif anticipates the doom motif of the beginning of the Fifth Symphony.

Sonata Op. 10 No. 1, 3rd movement, m. 55

In the Coda it is striking to see how he allows the second theme to come to rest, and like an improvisation, as in a recitative, reunites it in a final outburst with the first theme. The first theme itself, however, has the last word, its agitated tension being maintained right to the end.

Sonata Op. 10 No. 1, 3rd movement

The Sonata Op. 10 No. 2 in F major is different again in character. The sparkling first movement, Allegro, is light and cheerful and even assumes a comic character in the jumping alternations between the voices. The second movement is an Allegretto in F minor, in which, within its searching character, the polyphonic voicing attracts attention before being interrupted by an expansive chorale in D-flat major. After this, the beginning returns, even more mobile and varied.

This sonata is counted among Beethoven's most humorous, due mainly to the last movement, which begins as a somewhat farcical fugue before eventually wending its homophonic way. It is as if Beethoven wants to trick the listener by briefly disguising himself as "Bach." He must have been in a happy mood at the time, for the Rondo a capriccio known as *Die Wut über den verlorenen Groschen* (The Rage over the Lost Penny) hails from the same period, a similarly humorous piece that was later published as Op. 129.

The very substantial Sonata in D major, Op. 10 No. 3, once again in four movements, is the most impressive of the three. Not only is the sparkling virtuosity of the first movement or the capricious finale highly characteristic. It is above all the second movement, the Largo e mesto in D minor, that plucks at the heartstrings. It is the first time in Beethoven's sonatas that the expression of deep, even tragic feelings is encountered in this way. As Schindler reported, the composer said about this movement:

> Everyone [...] had sensed in the Largo the spiritual condition of a person consumed by melancholy and had felt the many nuances of light and shadow in this portrait of depression.
>
> SCHINDLER (II), p. 406

Is it just a coincidence or is it indeed to raise a salute to Mozart that in m. 17, at the moment the music turns from major to minor again, a theme arises that bears so much resemblance to the beginning of Mozart's tragic Adagio in B minor, K. 540?

Mozart, K. 540

Sonata Op. 10 No. 3, Largo e mesto, mm. 17–19

It is not inconceivable that Beethoven had already known this work for some years, because after it was probably published by Hoffmeister in 1788 (no copy has survived to document this, however), Artaria presented an edition in 1794, four years before Beethoven's Op. 10 was published by Eder in Vienna.[2]

Mozart wrote this Adagio in the key of B minor, a key that is rarely used by him, but a tonality that Beethoven describes as the "black key." Its character must have held a special significance for him.[3]

It is wondrously beautiful, too, how the next movement, a Minuet in D major, of which the Trio in G now also remains in major, blossoms from the last chord of this second movement.

With so many moods conjured up in Beethoven's sonatas, it was not difficult for his pupil Ferdinand Ries to comply with a special request of his. When a young lady visited Beethoven, who was staying in Baden, the composer, obviously in a somewhat overconfident mood, asked Ries to play something:

> One evening I went to Baden to continue my lessons with him. There I found a handsome young woman sitting beside him on the sofa. Feeling that I had come at an inopportune moment, I wanted to leave immediately, but Beethoven detained me and said: "Sit down and play for a while!"
>
> He and the lady remained seated behind me. I had already been playing for a long time when Beethoven suddenly called out, "Ries! Play something romantic!" Soon after:
>
> "Something melancholy!" Then: "Something passionate!" and so on. [. . .] Finally he jumped up and shouted: "Why, those are all things I have written!" I had been playing nothing but movements from his own works all the time, connecting them with small transition passages, which seemed to please him.
>
> WEGELER/RIES, p. 105

Maybe Ries chose for "something passionate" the first movement of the Sonata in C minor, Op. 13, the "Pathétique." That is most certainly passionate!

The idea of beginning this sonata with a Grave is something that Beethoven could have borrowed from Bach's Partita in C minor, BWV 826, which has the same key and the same rhythm, though naturally this rhythm also frequently occurs in the form of a French overture. He could also have had in mind something from an early sonata, published along with two others in the autumn of 1783 in Bonn without an opus number: the three "Kurfürsten" Sonatas. The Sonata in F minor[4] also begins with a slow introduction that returns, as in the “Pathétique,” in the adjoining fast continuation. There is even a thematic connection with the Allegro di molto e con brio from the “Pathétique.” Of course, there is a big difference between the two works, not only in the notes but also in the dynamics. While the Allegro assai from the second “Kurfürsten” Sonata opens right away in *forte*, the “Pathétique” treads another dynamic path. In contrast to the usual expectation that an ascending line is played with a slight *crescendo*, here, after four measures in *piano*, the *crescendo* takes place with fully articulated chords in a descending line. But despite the increasing tension, and although these measures are supported by an ascending bass also in *crescendo*, an outspoken *forte* is nowhere within reach.

Sonata WoO 47 No. 2, 1st movement

Sonata Op. 13, 1st movement

In this movement of the “Pathétique,” the many *tremoli* in the bass, together with the double melodic voicing and the dialogue in the second theme between treble and bass, suggest that Beethoven could originally have had a composition for orchestra in mind, but later decided that it was wonderfully suited to a sonata.

There is no doubt whatsoever that the second movement contributed to the work's instant popularity. This Adagio cantabile is indeed a sublimely simple song that to this day readily finds a place on the music stand of many an amateur. It is notable that the last movement, a Rondo: Allegro, although predominantly in the minor mode, attains real drama only in the Coda. The lightness of the writing, in stark contrast to the first movement, resembles that of the last movement of Beethoven's Third Piano Concerto, also in C minor.

In many sonatas it is clear that Beethoven's style of writing is most decidedly not always directly connected with the piano. The Sonata Op. 14 No. 1 in E major, for example, is highly suitable for the version for string quartet that he wrote several years later, albeit somewhat grudgingly. That it was not just a matter of transposing the sonata a half-tone higher, to F minor—the original key would have been too low for the violin and cello—but that the string-quartet version also made other demands, is apparent from Beethoven's letter of July 13, 1802, to his publisher Breitkopf & Härtel:

> The *unnatural mania*, now so prevalent, for transferring even *pianoforte compositions* to stringed instruments, instruments which in all respects are so utterly different from one another, should really be checked. I firmly maintain that only *Mozart* could arrange for other instruments the works he composed for the pianoforte; and *Haydn* could do this too—And without wishing to force company on those two great men, I make the same statement about *my own pianoforte sonatas also*, for not only would whole passages have to be entirely omitted or altered, but some would have to be added; and there one finds the nasty stumbling-block to *overcome that one must either be the composer himself* or at any rate possess the same *skill and inventiveness*—I have arranged only one of my sonatas for string quartet, because I was so earnestly implored to do so; and I am quite convinced that nobody else could do the same thing with ease.
>
> ANDERSON, Vol. I, pp. 74–75

Although that version of Op. 14 No. 1 is certainly successful, it has not achieved the fame of his original works for string quartet, and one can readily understand why the original piano sonata is performed much more frequently.

The following sonata, Op. 14 No. 2 in G major, certainly counts among Beethoven's frequently played sonatas. Indeed, the work has many musical assets to offer, such as the Andante, where he writes a series of variations on a funny and capricious, march-like theme. When the unexpected final *fortissimo* chord breaks out, he must have intended his audience to burst out laughing after the initial shock.

Sonata Op. 14 No. 2, 2nd movement

We have a description of the way to perform these two sonatas from the hand of Beethoven's volunteer secretary, Anton Schindler. After studying law and initially serving as a court clerk, Schindler chose to pursue a career in music. Being a good violinist, his first professional position was as Kapellmeister of the Viennese Theater in der Josefstadt, where he was engaged in September 1822.

It is probably not by chance that Schindler chose the two Sonatas Op. 14 for his description, because they are less demanding technically than Beethoven's other sonatas and can thus be played successfully by amateurs. Beethoven's admirers certainly read Schindler's commentary with some interest. It was known that Schindler always wanted to emphasize his importance to and friendly connection with Beethoven, and that he was prone to exaggeration in this respect. He even went so far as to falsify entries in Beethoven's conversation books. There is, however, no reason to suppose that he falsified everything. In his description of Op. 14 No. 2, he points very specifically to the contrasting characters of the musical material:

> Both these Sonatas have for their subject a dialogue between a husband and wife, or a lover and his mistress. In the second

Sonata, this dialogue, with its signification, is very forcibly expressed, the opposition of the two principal parts being more sensibly marked than in the first Sonata. By these two parts, Beethoven intended to represent two principles, which he designated the entreating and the resisting.

Even in the first measures, the contrary motion marks the opposition of these principles.

By a softly gliding transition from earnest gravity to tenderness and feeling, the eighth bar introduces the entreating principle alone.

This suing and flattering strain continues until the middle part is taken up in D major, when both principles are again brought into conflict, but not with the same degree of earnestness as at the commencement. The resisting principle now relaxes and allows the other to finish without interruption the phrase that has been begun.

In the following phrase—

—the two come closer together and the mutual understanding is rendered distinctly perceptible by the succeeding cadence on the dominant.

In the second section of the same movement the opposition is again resumed in the minor of the tonic, and the resisting principle is energetically expressed in the phrase in A-flat major. To this succeeds a pause on the chord of the dominant, and then in E-flat the conflict is again resumed till the tranquil phrase

comes in, as it were, like a preparation for mutual concord, for both repeat several times the same idea, resembling an interrogation, beginning slowly, and with lingering pauses, then over and over again in rapid succession. The introduction in the tonic of the principal motif renews the conflict, and the feelings alternate as in the first part; but, at the conclusion of the movement, the expected conciliation is still *in suspenso*. It is not completely brought about until the end of the sonata, when it is clearly indicated, and as it were expressed, on the final close of the piece, by a distinctly articulated "Yes!" from the resisting principle.

Then was not Beethoven justified in saying that the poetic idea which had stimulated his imagination in the composition of this work was quite obvious?

SCHINDLER (I), pp. 153–155

With his next sonata, in B-flat major, Op. 22, Beethoven returns to the four-movement form, and at the same time to a sonata in which the pianistic difficulties are very demanding. The title *Grande Sonate*, under which Hoffmeister had published this composition, indicates a large-scale work. Copious pianistic *tours de force* occur in the first movement, Allegro con brio, where the firm and terse theme is elaborated in all kinds of ways. The second movement, Adagio con molta espressione, is reminiscent of an aria from a Rossini opera in which the solo voice is notated in flowing 9/8 time. A light and gallant Minuet alternates with a polyphonically constructed Trio before the work is brought to a close with an extended Rondo: Allegretto, in which amicable themes are generously intertwined with sparkling passagework.

Although this sonata is not that innovative, Beethoven was highly pleased with it. In a letter to his publisher of January 15, 1801, he writes:

> This sonata has a clean face (literally "has washed itself"), my dear brother!
>
> KERST/KREHBIEL, p. 42

It is crystal clear, however, that his Sonata in A-flat major, Op. 26, is more innovative. A first movement of a sonata in variation form is not encountered all that often,[5] but it is really unusual to insert a *Marcia funebre sulla morte d'un eroe* into a sonata. From sketches made by Beethoven in 1800, it appears that writing a sonata with a funeral march was his intention from the very beginning, despite his pupils Ferdinand Ries and Carl Czerny having regaled the world with a more embellished story. They came up with the funeral march from Ferdinando Paer's opera *Achilles*, which was premiered in Vienna on July 6, 1801, and of which Beethoven was supposed to have said, "*That* I must compose!"

But a different connection is more plausible, namely that the idea for the *perpetuum mobile* finale is probably borrowed from Johann Baptist Cramer's Piano Sonata Op. 23 No. 2. Cramer was in Vienna in 1799 and enjoyed great success with his three sonatas dedicated to Joseph Haydn. Indeed, the last movement of Op. 23

No. 2 appears, like the last movement of Beethoven's Op. 26, to be constructed in an almost étude-like manner from continuous motifs. Whatever the case may be, by placing a march within the framework of a sonata, Beethoven was forced to move the Scherzo, which in sonatas prior to this had always come after the slow movement, to an earlier position. After all, a Scherzo immediately after a funeral march would be highly unusual. To finish the work after the funeral march with a *perpetuum mobile*, and to let all the tragedy fade into nothingness, demonstrates his expressive imagination.

The fact that Beethoven called both Sonatas Op. 27 *Sonata quasi una Fantasia* also reflects on their form, of course. The first one begins with a calm Andante, after which the further development is enacted like a story-telling in that all subsequent movements are no longer independent entities but, as indicated by the marking *attacca subito*, flow into each other without interruption.

While many of Beethoven's sonatas begin *piano*, it is remarkable that in these two "fantasia" sonatas the musical development arises from an even softer dynamic.

The lengthy *pianissimo* opening of Op. 27 No. 1 and the *sempre pp e senza sordino* of the first movement of the "Moonlight" create the exceptionally subdued atmosphere that contributes to the drive of the subsequent dynamic discourse. In Op. 27 No. 1 this is set with strong contrasts of tempo and dynamics, whereby the improvisatory "fantasia" element is emphasized by a retrospective on a previous movement, the Adagio con espressione: it reappears in the last movement as a Tempo I variant before the work is brought to a close by a short and snappy Presto.

A completely different approach can be discerned in Op. 27 No. 2. Here we see a gradual dynamic development from the sustained *pianissimo* of the first movement to the *piano* of the ensuing Allegretto, followed by a final Presto agitato in which the dynamic is extended from *piano* to *forte*, and even, if only for a few measures, to *fortissimo*.

Like the *attacca subito* in Op. 27 No. 1, the designation *attacca il sequente* at the end of the first movement of Op. 27 No. 2 means that here, too, a direct link must be made to the following movement. This is remarkable, for Beethoven originally composed this Adagio sostenuto as an independent piece. In his manuscript we notice that after the final chord he writes *il fine*, something that occurs after an individual movement in none of his other works, with the exception of the second movement of Op. 101. Clearly it was only later that he came up with the idea of using this music as the first movement of the "Moonlight" Sonata. In the autograph it can be seen that after the last chord the words *il fine* are crossed out and replaced by *attacca il sequente*, thus connecting the first and second movements. What a brilliant idea to transform the C-sharp minor of the Adagio into the illuminating D-flat major of the Allegretto, a world of difference constructed on the same foundation. When C-sharp minor returns in the subsequent Presto agitato, it produces an even more dramatic effect. Franz Liszt got to the heart of the matter when he described this Allegretto as "a flower between two abysses" (Stradal, p. 88).

It is remarkable how Beethoven yet again finds a totally different musical image for his next opus, the Sonata in D major, Op. 28, which, like his first sonatas, has four movements, now, as usual, again with the Scherzo after the slow movement.

The name "Pastorale" that it soon acquired is highly appropriate. A feeling of bucolic peace and space is invoked by a slow harmonic rhythm that supports the gently undulating melody on long organ points. Even as this first movement proceeds, the contrasts remain modest and it ends, in all peace and quiet, *pianissimo*. The Andante in D minor that follows is notable for a somewhat stately melody that is supported stepwise by quasi-*pizzicati*, after which the music's purposeful advance is interrupted by a D-major section, proud, light, rhythmic, and very pronounced. After the varied reprise of the beginning, fragments of the D-major theme return in the Coda, which flows away in *pianissimo*.

Beethoven loved to play this Andante. When, together with some other composers, he was invited by Friedrich Starke to add something to the latter's *Wiener Pianoforte-Schule* that was published in 1821, he chose, along with the last movement, a shortened form of the Andante and provided it with his fingering, thereby omitting the Scherzo (with a somewhat angular rhythm that alternates with the flowing motion of the Trio) that is placed between these two movements.

In the last movement, Rondo: Allegro ma non troppo, the mood of the first movement is revived, this time in a rocking 6/8 time and with an accompaniment reminiscent of bagpipes. Just briefly, as in a short summer thunderstorm, there is a more turbulent section, after which peace is soon restored. When at long last the Coda is reached, it seems as if Beethoven has had enough of all those rustic feelings, and plunges passionately into a sparkling Più allegro quasi presto.

It was not long before Beethoven composed his three Sonatas Op. 31, at which time he grumbled to his friend, the violinist Wenzel Krumpholz:

> I am not satisfied with my works I have written so far. From now on I am taking a new direction.
>
> CZERNY (II), p. 13

Such a remark prompts us to consider whether such a "new direction" can already be discerned in these sonatas: for example, in

Illustration of the young Ludwig van Beethoven by a contemporary master. Archives of the Strecker Foundation, Mainz.

the Sonata Op. 31 No. 1, with the humorous, hobbling structure of the first movement—as if someone has been a little too liberal with the wine—where the theme is always entering ahead of the bass, and a second movement that resembles an aria with light, sparkling coloratura performed by an Italian opera diva. Even the exceptionally lyrical last movement could count as a new direction not so often encountered in Beethoven's music. Even so, it is the Sonata in D minor, Op. 31 No. 2, that comes across as the most rejuvenating of the three. To Schindler's request that he say something about the sonata's musical content, Beethoven replied laconically, "Just read Shakespeare's *Tempest*" (Schindler [II], p. 406).

The expectant, interrogative opening of the first movement, including here, too, the first broken chord in *pianissimo*—hovering on a broken sixth chord of A major rather than in the home key of D minor—the dramatic sequel, and the recitatives sounding from afar, all give us reason to heed Beethoven's advice. Images in the recitatives of murmuring spirits surrounded by storm and water are never far off, and characters from Shakespeare's play are omnipresent. Beginning in m. 21, for instance, where bass and soprano engage in an engrossing dialogue, it takes little imagination to see Prospero and Ariel, surrounded by the rolling waters, expressed in the uninterrupted triplet passages.

Sonata Op. 31 No. 2, 1st movement

In the central movement, with the repeated short "timpani motif," the tension created by the first movement is never entirely dissipated.

Sonata Op. 31 No. 2, 2nd movement, m. 17

In the subsequent Allegretto, the sharply profiled rhythm from the "timpani" returns in the theme's agitated melodic shape that forms the core of this *perpetuum mobile.* For a successful performance, the tempo of the articulated thirty-second-note motif of the "timpani" needs to be adopted for the sixteenth notes of this final movement. Hence, this can not only be a real Allegretto but can also do justice to Beethoven's exceptional notation in the left hand, where the bass must be separated from the rest of the broken chord so that not the tonic but the dominant shines through and the music ascends from the ground. This image certainly fits Czerny's assertion that here Beethoven was inspired by the rhythmic cadence of a horseman galloping past his window.[6]

Sonata Op. 31 No. 2, 3rd movement

But a musical picture of spirits floating above the earth, drifting around aimlessly, ending in oblivion, comes even closer, especially because in the end everything disappears without leaving a trace, as Prospero says in *The Tempest:*[7]

The solemn temples, the great globe itself,
Yea, all which it inherit, shall dissolve.
And, like this insubstantial pageant faded,
Leave not a rack behind.

Sonata Op. 31 No. 2, 3rd movement, final measures

In the next sonata, Op. 31 No. 3, there is also something exceptional going on. It strikes us that a Scherzo and Minuet are to be found as the two middle movements of this four-movement sonata, but that a slow movement is missing. Will there be a reason for this? A Scherzo in 2/4 time is already rather unusual, but the answer can be found in the Minuet, where in the Coda the already somewhat melancholic mood that arises with the use of the Neapolitan second over a tonic pedal is emphasized, so that the last phrase assumes a tragic overtone. Indeed, the Coda is a sorrowful farewell to the Minuet, a dance that for Beethoven must have been symbolically linked to the "old" music of his predecessors Haydn and Mozart. The Presto con fuoco that follows the Minuet rushes excitedly into a new era.[8]

Sonata Op. 31 No. 3, 3rd movement, Coda

Sonata Op. 31 No. 3, 4th movement

Taking into consideration the order of the opus numbers, it is confusing to have to place the simple musical content of Beethoven's next two sonatas in the perspective of his Op. 31 No. 3. Indeed their opus number 49 came into being only because these *Deux sonates faciles* were not published until 1805 by the Bureau des Arts et d'Industrie in Vienna, even though they had been composed between 1795 and 1798. In 1802, Beethoven's brother Carl—perhaps without Beethoven's knowledge—went to some trouble to place them with various publishers, but without success.

It is clear that Beethoven wrote these sonatas for teaching purposes. The different moods are beautifully spread over their shortened two-movement spans, and because of the limited technical difficulties there is much to enjoy for everyone who plays the piano. Beethoven obviously found the popularity that the second movement of Op. 49 No. 2, Tempo di menuetto, soon gained so enticing that he used it again in his Septet Op. 20, published in 1802.

Before examining the following sonata, the "Waldstein," Op. 53, it is interesting to look at Beethoven's Sonata in F major, Op. 54, because here, too, a Minuet is to be found. While Beethoven was still kindly disposed to the Minuet when he wrote his two *Sonates faciles* Op. 49, times had changed, and after having taken leave of the Minuet in the course of Op. 31 No. 3, in Op. 54 he once again saw an opportunity.[9]

Greater contrasts than those in the first movement In tempo d'un Menuetto are scarcely imaginable. The recurring, ever more varied, and almost rococo theme is brought each time to an abrupt end by stamping *forte* octaves. Then the Minuet has the last word before, after a last, painful exclamation in *fortissimo* (m. 148), it disappears into obscurity. When the second movement, Allegretto, flows on in a sunny mood and the tempo is further increased to *più allegro* in the Coda, the mood of the first movement is totally left behind and the work concludes cheerfully. Even though this sonata has only two movements, both naturally form a coherent whole.[10]

Ever since his first compositions, Beethoven had been preoccupied by the balance between the overall structure of a work and the way in which separate movements could be connected.[11]

He also addressed this problem in the "Waldstein" Sonata, Op. 53, the original middle movement of which—later published as the *Andante favori*[12]—he upon reflection probably found too long.[13] Such an extremely long movement, lasting almost ten minutes, would have disturbed the sonata's equilibrium. Three long movements in one sonata were too much of a good thing, and it is indeed a splendid idea to insert a short Introduzione: Adagio molto, to allow the last movement, Allegretto moderato, to blossom out of it in *pianissimo*, and melting tonic and dominant to attain an ephemeral sound as the result of not changing the pedal in these measures. The outcome is so special that the French very soon came to dub this sonata "L'Aurore" (Dawn),[14] a characterization that perfectly fits the beginning of the first movement of this sonata, which, as in both Sonatas Op. 27, emerges almost surreptitiously from nothing.

Its overall design, with the two outer movements very substantial and long, again leads to a new structure. The musical center of gravity, traditionally lying mainly in the slow central movement of many sonatas, as is the case in a number of sonatas by Haydn and Mozart, has now been shifted to the outer movements.

A short central movement—here, too, arising out of *pianissimo*—is also to be found in the Sonata in F minor, Op. 57, the "Appassionata," although the variations in this peaceful Andante do last slightly longer than the Introduzione of the "Waldstein." However, while in the "Waldstein" the last movement sets out in a peaceful state of mind, in Op. 57 an exceptionally abrupt transition, by means of a single *fortissimo* diminished seventh chord, takes place. Indeed a shocking moment, totally in line with the passionate character of this work.[15] Ferdinand Ries described how, during a walk together, Beethoven became totally beside himself when the idea for the last movement occurred to him:

> During a similar walk we went so far astray that we didn't get back to Döbling, where Beethoven lived, until nearly eight o'clock. The entire way he had hummed, or sometimes even howled, to himself—up and down, up and down, without singing any definite notes. When I asked what this

> was, he replied: "A theme for the last Allegro of the sonata has occurred to me" (in F minor, Opus 57). When we entered the room, he rushed to the piano without taking off his hat. I took a seat in the corner and he soon forgot all about me. He stormed on for at least an hour with the new finale of this sonata, which is so beautiful. Finally he got up, was surprised to see me still there, and said: "I cannot give you a lesson today. I still have work to do."
>
> WEGELER/RIES, p. 87

It is not difficult to work out which theme this refers to. Up and down, "hummed" and "howled," without singing a specific, defining note: that must have been the idea behind the compelling sixteenth notes that give the theme of this last movement so much momentum.

Sonata Op. 57, 3rd movement

Over and over again, Beethoven finds solutions for the forms he wishes to express, something that is also to be seen in the Sonata in F-sharp major, Op. 78, which, like Op. 54, comprises just two movements. Concerning the beautiful introductory measures of the first movement, Hans von Bülow expressed himself with some malicious delight:

> If Ferdinand Hiller had composed these first four measures in a lady's album, he would be immortal; unfortunately, he failed to do it.
>
> PFEIFFER, p. 36

Beethoven himself was also pleased with this sonata, and when the popular "Moonlight" Sonata received rather too much praise in his opinion, he exclaimed to Czerny:

> Everybody is always talking about the C-sharp minor sonata! Surely I have written better things. There is the Sonata in F-sharp major—that is something very different!
>
> THAYER/FORBES, Vol. I, p. 297

His Op. 78 is dedicated to Countess Therese von Brunsvik, one of his pupils, of whom he was very fond and whose piano lessons, as Therese herself once remarked, tended to overrun. The unusual key of F-sharp major is reminiscent of the intimate lyricism of Bach's Prelude and Fugue in F-sharp major from the first book of *The Well-Tempered Clavier*, and the technique in the second movement, with its many virtuosic articulated sixteenth-note passages spread over both hands, would not be out of place as a special exercise in a piano lesson.

Sonata Op. 78, 2nd movement

Beethoven's next sonata, the Sonata in G major, Op. 79, was published as a "Sonatina" by Breitkopf & Härtel in Leipzig in 1810. In comparison with the other sonatas, with the exception of the two small Sonatas Op. 49, the modest length and the restrained level of difficulty are notable. The first movement, an energetic Presto alla tedesca, has the character of a German dance, and in the last movement, the theme is derived from what Beethoven refers to as a "German song" (*Deutscher Gesang*), such as the one he had composed in 1790–1791 for his *Ritterballet.*[16]

Ritterballet (Knight's Ballet), *Allegro molto*

Sonata Op. 79, 3rd movement

"Alla tedesca," *Deutscher Gesang*: headings that emphasize the national character of the music, and also a sonata that not for nothing must be playable by many. There must be a reason for this!

In Europe everything became precarious and turbulent once Napoleon Bonaparte had come to power after the French Revolution and declared himself emperor in December 1804.

French troops had rampaged through Europe, and on one occasion, in November 1805, had already taken Vienna. After their retreat, however, Napoleon was once again, in May 1809, at the city gates. In 1805 the city could be taken without resistance because French officers at the Tăbor Bridge, in those days the only crossing over the Danube, had been able to convince the Austrian commandant that the war was already over. Four years later, however, the city was indeed defended and the French progressed to a bombardment. It is understandable that Beethoven's initial admiration for Napoleon had cooled considerably. When the composer Wilhelm Karl Rust met Beethoven in a coffeehouse during the French occupation and a French officer passed by, the composer was not exactly reserved in expressing his opinion. A nephew of Rust described the event to one of Beethoven's first biographers, Alexander Wheelock Thayer:

> Beethoven doubled his fist and exclaimed, "If I, as a general, knew as much about strategy as I the composer know about counterpoint, I'd give you something to do!"
>
> THAYER/FORBES, Vol. I, p. 466

It is against this background that the energetic "Alla tedesca" can perhaps be explained in this apparently so light-footed sonata. After a short central movement in a gloomy mood, in the last movement the spiritual character dominates, the closing of which is perhaps soft, but hopeful.

A sonata of much greater significance that saw the light of day in the same period is the one in E-flat major, Op. 81a, "Das Lebewohl" ("Les Adieux"). Beethoven dedicated this work to Archduke Rudolph of Austria, who had fled Vienna when the French besieged the city. When the French left in November 1809, after a peace treaty had been signed, Rudolph returned with his family at the end of January 1810. In Op. 81a the various moods of the three movements are illustrative: the sorrowful departure, expressed toward the end by horn calls receding in the distance, the grief about the absentee, and the turbulent joy of the finale at the reunion. In a letter of April 12, 1811, to his publisher Breitkopf & Härtel, Beethoven made it clear that "the 'Lebewohl' and the 'Wiedersehen' can be dedicated to no-one but the Archduke Rudolph" (Anderson, Vol. I, p. 319).

So we see that the dedications were becoming more personal and could even be connected with the sonatas' musical content. Beethoven now also insisted that the title should be printed not only

Lebewohl, Abwesenheit und Wiedersehn.
Sonate für das Pianoforte
in Musik gesezt und
Seiner Kaiserl: Hoheit
dem Erzherzog Rudolph von Oesterreich
zugeeignet
von
L. v. BEETHOVEN.
Eigenthum der Verleger.
81e Werk ~ ~ Preis
Bey Breitkopf & Hartel in Leipzig.

Sonata Op. 81a, title page of the first edition

in French, the language of the court and of international relations, but also in German. In a letter to Breitkopf & Härtel dated May 20, 1811, he wrote:

> Your sonata is on its way [. . .] Print the title as I have written it, both in French and German—and the other headings in the same way.
>
> ANDERSON, Vol. I, p. 322

Breitkopf & Härtel, however, were not in favor of a bilingual title page, and the work appeared in two separate publications, one with a French, the other with a German title page, while in the separate sections the text remained bilingual.

The circumstances of that period probably persuaded Beethoven to provide his next sonata, too, with German instructions: for the first movement of the two-movement Sonata in E minor, Op. 90, *Mit Lebhaftigkeit und durchaus mit Empfindung und Ausdruck* (Lively and decidedly, with feeling and expression) and for the second movement, *Nicht zu geschwind und sehr singbar vorgetragen* (Not too fast and very singable). The first edition of this sonata was announced on June 9, 1815, by the publisher Steiner in the *Wiener Zeitung*. When Count Moritz von Lichnowsky, to whom the sonata is dedicated, asked Beethoven about its significance, his reply was, according to Schindler:

> He had set the Count's love-story to music, and if he wished to have names for the movements, the first could be "Conflict Between Head and Heart" and the second "Conversation with the Beloved."
>
> SCHINDLER (II), p. 210

A candid answer, for the count had plans to marry an admired opera singer, whom he did indeed marry in 1816 despite the opposition of his relatives.

Beethoven's answer, true or not—Schindler seems to be not always reliable in his declarations—is a beautiful thought. The first movement in minor is written with great contrasts in themes. In the major-key second movement, the feeling of perpetual happiness indeed flows, because in this Rondo the couplets are not written with great contrast and independence—as is usual in a Rondo form—but rather as an Intermezzo forming the link to the intensely vocal, frequently recurring theme.

Schindler's words gain extra significance through a letter from Beethoven to Johann Nepomuk Kaňka, a lawyer in Prague who had supported him in a number of legal actions—including one to retain the annuity promised by Prince Ferdinand Kinsky when, after the latter's death due to a fall from his horse, the family no longer wished to meet their obligations. In a letter dated April 8, 1815, Beethoven wrote to Kaňka:

> In what way can *I serve you with my art?* Tell me, do you want a musical setting of *the soliloquy* of a refugee king or a song about the perjury of a usurper—or about two friends living in adjacent houses who yet never see one another?
>
> ANDERSON, Vol. II, p. 508

With these words it appears that Beethoven was well aware of the events taking place in Europe. King Louis XVIII had indeed fled from France to Ghent (Flanders) upon receiving the notification that Napoleon Bonaparte, breaking his exile and residence on the island of Elba, had again appeared in the south of France, traveling with a small army toward Paris on March 1, 1815. His arrival and the resulting victory over Paris took place on March 20.

According to Beethoven, by doing this Napoleon was guilty of perjury because of the agreement made to decline any attempt to regain the throne following his banishment to Elba. At the time apparently for Beethoven no subject was too crazy to set to music, or was it just meant as an embarrassment for Kaňka?

But indeed, Beethoven was able to express all kinds of ideas in music, as he did in his Overture to *The Ruins of Athens*, a work he composed in 1811. Czerny explains:

> Beethoven attempted to portray concrete properties and ideas by musical means; this is seen in the Overture to *The Ruins of Athens*. The fragments of a once splendid pillar are illustrated in the first figure, played by the bass alone; then comes the wanderer's lament over vanished glory; next the doings of the (then) Turkish overlords, and in between, an innocent theme in which he modulates to the subdominant in the ancient Greek manner (instead of to the dominant), etc.
>
> CZERNY (II), p. 13

His next sonata, Op. 101 in A major, is yet again completely different in design. Beethoven worked on it from 1813, when the first sketches appeared, until its publication in 1817. It is an exceptionally difficult composition not only in a technical-pianistic sense but also with regard to the musical content. The instructions in German give Beethoven the possibility of making his intentions clear in a really refined way.

- I: *Etwas lebhaft, und mit der innigsten Empfindung* (Somewhat lively, and with innermost feeling)
- II: *Lebhaft Marschmäßig* (Lively, like a march)—a movement that must sound as if it is a march, but not with the character of a real march
- III: *Langsam und sehnsuchtsvoll* (Slow and full of longing)—the expression of unrequited desires
- IV: *Geschwinde, doch nicht zu sehr, und mit Entschlossenheit* (Fast, yet not too fast, and with determination).

For the realization of such nuances he had an excellent pianist in mind: Baroness Dorothea von Ertmann. Beethoven was extremely fond of his pupil, and in a letter of February 23, 1817, in which he dedicates this sonata to her, he addressed her with the following words of admiration:

> My dear and beloved Dorothea Caecilia!
>
> Please accept now what was often intended for you and what may be to you a proof of my devotion both to your artistic aspirations and to your person.
>
> ANDERSON, Vol. II, p. 671

The baroness, who studied with Beethoven from as early as 1803, was copiously praised by her contemporaries for the way in which she played his works. The composer Johann Friedrich Reichardt, former Kapellmeister at the court of Frederick the Great in Potsdam, recounts:

Dorothea von Ertmann (1781–1849), anonymous miniature. Beethoven-Haus, Bonn.

> A lofty noble manner and a beautiful face full of deep feeling increased my expectation still further at the first sight of the noble lady; and then as she performed a great Beethoven sonata I was surprised as almost never before. I have never seen such power and innermost tenderness combined even in the greatest virtuosi; from the tip of each finger her soul poured forth, and from her hands, both equally skillful and sure, what power and authority were brought to bear over the whole instrument. Everything that is great and beautiful in art was turned into song with ease and expression! And it was not one of those fine pianos that one finds so frequently here, but the great artist instilled her sensitive spirit into the instrument and forced it to serve her as perhaps no other hands have been able to do.
>
> THAYER/FORBES, Vol. I, pp. 412–413

Beethoven was aware of the problems that Op. 101 caused. In a letter of January 9, 1817, to the publisher of this work, Sigmund Anton Steiner, business partner of publisher Tobias Haslinger, he wrote:

> No doubt my excellent L[ieutenan]t G[eneral] will be taken aback, for he will think that 'difficult' is a relative term, e.g. what seems difficult to one person will seem easy to another, and that therefore the term has no precise meaning whatever. But the L[ieutenan]t G[enera]l must know that this term *has a very precise meaning, for what is difficult is also beautiful, good, great* and so forth. Hence everyone will realize that this is *the most lavish* praise that can be bestowed, since what is *difficult makes one sweat.*
>
> ANDERSON, Vol. II, p. 661

And just after that in an undated letter to Haslinger himself he noted:

> In particular, there are people who worry me about the sonata, which is technically difficult to perform.
>
> ANDERSON, Vol. II, p. 653

However, not only the technical difficulties are remarkable. In the structure of Op. 101, too, there arise numerous problems which give the interpreter a difficult task in lending unity to this work. For example, the poetic, almost ephemeral theme with which this sonata begins, not on the tonic A major, but on the dominant, is also used to connect the third and fourth movements, whereby a cyclic form is created—hereby already anticipating works by the Romantics, Liszt's Sonata in B minor, for example. The way Beethoven positions this theme in retrospect is highly expressive and this must be reflected in the interpretation. Continually interrupted by rests, made even more significant by giving these a fermata, the theme dissolves like a memory, leaving just shreds.

Sonata Op. 101, 1st movement

Sonata Op. 101, transition to the 4th movement

It is also remarkable that in this sonata an increasingly polyphonic style of writing is used to convey more contrasting possibilities regarding character. Although Beethoven regularly writes polyphonically, this is the first time it occurs extensively. Note, for example, how the firm rhythm of the second movement, from m. 55 onward, is completely and unexpectedly interrupted by a tenderly singing canon.

Sonata Op. 101, 2nd movement

Indeed a very contrasting emotion, such as we notice also in the last movement, where a fully worked-out fugato appears for the first time. Beethoven may have come upon this idea through his admiration for Bach, and in this case even more specifically Handel. After the deeply felt sorrow of the third movement, the contrast with the outburst of unrestrained joy in the last movement is immense. It is with the upbeat of m. 33 in the Exposition of this sonata form that the spirit of the main theme breaks out in full confidence. *Geschwinde, doch nicht zu sehr, und mit Entschlossenheit* (Fast, yet not too fast, and with determination) is Beethoven's notation at the beginning of this Allegro. The polyphonic writing, the sixteenth notes, quasi-Baroque in their motion, the outburst of freedom, all seem to be inspired by a Handelian optimism. A sudden change of mood takes place only when the main theme, now as the subject for an audacious fugato, appears in m. 123; here the ingenious complexity of the further polyphonic elaboration is even more reminiscent of Bach than of Handel. Exceptionally significant is also the point at which Beethoven employs this fugato: it is in the Development, the ideal place for conjuring up musical tension by the use of complex structures.[17] Immediately at the beginning, in mm. 121–122, an abrupt change takes place from A major to A minor, a tonality with a gloomy expression, like the second movement of his Seventh Symphony. Note also the appearance of the theme in *pianissimo*, a dynamic indication that for Beethoven always is an expression for something unusual, mysterious, divorced from reality.

From then on, all efforts are expended in striving to regain the optimistic A major character of the Exposition. In parallel with the dynamic discourse, the fugato theme, built up to four voices, finds the dominant at first in a radiant *fortissimo* outburst in m. 223, emphasized by Beethoven's notation "Contra E" and the appearance of the head of the theme in a gigantic augmentation, hidden between the tied octaves in the bass. Then, in m. 232—a long arpeggio, spanning almost the entire keyboard of the most recent instruments of that time—A major returns in a glorious Recapitulation. From then on it seems that all negative, oppressed, and disturbing elements are left behind and that the unbroken spirit of the Exposition can revive. With Beethoven, however, we never find such a literal procedure, as can also be noticed in m. 240, where for the first time the theme appears softly with the indication *dolce poco espressivo* in a very low bass, whirling with the other voices around a pedal point in a new counterpoint. A long, floating chain of sixteenths, leading again to a *dolce* in m. 252, introduces new lightness into this finale until m. 313 in the Coda, when, completely unexpectedly, the exclamation from the beginning of the Exposition, now in *fortissimo*, brings everything to a dramatic standstill.

When the answer is in *piano*, and even the theme of the dark fugato appears anew in *pianissimo*, it looks as if the negative feelings will start all over again. However, the reaction in mm. 319–321 is a gentle one, and as in retrospect, looking back from a distance, almost like an improvisation playing around with fragments of the theme, everything fades away in *pianissimo* and a long *ritardando*. Must this be the ultimate destination? No! *Fortissimo* A-major chords are energetically pushing upward.

Although it seemed that Beethoven had reached the limits in Op. 101 with regard to expression and pianistics, in his Sonata Op. 106, the "Hammerklavier," composed in the years 1817/1818, he goes even further. It must have given him some pleasure to state that pianists would have a hard time with his Op. 106. To his publisher Artaria he allegedly uttered the following prophetic words:

> There you have a sonata, he told him, that will give pianists something to do (and) will be played 50 years hence.
>
> PROD'HOMME (1), p. 245

However, for a pianist like Franz Liszt it did not take that long. For him no challenge was too great. Not only did he play the work for a small circle of his friends, in May 1836 he also did so for a large audience in the salon of Érard in Paris.[18]

Hector Berlioz was present on that occasion and wrote in the *Critique musicale* of June 12, 1836, the following words of praise:

> [. . .] this sublime poem which, for almost the totality of pianists, was until this day only the enigma of the Sphinx. A New Oedipus, Liszt explained it in such a way that the author, had he been able to hear it, must have shuddered with pleasure and pride in his tomb. [. . .] Not one note was omitted, not a note added (I followed the score with my eyes), not one alteration in tempo that was added to the movement, not one turn or thought that was indicated in the text was weakened, not an inflection, not an idea was enfeebled or twisted from its true sense. Particularly in the Adagio, in the reproduction of this amazing Hymn that the genius of Beethoven seems to have sung to himself while gliding solitarily in the immensity, he maintained himself constantly on the level of the author's ideas. One can say no more, I know, but one must not say less, either, because it is true. It is the ideal performance of a work reputed to be unplayable. By reproducing thus a work still not understood, Liszt has proven that he is the pianist of the future. Honor to him!
>
> BERLIOZ, *Critique musicale*, Vol. II, pp. 474–475

As in the case of Op. 81a, Beethoven dedicated this sonata to Archduke Rudolph of Austria. While in "Das Lebewohl" it is clear what feelings are being expressed, the musical content of Op. 106 is of a totally different dimension. Especially in the almost twenty-minute-long Adagio sostenuto and in the colossal fugue, Allegro risoluto—two movements of almost Brucknerian proportions—the interpreter has to exploit unprecedented musical and technical powers. With the intensity of the Adagio sostenuto in F-sharp minor, the key of affliction, the first measures of which must be played *mezza voce* but at the same time "appassionato e con molto sentimento," a tension is created that must be maintained right up to the last chord.[19]

The Russian pianist Wilhelm von Lenz, one of Beethoven's first biographers, waxed lyrical over this movement:

> The adagio (6/8 in F-sharp minor) has something of the biblical wailings of Sion. It is an immense lamentation set on the ruins of all happiness.
>
> LENZ (I), p. 250

He later formulated his opinion succinctly:

> A mausoleum of the collective sorrow of the world.
>
> LENZ (II), Vol. 5, p. 41

It goes without saying that Beethoven also employed for the expression of this suffering what he called the "black key." The B minor comes to the fore in all the movements at highly dramatic moments—for example, the close of the Scherzo, where the way back to B major must be found; the *cancrizans* development of the fugue, where in mm. 143–151 the theme appears note by note backward; or in mm. 117–121 of the Adagio.

Sonata, Op. 106, 3rd movement

Nothing of this dark mood is to be heard in the first movement. This music is bold and pervaded with daring vitality. It begins with a salute to Rudolph,[20] the implied text and the theme of which correspond to a sketch by Beethoven for a tribute cantata for four-part chorus intended to be performed on the occasion of Rudolph's appointment as Archbishop of Olmütz. It is as if Beethoven is throwing his hat in the air and, just as in the choral work, calling out, "Vivat, vivat Rudolphus!"[21]

Sonata Op. 106, 1st movement

In this sonata, too, he positions the Scherzo, just as in the Ninth Symphony, before the slow movement, thereby moving the central point of the sonata to the Adagio sostenuto. To keep the total work in balance, a long and substantial Finale has to follow. Because Beethoven probably considered the transition from the Adagio to such a Finale too direct, he found a solution by writing a brief Largo as a link. Arising out of the Adagio, it sounds like the proclamation of new life.

In a free notation in which even the bar lines disappear, a written-out improvisation, the tension is built up that is discharged in the colossal fugue that, full of energy, breaks out in a liberating Allegro risoluto.

Is it not striking that when the theme in its original form arises for the first time in m. 16, the descending thirds that mark the first note of each beat, B-flat, G, E-flat, are also the main notes of the melody that mark the words "And <u>H</u>e shall <u>r</u>eign for <u>e</u>ver and <u>e</u>ver" from the "Hallelujah" chorus in *Messiah* by Handel,[22] a composer Beethoven deeply admired and had been studying for many years?[23] And how beautiful it is that after the eighth-note rests in this theme, the theme is completed by a long line of uninterrupted sixteenth notes, indeed reflecting "for ever and ever" (see Chapter 4, "Tempo").

After the joyful beginning of this fugue, an abundance of expression is exploited over a broad spectrum of keys and counterpoint. For example: the theme appears in augmentation (stretching it out, E-flat minor, mm. 94–129), in retrograde (backward, B minor, mm. 153–195), and in inversion (turning it upside down, G major, mm. 208–249). Even so, it is not the art of the fugue that is superb, but rather the inaccessibility, the boldness, the ever more intensely compulsive energy.

However, in this case, too, Beethoven finds a contrast in a serene, polyphonically constructed section in D major marked *sempre dolce cantabile en una corda*, a prayer of thanksgiving, the theme of which relates to the Gratias and the Benedictus of the *Missa Solemnis*, composed a few years later. When this theme is combined from m. 279 with the first notes of the fugue theme, it disappears as quickly as it arose, and the unrestrained energy returns even more unbridled. In the end, the inevitable happens: the fugue bursts out in an explosion of trills and only comes to rest in *piano* in just a few measures, marked *poco adagio*. Then the theme arises in *pianissimo*, like a phoenix from its ashes, before jubilant trills and four chords, all in full *fortissimo*, conclude this immense work. In a letter from Beethoven's friend, the civil servant and violinist Karl Holz, to Lenz we can read how Beethoven saw the form of the Fugue in the perspective of a new era:

> To write a fugue is no great art. When I was a student, I made dozens of them. But the fancy wishes also to assert its privileges, and today a new and really poetical element must be introduced into the traditional form.[24]
>
> KOPITZ/CADENBACH, Vol. I, p. 471

That he succeeded in such an approach is also apparent from the two fugues in the Sonata in A-flat major, Op. 110, the middle of three sonatas with consecutive opus numbers: Op. 109 in E major, Op. 110 in A-flat major, and Op. 111 in C minor. These are the last piano sonatas that he composed and, however different they may be, the musical content appears to have its source in a single innermost urge. They were composed between 1820 and 1822, the years when he was working on the *Missa Solemnis.* One might say that the religious significance of that composition is reflected in these sonatas.

The first movement of the Sonata in E major, Op. 109, Vivace ma non troppo, begins lightly and "inquisitively" because the progression of intervals in the first theme is continually ascending and descending, seemingly never finding a firm foothold. The immediately connected *adagio espressivo*[25] is in the form of a recitative, which, however, provides no answer to the questions posed, after which the process is repeated.[26]

Sonata Op. 109, 1st movement

In the last measures of the Coda, a solution is still far off, which results in an agitated outburst of emotion in the Prestissimo in E minor that is immediately connected. A short chorale, sounding from afar—Beethoven's marking here is *sul una corda*—attempts to restore peace, but in vain: the movement ends dramatically. The key of E major that returns in the third movement is often seen as a key of mysticism, meditation, prayer, and purity, as used by Haydn in his portrayal of Paradise in *The Creation*, or the two Preludes in E major from Bach's *Well-Tempered Clavier* that give rise to similar feelings.

The association with Bach is even clearer because in this last movement the theme possesses similarities to a sarabande. Not just because its motion, as in a sarabande, often pauses on the second beat, but also through the subdued mood—*Gesangvoll, mit innigster Empfindung* (Singing, with the most profound feeling).

In the original manuscript of this sonata, we notice that below the Italian indication *Andante molto cantabile ed espressivo* is written *Gesang* (song) *mit innigster Empfindung.*

This is indeed a remarkable change, because in the printed version it indeed reads, *Gesangvoll, mit innigster Empfindung.* Only the slightest difference, and apparently arising only at the printing stage. While the original indication seems to concern "simplicity," the final notation seems to refer to this theme's expressiveness. It is, however, clear that the musical expression in this movement is a reaction to the emotional outburst of the preceding Prestissimo. Here, too, there is something remarkable in the manuscript. Originally, the indication "Presto" was written in ink there, after which Beethoven deleted the "o" and added "issimo" in pencil to change it into Prestissimo, maybe with the intention of further emphasizing its contrasting character with those of the outer movements.[27]

After the theme of the final movement has been introduced, all kinds of moods are evoked in the Variations—hopeful in Variation I, searching in Variations II and IV, decisive in Variations III and V. A solution must be found. A last attempt is made in Variation VI, in which the first theme returns in an extremely compact form and then, supported by increasingly turbulent passages, ends in trills, striving for happiness. However, the vigor decreases and the attempt fails. Acquiescence is to be found only in the voice of the sarabande. Beethoven dedicated the work to Maximiliano Brentano and wrote in a letter of December 6, 1821, the following:

> A dedication!!! Well, this is not one of those dedications which are used and abused by thousands of people—It is the spirit which unites the noble and finer people on this earth and which *time* can *never* destroy. It is this spirit which now speaks to you . . .
>
> ANDERSON, Vol. II, pp. 931–932

Just as this sonata might be "read" as a series of events that lead to a solution, the first two movements can be seen as a preparation for the third one, where the "Spirit" finds its ultimate destination.[28]

Such a development is even more noticeable in Beethoven's next sonata, the Sonata in A-flat major, Op. 110. The first movement, Moderato cantabile molto espressivo, has, as Beethoven specifies, a *con amabilita* (*sanft*) character, evoking a mood of peace and tranquility. Only in the penultimate measure does the color change like a shadow, auguring the imminent dramatic developments.

Sonata Op. 110, 1st movement

Intense emotions burst out in the subsequent Allegro molto, where great dynamic contrasts confront each other like question and answer. In the middle section we see the voices literally crossing in a suggestive manner by the downward-whirling eighth notes contrasting with the upward drive of the syncopated quarter notes, all of this reinforced by marking each phrase *sforzato* and *fortissimo*.

Sonata Op. 110, 2nd movement

When this Allegro molto moves via a short Adagio ma non troppo to a recitative, the content becomes increasingly personal.

Words in fits and starts, even stammering, lead to a "Klagender Gesang" ("lament"), as Beethoven denotes this, an *Arioso dolente* in which the opening of the aria "Es ist vollbracht" (It is finished) from Bach's *St. John Passion* is cited literally:

Bach, St. John Passion, *Aria "Es ist vollbracht"*

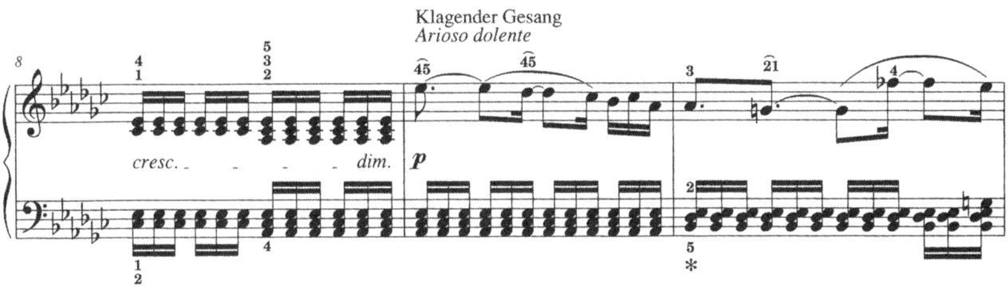

Sonata Op. 110, 3rd movement

Through this explicit reference, the strikingly emphatic vocal transitions in the previous movement gain their deep significance. Right at the beginning of the *St. John Passion*, in the chorale "Herr, unser Herrscher" (Lord, our ruler), Bach employs the symbolism of constantly intertwining voices (flutes and oboes) to depict most impressively the musical image of the crucifixion scene. By means of such allusions, in his Op. 110 Beethoven confers an ever-present Passion ambience.

When the way back from the Arioso dolente has to be found, Beethoven employs an extensive fugue, the theme of which soars from *piano* in ascending quarter notes and, with the use of ever more voices, is sung with increasing force and conviction. The structural design he chooses from the recitative onwards corresponds to the way Bach does that in his cantatas, namely in the order recitative, aria, and then chorus. With Beethoven, too, this fugue is much more a choir of human voices than a fugue in the technical sense. As he said to Karl Holz, a poetic element has been added.

The musical significance of this work is emphasized even more when Beethoven suddenly interrupts the fugue, and the *Arioso*, marked *Ermattet, klagend* (wearily plaintive), returns for the second time, even more intense, due not only to its being transposed half a tone lower, to G minor, but more especially because of the melody disintegrating due to the notated rests, feeling as though the heart stops beating. In mm. 132–136, with a last supreme effort, an egress is sought whereby the short full chords are placed off-beat, striving upward and with the consequence that the increasing tension is even more compelling. However, this effort does not succeed, and when the fugue is reached again, it seems that it has been drained of all its energy, not only because Beethoven's dynamic indication is no longer *piano* but *sempre una corda*, but more specifically because the theme appears in its inversion, so that the strength of the intervals is diminished due to their descent. Beethoven writes *Nach und nach wieder auflebend sempre una corda* (little by little reviving again, always *una corda*), and in Italian *poi a poi di nuovo vivente* (reviving little by little); the path to the new life arises out of emptiness. Coming out of the *una corda* (m. 137), the dynamic discourse changes only in m. 165, where Beethoven writes *poi a poi tutte le corde* (little by little all the strings, meaning lift the *una corda* pedal gradually). Then, after a chaotic quest with voices falling over each other, in which the dynamic level changes to *piano* and the tempo pushes forward—finally, in m. 174, the original fugue theme appears in *forte* and, for the very first time, the accentuation now corresponds to the customary metrical proportions emphasized by *sforzati* on the first beat. From then on, with all the voices finally united, the music drives homophonically, irresistibly upward and soars ecstatically to a liberating conclusion.

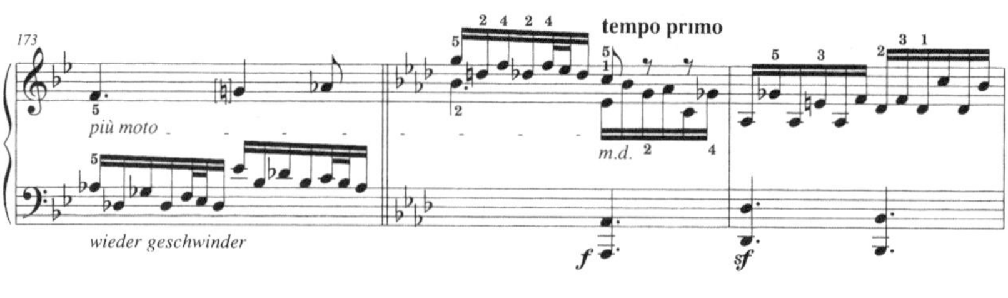

Sonata Op. 110, 4th movement

Upon reflection, it must be concluded that in this sonata Beethoven is expressing an image of Christ's Passion: the first movement as his birth, with the foreboding of his fate expressed in the final measures, then the persecution, the crucifixion, the suffering, and in the end the resurrection. It is most striking that this is the only sonata for which Beethoven gives a specific date. At the top of the first page of the autograph he writes, "Den 25sten December 1821." Indeed, Christmas Day, the birthday of Christ.[29]

The significance seems to stretch even further, because it is the only one of his very last piano sonatas that is not dedicated to anyone. It is a work written for himself with the significance of a *document humain.*

While Beethoven needs several movements to formulate his ideas in Op. 110, in his last sonata, Op. 111 in C minor, it appears that just two movements achieve his goal. In the first movement, a Maestoso is combined with an Allegro con brio ed appassionato; the final movement is an Arietta with variations, marked *adagio, molto semplice e cantabile*. It is as if the pent-up tension is already present before the Maestoso begins and dissipates in an outburst of two consecutive diminished seventh chords. After a third outbreak, the music suddenly turns inward in chromatically descending chords before piercing dissonances dissolve in a long trill that breaks out in the Allegro con brio ed appassionato. The concerted tension that Beethoven has created in the sixteen measures of the Maestoso then explodes in all intensity. The rugged theme of this movement, the driving sixteenth-note passages, the voices forced ever further apart between the high and low registers of the piano, at last reach the second theme, as a recitative that calls in vain for peace. After the repeat, it is only in the Development that a fugal way of writing with the early measures of the theme (m. 76) provides some retrospection in *piano*. However, the theme soon reappears in full chords, where even some *sforzati* support the *forte* dynamics. When ultimately all cumulates in *fortissimo* octaves played by both hands, the full extent of the catastrophe becomes clear. However, even now no solution is to be found, and all elements return even more violently due to the lower setting of the music, where the high and low registers are being driven even further apart.

A possible way out of this tragedy is found only in the final measures of this movement, the Coda, in which Beethoven turns wondrously toward C major, the "key of liberation"! In this key he wrote the three *Leonora* overtures and the jubilant finale of his opera *Fidelio*, literally a rescue opera. The concept behind his Fifth Symphony, with its motto *per aspera ad astra* (through adversity to the stars), is also based on the transition from C minor to C major. Here in Op. 111 the C major appears in the Coda that links the first movement to the second, opening the portal to internal liberation.

In a subtle and evocative way, Beethoven connects the *pianissimo* ending of the first movement to the *piano* beginning of the second. He places the first C-major chord of the Arietta precisely between the last notes that the right and left hands have just played: they are lying very far apart from each other on the keyboard. The gate opens and the Arietta steps softly forth from its center. With this gesture it is of course necessary to maintain the tension between the two movements; an interruption would completely destroy the expression.

In this way the Arietta begins: not as a *bravura*, but rather as a "small," intimately sung aria, written in the unusual 9/16 meter that, due to the small note values used, makes for a light character.

The designation *Adagio, molto semplice e cantabile* also demands particular attention. From Beethoven's handwriting it appears that what he intended is not *Adagio molto* but *molto semplice*. In the autograph the words *molto semplice e cantabile* are written smaller and more hastily than *Adagio*.

By the use of C major, the light character, and the *molto semplice*, the Arietta is as it were uplifted. In the first variations, the theme gains in vitality due to the introduction of ever-shorter note values. This leads to a joyful outburst in the third variation, which, however, as quickly as it arose, disappears into an inquisitive theme in m. 65 where the subdued chords are continually briefly interrupted by rests like breaths. In a *leggiermente* the theme ascends, an attempt that for a moment has to make way for heartrending chromatic chords (m. 81) but then takes off as in an improvisation. Discharging into the head of the theme and surrounded by trills, the two voices search for a solution: a dialogue, the most extreme intensity of which is rendered by the great distance between the registers (m. 114). In vain. The forces diminish and, in total tragedy, the theme now sounds in E-flat major, which, with the stalling rests, is reminiscent of the second Arioso in the Sonata Op. 110. However, Beethoven's optimism wins. In a forceful modulation, the theme is rediscovered (m. 130). Uninterrupted and of course in C major, thrust on by mobile passages, it ascends. When Beethoven adds a single note, a C-sharp, to the theme as a sigh of surrender (m. 171), a solution is near.[30] Two voices unite in the last measures—inner liberation and peace are ultimately found.

CHAPTER TWO

Beethoven's Pianism

> My pianoforte playing has considerably improved.
>
> —BEETHOVEN IN A LETTER TO CARL AMENDA, JULY 4, 1801; ANDERSON, Vol. I, p. 65

IT HAS ALREADY BEEN mentioned in the previous chapter how, in addition to a pianistic style of writing, in the diversity of Beethoven's notations, part writing (voice leading) can be observed that is reminiscent of a string quartet or that conveys an orchestral or vocal expression. The performing pianist should have a broad palette of colors at his disposal to express all this on the piano. For Beethoven, the sound of the piano in itself seems not to be the central point, but rather has to correspond to the texture within which the interpreter is invited to search for a sound for strings, for winds, or for the *tutti* sound of an orchestra. If the notation is a "vocal" one, as for a choir, all voices must be taken into consideration and the soprano must not be allowed to dominate the scene, as many pianists these days seem to favor. After all, the altos, tenors, and basses are also singing along! Moreover, it seems that for Beethoven a beautiful sound in itself could even distract him from his musical intentions.

When the Viennese builder Andreas Streicher offered him a wonderful instrument and had it delivered to his house, he responded in a letter of November 19, 1796, as follows:

Dear Streicher!

I received the day before yesterday your fortepiano, which is really an excellent instrument. Anyone else would try to keep it for himself; but I—now you must have a good laugh—I should be deceiving you if I didn't tell you that in my opinion it is far too good for me, and why?—Well, because it robs me of the freedom to produce my own tone. But of course this must not deter you from making all your fortepianos in the same way. For no doubt there are few people who cherish such whims as mine.

ANDERSON, Vol. I, p. 24

Beethoven wrote this letter several months after his Sonatas Op. 2 had been published by Artaria, and indeed there are examples in the texture which suggest that he is concerned with something more than an already established piano sound. The first theme of the Largo appassionato from the Sonata Op. 2 No. 2, for instance, can easily be envisaged as music for a string quartet, but even the sound of two trombones accompanied by a cello and the *pizzicati* of a double bass, as the Swiss pianist Edwin Fischer had in mind, could also be possible and could even emphasize the theme's religious and chorale-like character, as Carl Czerny characterized it.[1]

Sonata Op. 2 No. 2, 2nd movement

In the "Pathétique" Sonata, Op. 13, composed some years later, not only is the first movement exceptionally orchestral in design, but, additionally, the central part of the second movement could easily be set in the context of an oboe and a bassoon decorated by two clarinets, as the Austrian pianist Jörg Demus imagined.[2]

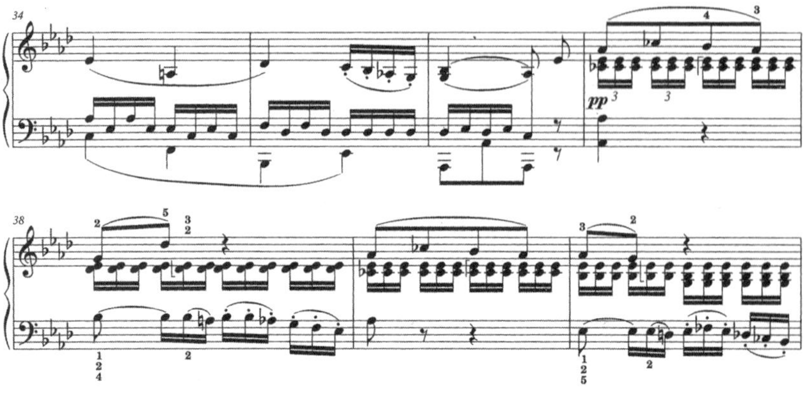

Sonata Op. 13, 2nd movement

Wind instruments and "drum rolls" can of course be heard in the Marcia funebre of the Sonata in A-flat major, Op. 26. Fifteen years later, at the request of Friedrich Dunckler, the secretary to King Friedrich Wilhelm III of Prussia, who needed music for a stage tragedy, Beethoven arranged this movement for a relatively limited orchestra in a setting without trumpets and timpani. He did, however, then transpose the music to B minor, the "black key" as Beethoven called it, which emphasizes that the character of a particular key had by then gained even more significance for him.

Sonata Op. 26, 3rd movement

Quasi-string-quartet settings can be found in many of Beethoven's sonatas. The English pianist Denis Matthews, for instance, remarked with reference to the first movement of the Sonata Op. 2 No. 3 that the opening could just as well have been written for string quartet, where in m. 8 the cello takes the lead.[3]

Sonata Op. 2 No. 3, 1st movement

The string-quartet version of Op. 14 No. 1 has been mentioned earlier, and how beautifully this arises in m. 62 of the second movement, Allegretto, where the *crescendo* on one single note cannot be realized on the piano.[4]

Sonata Op. 14 No. 1, 2nd movement

A similarly impossible notation occurs in m. 39 of the slow movement of the Sonata in E-flat major, Op. 7, where, from the dynamic indication *piano* on the first beat, the *crescendo* leads to the *sf* for both octaves on the last beat of the measure.

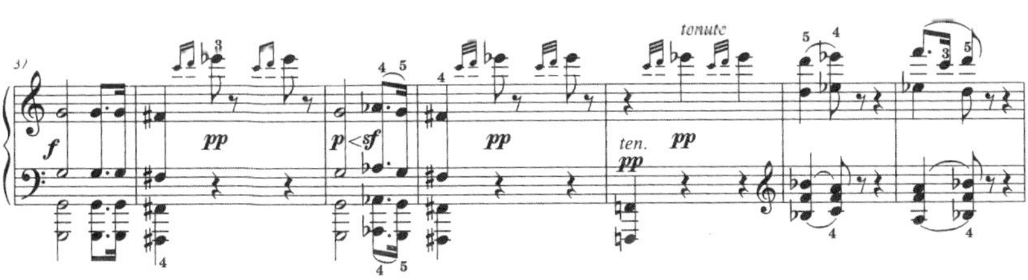

Sonata Op. 7, 2nd movement

Such power of imagination we also notice in mm. 193–195 from the first movement of Op. 81a, "Les Adieux."

Sonata Op. 81a, 1st movement

Alongside these instrumental forms of expression, there are also many "vocal" notations to be found in Beethoven's sonatas, not only in rhetorically designed themes such as in the recitatives in Op. 31 No. 2 and Op. 110, but for example also in the effusive expression of themes with rhetorical rests, such as the first theme of the Adagio of Op. 2 No. 3 and the first theme in the Largo con gran espressione from his Sonata Op. 7.

There are also "real" arias to be found in a number of sonatas, embellished with coloraturas and lengthily phrased themes above a simple accompaniment, for example in the slow movements of the Sonata in B-flat major, Op. 22, and the Sonata in G major, Op. 31 No. 1, or the duet in the Andante of the Sonata Op. 79. Naturally, the Ariosos from Op. 110 are also conceived vocally—as the title "Arioso" already reveals. Furthermore, the vocal approach is eminently present in the fugues of Op. 110, as discussed in Chapter 1, although a fugue can also be more instrumental in design, as the fugue in Op. 106, even though in mm. 250–279, in a flourishing D major, one can also think of a vocal intermezzo. In addition to this, mm. 89–104 from the Prestissimo of Sonata Op. 109 sound like a chorale, and the second theme in the first movement of the "Waldstein" Sonata can also be easily envisaged in the same way.

Beethoven's approach to piano sound did not, of course, go unnoticed by contemporaries such as Friedrich Wieck, Schumann's future father-in-law, who heard him improvising in July 1823:

> Then he improvised for me during an hour, after he had mounted his ear-trumpet and placed it on the resonance-plate

> on which already stood the pretty well battered, large grand piano, with its very powerful, rough tone, which had been presented to him by the city of London. He played in a flowing, genial manner, for the most part orchestrally, and was still quite adept in the passing over the right and left hands (a few times he missed the mark), weaving in the clearest and most charming melodies, which seemed to stream to him unsought, most of the time keeping his eyes turned upward, and with close-gathered fingers.
>
> SONNECK (ED.), p. 208

Naturally, it did not escape this excellent piano pedagogue that Beethoven was playing with "dichten Fingern," a closed hand whereby the fingers, through their clenching, are held close to each other, a position that was also noticed by Gerhard von Breuning, the son of Beethoven's friend Stephan von Breuning. Gerhard, who visited the composer frequently in his last years, wrote:

> He held his fingers very curved, so much so that they were completely hidden by the hand, what is called the old position, in brief, as contrasted to the present way, in which the fingers are characteristically more extended.[5]
>
> VON BREUNING, p. 78

This also comes to the fore in his lessons with his pupil Countess Therese von Brunsvik:

> He came regularly, but instead of an hour frequently stayed from twelve to four or five o'clock, and never grew weary of holding down and bending my fingers, which I had been taught to lift high and hold straight.
>
> THAYER/FORBES, Vol. I, p. 235

This hand posture was also propagated by Andreas Streicher, not only an excellent pianist, composer, and piano teacher, but also one of Beethoven's pupils. Together with his wife, Nannette Streicher-Stein, he owned one of Vienna's foremost piano-manufacturing workshops.[6] Streicher wrote in his book, published in 1801:

> *The arm* must support the hand; *the hand*, its fingers. The more restful the arm and hand the surer the motion of the fingers, the greater the dexterity, and the more beautiful the tone.
>
> The *fingers* must be curved when playing. That is to say: one needs to retract them so far until they form one line with the naturally extended thumb.
>
> *The finger must touch the key only with its foremost, fleshy part, but never with the nail.*
>
> STREICHER, p. 7

Finally, such a compact hand posture can be gathered from an exercise that Beethoven himself notated with the comment "Zur Übung der Faust" (For practicing the fist).

CRAMER (II), p. xii

Beethoven's hands. Drawing by August von Kloeber (1818).
H. C. Bodmer Collection, Beethoven-Haus, Bonn.

Also in an ascending sequence of notes to be played absolutely legato, Beethoven demands that "*the hand should remain as closed as possible.*"

CRAMER (II), p. xii

For an exercise in which each note should be *fortissimo*, the choice to use the third finger only is logical, it being the strongest finger in the middle of the hand. A typical pianistic solution to achieve a full, firm sound can also be seen in his advice for the next exercise: play the jumping notes in the bass with the third and fourth fingers simultaneously.

CRAMER (II), p. xii

That such a firm, compact approach is also needed for playing full chords is clear. This is a way of writing that occurs frequently in Beethoven's sonatas. Examples are the opening chords of the Sonata in C minor, Op. 10 No. 1; Op. 13; the theme of the last movement of Op. 2 No. 1; the middle section of the last movement of the Sonata in A major, Op. 2 No. 2; and the first movement of the "Appassionata," Op. 57.

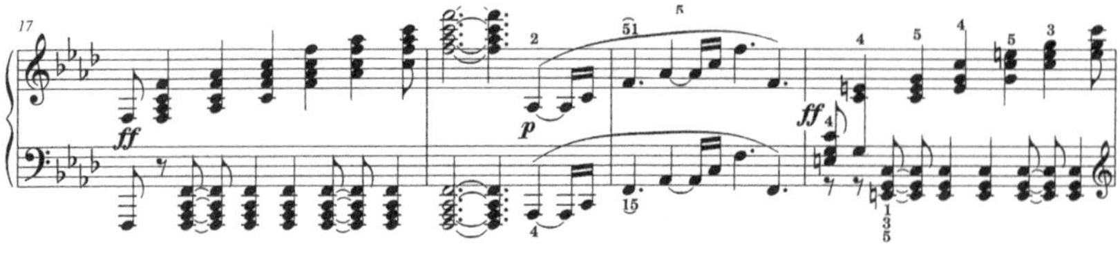

Sonata Op. 57, 1st movement

This applies not just to playing chords; for playing octaves, too, a firm hand is a condition *sine qua non*. Although examples of octave playing are to be found in Haydn's sonatas, as in the first movement of the Sonata in D major, Hob. XVI/51, it was Beethoven who developed the full expressiveness of this in his piano works, for which we have to think only of the *staccato* octave passages of his Fifth Piano Concerto.

Piano Concerto Op. 73, 1st movement

Striking examples are also to be found in his sonatas, as was already discussed in Chapter 1 in relation to the middle section of the In tempo d'un Menuetto from the Sonata Op. 54. A fine example, the writing style of which anticipates that of Schubert, can also be seen in the Development of the first movement of Op. 14 No. 1, where the melody must be played *legato* in octaves for no fewer than fifteen measures. Other examples can be seen in the polyphonic structure of mm. 147–154 from the first movement of the Sonata Op. 2 No. 3, or in a highly virtuosic combination with fast triplets in the last movement of the "Waldstein," Op. 53.

Sonata Op. 53, 3rd movement

Another pianistic effect that Beethoven applied is the octave *glissando.* This was indeed not new, for the double *glissando* had been encountered earlier on, for instance in the last variation of Mozart's "Lison dormait," K. 264, with shifting sixths, but the way in which Beethoven used this effect in the first movement of the First Piano Concerto upon the return to the Recapitulation is indeed most compelling. That he left no room for any misunderstanding about a possible intention to divide the octave passage over two hands is apparent from the added low bass.

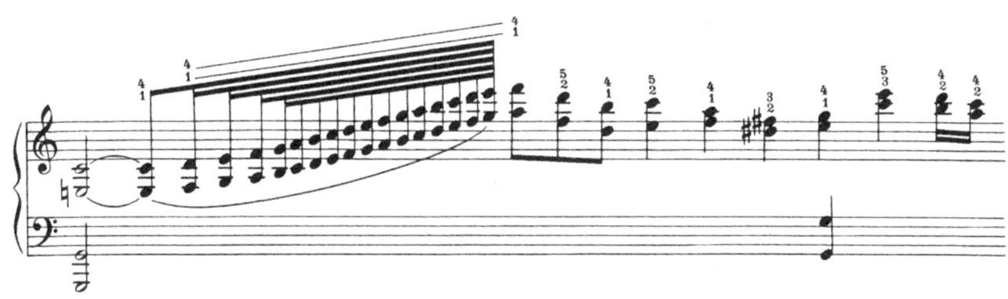

Mozart, Variations K. 264

Piano Concerto Op. 15, 1st movement

In the Coda of the last movement of the "Waldstein" Sonata, Beethoven elevates this concept to an artistically higher plane. Of course, the effect is no less pianistic, but this specific *pianissimo* octave *glissando* on the 6/4 chord indeed also results in a distinct expression of wondrous elation.

Sonata Op. 53, 3rd movement

Of course, Wieck also spoke about the crossing of the hands, perhaps with some perverse pleasure, for Beethoven missed quite a few of these. Even though this is not a new technique—it can be found in the sonatas of Domenico Scarlatti, in the Gigue of Bach's First Partita, BWV 825, in the first movement of Mozart's Sonata in D major, K. 311, and in the fourth variation from the first movement of the Sonata in A major, K. 331—Beethoven applied it on a much larger scale, as in the tarantella-like finale of Op. 31 No. 3.

Sonata Op. 31 No. 3, 4th movement

Or in the second theme of the first movement of the "Pathétique," where the high and low "string instruments" spin around the "wind instruments."

Sonata Op. 13, 1st movement

That this technique was not something simply for showing off is apparent from the fact that Beethoven also applied it in slow movements, such as the expressive Adagio of his Sonata Op. 2 No. 3, where the treble and bass conduct a dialogue in various colors with the middle voice.

Sonata Op. 2 No. 3, 2nd movement

Beethoven's brilliant performance of fast scales, double-note trills, and leaps must also have been remarkable. In any event, Carl Czerny mentions it when he compares the playing of Beethoven with that of Hummel:

> No one matched him in the speed of his scales, double trills, leaps, etc. (not even Hummel).
>
> CZERNY (II), p. 15

We can already find examples of this in a number of early sonatas.

Sonata Op. 2 No. 2, 1st movement: fast scales

Sonata Op. 7, 1st movement: leaps

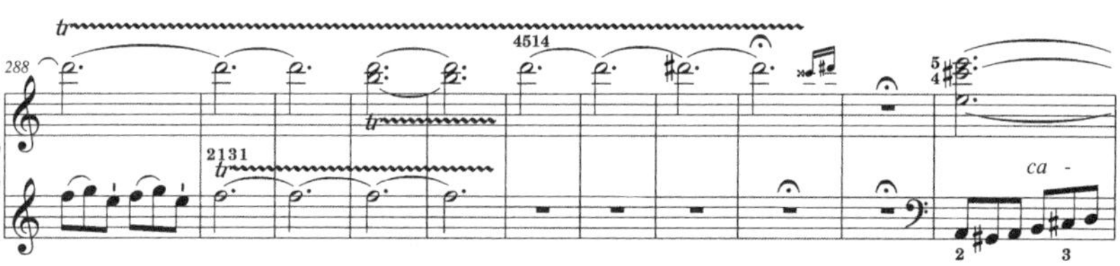

Sonata Op. 2 No. 3, 4th movement: double-note trills

An exceptional innovation in piano technique was also to play the melody and trills simultaneously with one hand. From a letter Beethoven wrote to his pupil Eleonore von Breuning, dated November 2, 1793, it is apparent that he had applied this idea during his improvising and was now worried that the pianists in his audience would steal the idea. It was better to beat them at their own game and to use this technique immediately in a composition so that his enemies could be suitably impressed.

When in 1793 he wrote his variations for violin and piano on Leporello's aria "Se vuol ballare" from Mozart's opera *Don Giovanni* (WoO 40), he was twenty-three years old and in fierce competition with a good 300 other pianists who then presented themselves in Vienna. In Beethoven's letter to Eleonore, we read:

> The v[ariations] will be rather difficult to play, and particularly the trills in the coda. But this must not intimidate and discourage you. For the composition is so arranged that you need only play the trill and can leave out the other notes, since these appear in the violin part as well. I should never have written down this kind of piece, had I not already noticed fairly often how some people in Vienna after hearing me extemporize of an evening would note down on the following day several peculiarities of my style and palm them off with pride as their own. Well, as I foresaw that their pieces would soon be published, I resolved to forestall those people. But there was yet another reason, namely, my desire to embarrass those Viennese pianists, some of whom are my sworn enemies. I wanted to revenge myself on them in this way, because I knew beforehand that my variations would here and there be put before the said gentlemen and that they would cut a sorry figure with them.
>
> ANDERSON, Vol. I, pp. 14–15

Variations WoO 40

It appears that this technique had a special significance for him.[7] Whereas it was then to demonstrate his virtuosity, in his later works it is the expression of an inner motivation such as in the last movement of the "Waldstein" Sonata, the first and last movements of the "Hammerklavier," the last movement of Op. 109, and the Arietta of his very last piano sonata, Op. 111. Thus, an idea from his youth continued to play a significant role throughout the rest of his life.

Sonata Op. 111, 2nd movement

For a thorough understanding of Beethoven's pianism, his handling of passage playing is also of great importance. It appears that he found it important to introduce clear patterns into this, so that knowledge of prosody must be applied. This knowledge, which played a significant role in the Baroque, was instilled into him at a young age by his teacher Christian Gottlob Neefe, a real Bach devotee who even in those days possessed an autograph copy of Bach's *Well-Tempered Clavier.*[8]

There are, for example, instances known from as early as Beethoven's time in Bonn of his being intensively involved with prosody, and that this always was a leading objective during his life. Good examples can be found in vocal music, where the expression of the text had to fit the music correctly in accordance with the metrical laws and signs, accentuation, and rhythm of prosody.

This is how he marked in a sketchbook the first stanzas of his song "Der Gesang der Nachtigall":[9]

Tūrtĕltāubĕ dŭ klāgĕst sŏ lāut ŭnd rāubĕst dĕm unw.
Wēißt dŭ wās dĭe Nāchtĭgăll sīngt? unw.

Turtle dove you wail so loud and steal the etc.
Do you know what the nightingale is singing? etc.

Another example, where he was keen to provide similarly metrical feet for the verses, is the "Opferlied," Op. 121b, a composition on a text by Friedrich von Matthisson that occupied him for many years. Three different versions were published over the years, the last one for voice and orchestra in 1825 by Schott in Mainz.

Knowledge of poetic feet, as shown by indications of long and short syllables and verse meter, can also be seen in annotations that were added in a Haslinger edition of the eighty-four Etudes of Johann Baptist Cramer, an edition that was almost certainly published in 1826,[10] shortly before Beethoven's death.

This edition, which came from the estate of Anton Schindler and is now in the collection of the Deutsche Staatsbibliothek in Berlin, was discovered by the British scholar J. S. Shedlock and published for the first time in 1893 by Augener in London.

Since then, it has been a regularly recurring subject of discussion.[11] The question is: are the additional comments with Beethoven's name for twenty-one etudes in this edition—all written in Schindler's hand—indeed referring to Beethoven, or are they another forgery by Schindler?

As mentioned earlier, Schindler was keen to show off his connection with Beethoven, and therefore some doubt is not out of place, but to pass these annotations off as a forgery on these grounds seems a little far-fetched. Shedlock spoke in 1893 about the "boldness and originality" of the annotations, a view that was repeated by Hans Kann, the editor of the edition published by Universal in 1974. Kann pointed in his preface to the "originality and directness of the text" for the twenty-one etudes identified by Beethoven's name, in comparison with the "stereotypical repetitions" for many other etudes where Schindler wrote his own comments, signed "A.S."[12]

It is interesting, as can be seen in the following examples from these annotations, that besides prosody, many other topics are mentioned: a polyphonic approach in general, and more specifically pseudopolyphony in passagework; prolonged touch; different rhythmic groupings; and of course some suggestions about piano technique. All of these are regular points of attention in a piano lesson, and many belong to the regular performance practice of the time. (See Chapter 4 and the examples by Leopold Mozart in this chapter below.)

We know from the painter August Karl Friedrich von Kloeber, who in August 1818 was an eyewitness, that Beethoven gave a piano lesson to his nephew Karl, who was at the time twelve years old.[13]

For such lessons, Cramer's etudes would be ideal material. They were not as difficult as the recently published etudes from the *Gradus ad Parnassum* by Clementi,[14] and, contrary to Czerny's style, they were much more expressive. Above all, Beethoven admired Cramer not only as a fine pianist, but specifically for his legato touch, something for which he had himself been praised since his youth. The choice for him to use Cramer's etudes would not have been a difficult one.[15]

Additionally, it would be very natural for Schindler, who had known Beethoven from 1814 on and had been his amanuensis since 1822, to be interested if Beethoven had made remarks, because during his study in law he had also begun with piano lessons. Perhaps he collected remarks Beethoven made, or got information from Karl, or recalled it years later, or even had access to another source as yet unknown to us, and put all he knew into the Haslinger edition.

In short, the question of whether these annotations are a complete forgery or not will be unsolved until new information comes to light. For now, it is interesting to become acquainted with them, beginning with a remark about prosody for the Etude in E-flat major (Cramer No. 15), where all notes that bear the melody are explained from the prosodic point of view:[16]

From the thirteenth to the sixteenth measure the melody lies in the highest notes; the accentuation here resembles iambic scansion. [. . .]

BEETHOVEN

Cramer, Etude No. 15

From m. 21 onward we see that the usual marks are notated.

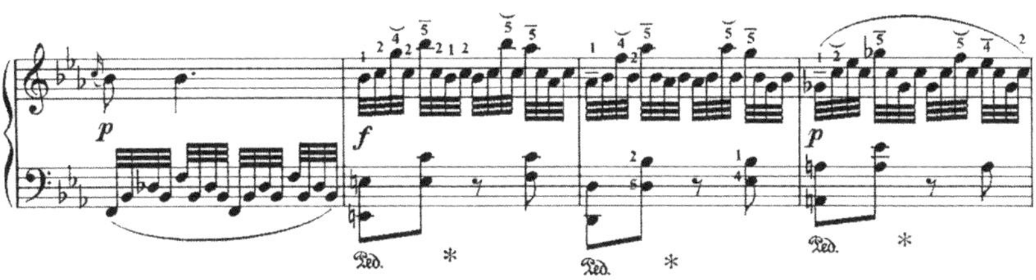

Cramer, Etude No. 15

In the Etude in C minor (Cramer No. 4), it is noticeable that these marks are not applied consistently, but are replaced by ∨ and ∧, whereby mention is also made of the *Längen* and *Kürtzen* and the possibility of some agogics.

Here, the longs and shorts must be attended to throughout, i.e. the 1st note long (–), the 2nd short (◡), the 3rd in its turn also long, and the 4th short again: the same as in scansion of trochaic measure. At first, the 1st, and also 3rd note, is to be intentionally lengthened so that the long may be perceptibly distinguished from short, but without

> prolonging the 1st and 3rd notes as if they were dotted. The tempo should only be increased later on, and then the sharp edges will easily be smoothened down. The intelligence of the pupil becoming gradually more formed will help, and proper binding will be obtained. The hands to be somewhat spread out.
>
> BEETHOVEN

Cramer, Etude No. 4

In the Etude in G major (Cramer No. 21), both kinds of mark are used alongside each other.

> Attention must be paid to the accent of the fifth note of each group which mostly appears as a minor second. Trochaic measure forms the basis of each group: the first note accented and long, but less so the fifth.
>
> BEETHOVEN[17]

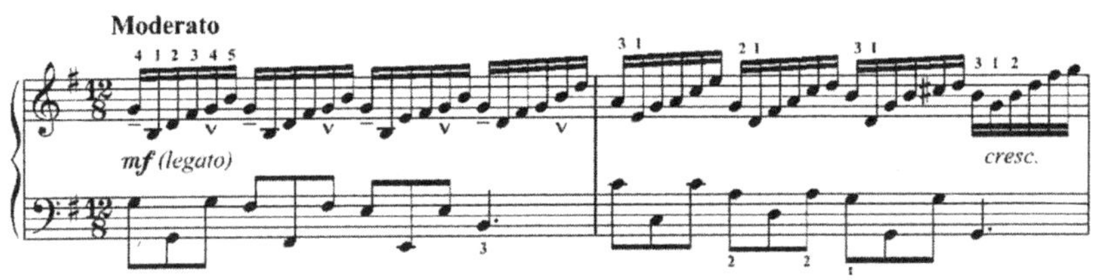

Cramer, Etude No. 21

In the Etude in B-flat major (Cramer No. 7) it is noticeable that this can also be used in combination with another playing custom from that era, the so-called prolonged touch, also known as super-*legato* or finger pedal (see Chapter 4). Along with this, attention is still paid to the balance between the right and the left hand.

> Here the 1st and 3rd notes of each group carry the melody (in trochaic measure). The finger continues to dwell for the space of two eighths, on the long syllable (1st note). The tenor seconds the soprano; therefore, alto and bass should not be given out with equal strength.
>
> BEETHOVEN

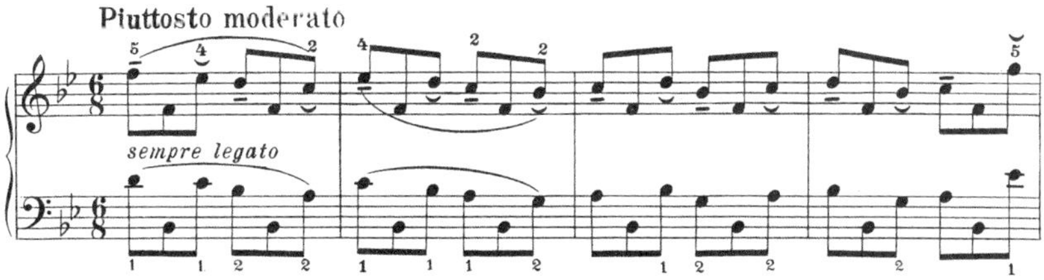

Cramer, Etude No. 7

Besides introducing a specific design into passages in this way, attention is also paid in the notes to the "rhythmical accent." This appears to be associated mostly with the pulsing that is connected to the given meter, but not always. It is sometimes more, sometimes less frequently applied than the chosen meter would imply, and therefore seems to arise more from musical practice than from theoretical considerations.

In the Etude in C major (Cramer No. 1) it appears that the light accentuation of the first sixteenth note of each beat unit characterizes the melodic line. It also appears that the rhythmic accent does not differentiate between heavy and light parts of a measure. Each change in the harmony is supported.

> The rhythmical accent is the same on all beats. In this way, it appears in scale-like progressions.
>
> BEETHOVEN

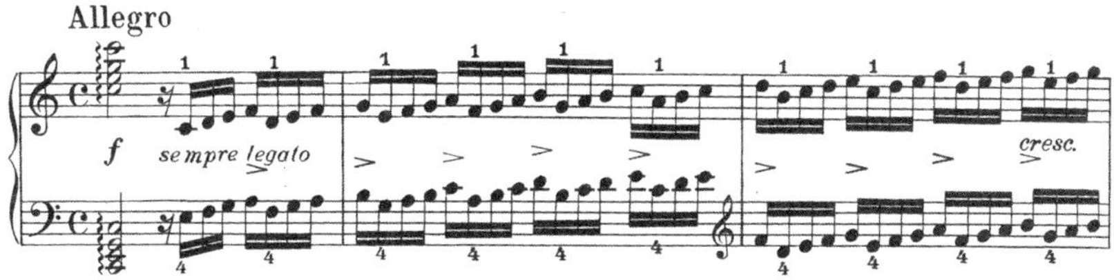

Cramer, Etude No. 1

The same principle is mentioned by Leopold Mozart in his *Violinschule*, published in 1756.

> Consecutive and continuous rapid notes are subject to many variations. I will here set down a single passage which from the first can be played quite smoothly and easily, and in which each note may be performed with its own separate stroke. Great pain must be taken with their exact equality, and the first note of each quarter must be marked with a vigor which inspires the whole performance. For example:

L. MOZART, p. 114

In the case of a *legato* style of playing, too, Leopold Mozart wanted the accentuations to be maintained.

> In a very quick tempo, and in order to make a new exercise and tenth variation, one can even play a whole measure in one stroke. But here also, as in the previous style, the first notes of each quarter must be marked by an emphasis. For example:

L. MOZART, p. 117

It can be seen in the Etude in E minor (Cramer No. 2) that the alternation between ascent and descent in the course of the melody is so very important that four accentuations are given in each measure, which indicate the pivots of the melodic line, despite the fact that the harmonies do not change. The prolonged touch is also applied here.

Again the rhythmical accent must be uniformly placed on the first note of each triplet. In the four introductory measures the thumb adheres firmly to the fundamental note, so that the broken third, and in a similar manner all broken chords, may be made clear. In order to obtain binding, the triple figure in the left hand must be dealt with in the same way.

BEETHOVEN

Cramer, Etude No. 2

In the Etude in A major (Cramer No. 13) it is apparent that the rhythmical accent is not automatically applied to each beat unit. In the first measure, all form of accentuation is missing, probably because the harmony that forms its basis does not change and neither does the direction of the melodic line. The tone repetition in the middle of the measure already provides for some accentuation of its own accord. In m. 2 the situation changes, however. Now each beat unit has another harmony, while furthermore at every other note there is a change in the direction in which the sixteenth notes move.

The study of longs and shorts in passages is here the aim. The rhythmical accent occurs on almost all beats of the measure, for example from the 2nd to the 5th measure inclusive—from the 7th to the 11th measure inclusive. Longs and shorts, the first of which I mark V, placing it under the note, which has to be accented. By paying attention to the longs and shorts the melodic movement stands out in the passages; without so doing, every passage loses its meaning.

BEETHOVEN

Cramer, Etude No. 13, mm. 1–4

Cramer, Etude No. 13, mm. 7–11

From the comment accompanying the Etude in A minor (Cramer No. 6), it appears that the rhythmical accent initially stresses the first note of each triplet, but then must clarify the *rhythmische Gliederungen* (rhythmical structures) that assume a totally different pattern of movement, whereby groups of two or four sixteenth notes are formed, despite everything being notated in groups of three notes. From this it appears that a *falsche rhythmische Fortschreitung in der Melodie* (false rhythmical progression in the melody) is regarded as so disturbing that the demands of meter must be ignored. Such an arrangement is, for example, clear from m. 15 onward.

> The rhythmical accent on the 1st note of each triplet. In addition, here the rhythmical articulations, now long, now short, must be well attended to, for without this a false rhythmical progression would become perceptible in the melody. [. . .]
>
> BEETHOVEN

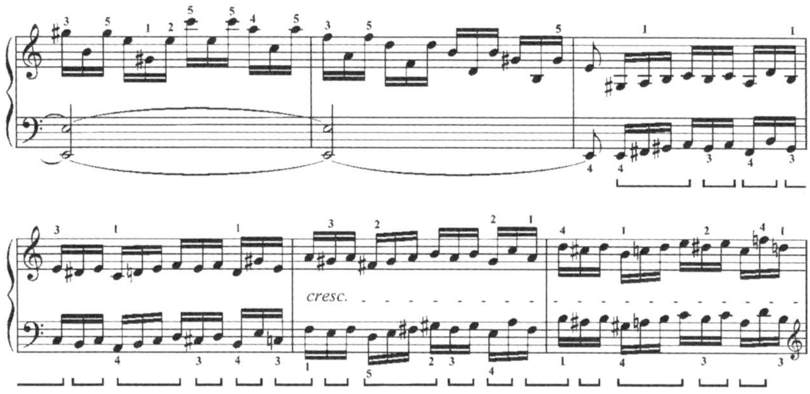

Cramer, Etude No. 6

Beethoven also adheres to this principle in the Etude in E minor (Cramer No. 2) by continually stressing the third and highest note of the melody in the triplet passage.

Cramer, Etude No. 2

Beethoven's piano sonatas offer many possibilities for applying these instructions. In the last movement of the Sonata Op. 26, for instance, where a distinct outline can easily be introduced in the sixteenth-note passages by using the *Längen* and *Kürzen*.

Sonata Op. 26, 4th movement

Or, in the same way, from m. 23 onward in the first movement of the "Waldstein."

Sonata Op. 53, 1st movement

In the first movement, Allegro con brio, of his Sonata Op. 111, Beethoven emphasizes the rhythmical accent by means of *sforzati*, which makes it even clearer that this has to do with a special emphasis and that it is not his intention to let the accentuation flow from the highest note in each sixteenth-note group.

Sonata Op. 111, 1st movement

Examples of passages with triplets are to be found in the last movement of his Op. 2 No. 1, in the Trio in the third movement of his Sonata Op. 2 No. 3, and in the Minore in the third movement of his Sonata Op. 7, where, as in Cramer's Etudes Nos. 2 and 7, prolonged touch can be used. For a shift in the meter, too, such as in Cramer's Etude No. 6, parallels are to be found—for example, in mm. 122–133 of the first movement of the "Waldstein" Sonata or mm. 32–37 of the first movement of the "Moonlight" Sonata, a passage that also returns toward the end. Here, too, the triplet movement is divided into groups of two.

Sonata Op. 27 No. 2, first movement

When the new virtuoso style appeared in Beethoven's time in works of, for example, Czerny and Hummel, where slick, fast, and more decorative passages were becoming more fashionable, he complained about Czerny's playing: "Czerny never sustains his notes and articulates badly" (Schindler [II] p. 416). His aversion to the new virtuosity is expressed even more vehemently in a conversation with the Prague pianist and composer Václav Jan Tomášek (Wenzel Johann Tomaschek) which he noted verbatim on November 24, 1814:

> T: Were you at [Meyerbeer]'s opera?
> B: No; it is said to have turned out very badly. [. . .]
> T: I was at the opera; it began with hallelujah and ended with requiem.
> B: Ha, ha, ha, ha, ha! It's the same with his playing. I am often asked if I have heard him—I say no; but from the opinion of my acquaintances who are capable of judging such things I

could tell that he has agility indeed, but otherwise is a very superficial person. [. . .]

T: I heard that before he went away he played at Herr ———'s and pleased much less.

B: Ha, ha, ha, ha, ha! What did I tell you?—I understand that. Let him settle down here for half a year and then let us hear what will be said of his playing. All this signifies nothing. It has always been known that the greatest pianoforte players were also the greatest composers; but how did they play? Not like the pianists of to-day, who prance up and down the keyboard with passages which they have practiced—*putsch, putsch, putsch;*—what does that mean? Nothing! When true pianoforte virtuosi played it was always something homogeneous, an entity; if written down it would appear as a well-thought-out work. That is pianoforte playing; the other thing is nothing!

THAYER/FORBES, Vol. I, pp. 598–599

Running to and fro was nothing for Beethoven, as is also to be observed from his sometimes unusual fingering, which made fast playing impossible. Take, for example, his fingering in the triplet passage in mm. 88–89 of the first movement of the Sonata in A major, Op. 2 No. 2. Carl Czerny also noticed that it is easier to spread this passage over two hands.

Sonata Op. 2 No. 2, 1st movement, Artaria edition

Spirited and vivacious, energetic and resolute, and the more tranquil passages with much feeling. An octave-passage (bar 84 &c) is so difficult, that, for small hands, we advise the following mode of performance:

Sonata Op. 2 No. 2, 1st movement, Czerny (II), p. 36

That musical expression was paramount for Beethoven is also to be seen from his reaction to a request from the English publisher Thomas Boosey to contribute to a proposed collection of virtuoso piano pieces (*Allegri di bravura*).[18] When his pupil Ferdinand Ries presented this request to him in a letter dated July 16, 1823, he rejected the idea completely.

> As for the Allegri di Bravura I must have a look at yours.—To be candid, I must confess that I am not partial to this type of composition, for it only encourages mechanical playing to an undue extent; I am referring, of course, to the Allegri I have come across.
>
> ANDERSON, Vol. III, p. 1064

Beethoven had other priorities. In a letter he addressed in the summer of 1817 to Marie Pachler-Koschak, a distinguished pianist who also composed, he wrote:

> Surely you will play for me the sonatas in F major [Op. 54?] and C minor [Op. 13], won't you? I have not yet found anyone who performs my compositions as well as you do; and I am not excluding the great pianists, who often have merely mechanical ability or affectation.
>
> ANDERSON, Vol. II, p. 708

Indeed, his own ideas even went so far that he intended to write a piano method himself. In a letter Gerhard von Breuning wrote to Franz Wegeler we read:

> I [Gerhard] was using Pleyel's pianoforte studies; but with this, as with all the others, he [Beethoven] was not satisfied. He said to me once when I was sitting at his bedside: "I felt like writing a set of pianoforte exercises myself once, but never found the time for it; I would have written something quite unconventional though."
>
> WEGELER/RIES, p. 158

Beethoven's musical preferences lay elsewhere, as Ferdinand Ries discovered during a piano lesson:

> I received nearly two full hours of instruction that day. If I made a mistake somewhere in a passage, or struck wrong notes, or missed intervals—which he often wanted strongly emphasized—he rarely said anything. However, if I lacked expression in crescendos, etc. or in the character of a piece, he became angry because, he maintained, the first was accident, while the latter resulted from inadequate knowledge, feeling, or attention. The first happened quite frequently to him, too, even when he played in public.
>
> WEGELER/RIES, p. 83

However, times had changed and that pure virtuosity was competing for center stage was also noticed by Wilhelm Christian Müller, a writer and teacher who, with his daughter, a pianist, visited Vienna in October 1820 and heard various pianists play, including Beethoven's favorite pianist, Dorothea von Ertmann:

> The Baroness Erdmann [sic], who studied with Beethoven, seemed to surpass all with regard to performance. Others reel off with sorcerous speed the most daunting multitudes of notes; but they remain oblivious to the spirit, even the character of the composition; they act neither on the emotions nor on the imagination.
>
> KOPITZ/CADENBACH, Vol. II, p. 600

Who cannot help thinking that it could seem as if Müller's words were spoken just recently and have still not lost any of their significance?

CHAPTER THREE

The Piano in Beethoven's Time

> The whole tribe of pianoforte manufacturers have been swarming around me in their anxiety to serve me—and all for nothing. Each of them wants to make me a pianoforte exactly as I should like it.
>
> —BEETHOVEN IN A LETTER TO NIKOLAUS ZMESKALL, NOVEMBER 1802; ANDERSON, Vol. I, p. 82

"THIS YOUTHFUL GENIUS IS deserving of help to enable him to travel," wrote Beethoven's teacher Christian Gottlob Neefe on March 2, 1783, in Cramer's *Magazin der Musik*, and now that, four years later, Beethoven had reached the age of sixteen, the time had come. Of course, the journey would be to Vienna, the center of music and the city where Mozart was living, whom he was eager to visit. For such an expensive journey he not only drew on his savings, accrued with difficulty from his position as second organist alongside Neefe at the court of Elector Maximillian Franz, but probably on his musical resources as well.[1] It is not unimaginable that his song "Wenn jemand eine Reise tut" (If someone goes on a trip), composed in 1786, was intended as a hint for several maecenases in Bonn to support him in this proposed plan.[2]

Be that as it may, at the end of 1786, in the company of a good friend of the family, Johann Ignaz Willmann,[3] he boarded the stagecoach and reached Vienna several weeks later.

His proposed visit to Mozart had, however, to be postponed, for the composer was still in Prague, where his opera *Le Nozze di Figaro* had been received with unprecedented approval.

Mozart arrived in Vienna on February 12, 1787, and, inspired by this triumph and in the possession of a new libretto by Lorenzo Da Ponte, was already busy with his next opera, *Don Giovanni*. Of course, he could spare some time to hear a talented youngster from Bonn who had traveled over 550 miles, but he was not really in the right mood for giving lessons. Even so, it appears that, after Beethoven had improvised on a theme given by him, he is held to have exclaimed:

> Keep your eyes on him; some day he will give the world something to talk about.
>
> SONNECK (ED.), p. 11

Beethoven's sojourn in the capital was, however, quite short. After only a few months he must have packed his bags again for his journey back home, for on April 26 he appeared in Augsburg, where he took up lodgings in the "Weißen Lamm."[4]

This stay also gave him the opportunity to arrange another interesting meeting. Johann Andreas Stein, the famous fortepiano manufacturer, had his workshop in the city. Beethoven knew his instruments very well, because several of them were used at the court in Bonn,[5] but now he could ask the man in person if he might try his most recent instruments. Furthermore, something even more personal could be a reason for visiting the almost-sixty-year-old Stein: perhaps Mozart had asked him to fulfill a special wish, giving the fortepiano maker his best regards.

Mozart was a great admirer of Stein's instruments. After he had visited the manufacturer in 1777, he wrote on October 17 to his father:

> This time I shall begin at once with Stein's pianofortes. Before I had seen any of his make, Spath's claviers had always been my favorites. But now I much prefer Stein's, for they damp ever so much better than the Regensburg instruments. When I strike hard, I can keep my finger on the note or raise

> it, but the sound ceases the moment I have produced it. In whatever way I touch the keys, the tone is always even. It never jars, it is never stronger or weaker or entirely absent; in a word, it is always even. It is true that he does not sell a pianoforte of this kind for less than three hundred gulden, but the trouble and the labor which Stein puts into the making of it cannot be paid for. His instruments have this special advantage over others that they are made with escape action. Only one maker in a hundred bothers about this. But without an escapement it is impossible to avoid jangling and vibration after the note is struck. When you touch the keys, the hammers fall back again the moment after they have struck the strings, whether you hold down the keys or release them.
>
> ANDERSON, Vol. I, p. 328

Mozart's comparison of Stein's instruments with those of Franz Jakob Spath favors those of Stein.[6] Fourteen years later it appears that Beethoven held the same opinion, judging from an article by Carl Ludwig Junker in the *Musikalische Korrepondenz der teutschen Filharmonischen Gesellschaft* of November 30, 1791:

> Although he [Beethoven] did not perform in public, perhaps because the instrument did not meet his wishes; it was a Spath grand piano, and he is accustomed in Bonn to only playing on one by Stein.
>
> KOPITZ/CADENBACH, Vol. I, p. 498

Stein, who had begun as an organ builder's mate with Johann Andreas Silbermann in Strasbourg, had opened his own workshop in Augsburg in 1750 at the age of twenty-two, after having spent the previous year learning the trade even further with Spath in Regensburg. Originally specializing in organ building, his interest in the fortepiano steadily increased.

This instrument had taken Europe by storm after the Italian Bartolomeo Cristofori in, or just before, the year 1700 had developed a hammer mechanism and had created his first "gravicembalo col piano e forte." On this it was possible to vary the dynamic from "piano" to "forte" just by varying the touch. The instrument was modeled on the traditional Italian harpsichords from the seventeenth century, whereby the loose instrument itself was always installed in a case. This seems to have been so with Cristofori's early instruments, too, but in reality the inner and outer cases form one solid unit.

It goes without saying that with such a new instrument the builders were constantly experimenting to improve the functioning of all the various components. Stein, for instance, wanted very precise damping, in which, it appears from Mozart's letter, he was more successful than Spath. Mozart was especially pleased with the escapement mechanism (*Auslösung*), which made it possible for the hammer to return immediately to its original position, to be ready to strike again. The escapement, in Stein's case comprising a separate, movable catch (the so-called *Prellzungen* action), was not present in the instruments of Spath, who was still using an overhead rail or ledge.

Another component to which much attention was paid was the soundboard. The spruce wood used had to come from trees growing at above 3,000 feet (about 900 meters) because, due to the low temperatures in those regions, the growth is slow enough for the rings to be formed close to each other. For the soundboard must be sturdy but also elastic enough to amplify the vibrations of the strings. Stein paid extra attention to this. Mozart continues in the letter to his father:

> He [Stein] often says: "If I were not myself such a passionate lover of music and had not myself some slight skill on the clavier, I should certainly long ago have lost patience with my work. But I do like an instrument which never lets the player down and which is durable." And his claviers certainly do last. He guarantees that the sounding-board will neither break nor split. When he has finished making one for a clavier, he places it in the open air, exposing it to rain, snow, the heat of the sun and all the devils in order that it may crack. Then he inserts wedges and glues them in to make the instrument very strong and firm. He is delighted when

> it cracks, for he can then be sure that nothing more can happen to it. Indeed he often cuts into it himself and then glues it together again and strengthens it in this way. He has finished making three pianofortes of this kind. Today I played on one again.
>
> ANDERSON, Vol. I, pp. 328–329

Johann Peter Milchmeyer remarked that the quality of the soundboard contributes significantly to that of the sound. In his method *Die wahre Art das Pianoforte zu spielen* of 1797, he writes:

> Above all, the player who examines a pianoforte must listen closely whether the tones are clear and cantabile and the echo is of long duration when he strikes and holds a chord with the topmost notes, for from this one may make an inference about the quality of the soundboard, and furthermore whether these notes resemble a beautiful female voice and take on something of the tone of a clarinet.
>
> MILCHMEYER, p. 57

It is not for nothing that Milchmeyer chooses as an example the striking of a chord in the upper register, because it is there that the quality of the instrument can best be judged. In the treble the strings are of limited length. Because the instruments are built according to the straight-stringing (or parallel-stringing) principle, these strings benefit from only a small section of the soundboard, so that the tone becomes steadily thinner toward the top.[7] The differences between the instruments of around 1800 and those of the present day can, however, also be more easily established.

A modern Steinway grand 67 inches (170 cm) in length, weighs 606 pounds (275 kg), and a 108-inch (274 cm) concert grand weighs 1,058 pounds (480 kg). By contrast, Stein's instruments are more than six feet long—a distance necessary to allow sufficient room for the bass strings—and weigh no more than 176 pounds (80 kg).[8] With a keyboard range from FF to f³, the wooden frame can bear a string tension of around 3,300 pounds (1,500 kg). This is nothing in comparison with the modern concert grand, in which, with a range from AAA to c^5, the tension on the cast-iron frame can reach more than 46,000 pounds (21,000 kg). It was on the instruments of Stein and other manufacturers of that era that Beethoven's qualities as a pianist and accomplished improviser were first noticed. To do justice to his rapidly developed reputation in this area, and also for his further development as a composer, a second visit to Vienna was inevitable. In December 1792, a year after Mozart's death, Beethoven again arrived in the capital, this time bearing letters of recommendation from the aristocracy, including Count Waldstein. There he not only contacted Haydn for composition lessons but also immediately started comparing himself with others as a pianist.[9] Abbé Joseph Gelinek, who had a formidable reputation as a pianist, was the first to experience this. Czerny described the occasion:

> I can still remember how Gelinek told my father one day that he was invited to a private party that evening where he was to cross swords with an unknown pianist. "We are going to thrash him soundly!" Gelinek added. The next day my father asked Gelinek how the battle had gone. "Oh!" said Gelinek, completely dejected, "I won't forget yesterday! That young man is possessed of the devil. Never have I heard such playing! He improvised on a theme I proposed like I never heard even Mozart improvise. Then he played compositions of his own, which are wonderful and grandioso to the highest degree, and he achieves difficulties and effects at the piano such as we have never even dreamed of."
>
> CZERNY (II), p. 4

Such competitions were quite usual in those days. Mozart, for instance, competed as a matter of honor with Muzio Clementi—a contest that finished inconclusively.[10] Any pianist who wanted to be counted as such had to prove himself not only by playing his own compositions, but also through his skills in sight-reading and, of course, improvisation.

Beethoven found a worthy contender in Joseph Wölfl, a pupil of Mozart. The composer Ignaz Xaver von Seyfried, who had also studied under Mozart, was present:

> There the interesting combats of the two athletes not infrequently offered an indescribable artistic treat to the numerous and thoroughly select gathering. Each brought forward the latest product of his mind. Now one and anon the other gave free rein to his glowing fancy; sometimes they would seat themselves at two pianofortes and improvise alternately on themes which they gave each other, and thus created many a four-hand Capriccio which if it could have been put upon paper at the moment would surely have bidden defiance to time. [. . .] In his improvisations even then Beethoven did not deny his tendency toward the mysterious and gloomy. When once he began to revel in the infinite world of tones, he was transported also above all earthly things;—his spirit had burst all restricted bonds, shaken of the yoke of servitude, and soared triumphantly and jubilantly into the luminous spaces of the higher aether. Now his playing tore along like a wildly foaming cataract, and the conjurer constrained his instrument to an utterance so forceful that the stoutest structure was scarcely able to withstand it; and anon he sank down, exhausted, exhaling gentle plaints, dissolving in melancholy. Again the spirit would soar aloft, triumphing over transitory terrestrial sufferings, turn its glance upward in reverent sounds and find rest and comfort on the innocent bosom of holy nature. But who shall sound the depths of the sea? It was the mystical Sanscrit language whose hieroglyphs can be read only by the initiated. Wölfl, on the contrary, trained in the school of Mozart, was always equable; never superficial but always clear and thus more accessible to the multitude. [. . .]
>
> THAYER/FORBES, Vol. I, pp. 206–207

As can be gathered from von Seyfried's words, Beethoven made the most extreme demands on the instrument with his passionate playing. Luigi Cherubini once said to Czerny that he found that Beethoven mishandled the fortepiano. This did not bother Beethoven one iota. When playing the full chords in the first movement of his Sonata in D minor, Op. 31 No. 2, he shouted: "The piano must break!" (Fischer [II], p. 29).[11]

Sonata Op. 31 No. 2, 1st movement

Anton Reicha observed the consequences when he turned the pages for Beethoven during a concert at the court in Bonn:[12]

> One evening when Beethoven was playing a Mozart concerto at the Court, he asked me to turn the pages for him. But I was mostly occupied in wrenching out the strings of the piano, which snapped, while the hammers stuck among the broken strings. Beethoven insisted upon finishing the concerto, so back and forth I leaped, jerking out a string, disentangling a hammer, turning a page, and I worked harder than did Beethoven.
>
> PROD'HOMME (II), p. 351

Although it is apparent from this report that Beethoven regularly exceeded the bounds of the possible, the ravage was not totally his fault. The handcrafted wrought-iron stringing for the treble and that of brass for the bass were highly vulnerable,[13] meaning that strings often broke.[14] This cannot be compared with the strong and flexible steel core material covered with copper wire in the bass that is used in modern piano construction.

In Vienna, Anton Walter was one of the best-known piano builders. Beethoven had already played an instrument of his when he visited Mozart for the first time in 1787. In any case, Carl Czerny found one of this builder's instruments at Beethoven's when he visited him early in 1801:

> I was about ten years old when Krumpholz took me to see Beethoven. With what joy and terror I greeted the day on which I was to meet the admired master! Even now this moment is still vividly present in my memory. It was a winter's

> day when my father, Krumpholz and I took our way from Leopoldstadt (where we still were living) to Vienna proper, to a street called *der tiefe Graben* (the Deep Ditch), and climbed endless flights to the fifth and sixth stories, where a rather untidy-looking servant announced us to Beethoven and then admitted us. The room presented a most disorderly appearance; papers and articles of clothing were scattered about everywhere, some trunks, bare walls, hardly a chair, save the wobbly one at the Walter Fortepiano (then the best). [. . .]
>
> SONNECK (ED.), pp. 25–26

Walter was the first Viennese piano manufacturer to provide his mechanism with a hammer check, which was still absent from Stein's instruments. The check catches the hammer on its rebound from the attack, preventing it from bouncing up again and striking the string twice. A mechanism with a hammer check is also more suitable for forceful playing. Only when the pianist allows the key to rise fully does the hammer return to its original position.

In this fragile instrument, the largest wooden hammer in the bass, covered with a thin coating of leather, weighs only 0.04 ounce (1.2 grams), the smallest in the treble 0.02 ounce (0.6 gram). This is a huge difference compared with the modern grand piano, the largest hammer head of which, depending on the density of the compressed felt, weighs around 0.5 ounce (14 grams) and the smallest around 0.2 ounce (5–6 grams).

The result is that on the modern piano the intensity and duration of the tone have increased, but the number and intensity of the overtones have decreased. In general, on the present-day piano the tone is denser and more uniform in color than is the case for the instruments of Stein and his contemporaries.

Although these early fortepianos required a lot of maintenance and had to be regularly adjusted and tuned, the harpsichord was soon banished into relative obscurity and the new instrument quickly gained in popularity with both the aristocracy and the newly rich in society. This resulted in a tremendous blossoming of the sector.

While early in 1800 there were approximately forty fortepiano manufacturers in Vienna, between 1815 and 1833 as many as 200 workshops could be counted.[15] It was thus no coincidence that in Vienna Beethoven again met Nannette Stein, whom he knew from his visit to her father in Augsburg.

Nannette, the same age as Beethoven and a talented pianist, had been thoroughly schooled by her father in the building of fortepianos. After the death of her father in 1792 and her marriage in 1794 to the pianist and music teacher Andreas Streicher, she had decided to move to the capital, where, together with her younger brother Matthäus Andreas Stein, she continued with the workshop under the name "Frère et Soeur Stein à Vienne." This meant that the acquaintance with Beethoven could quickly be resumed.

Now he could also let them know about one of his main concerns about these early instruments: the quality of the sound. In an undated letter to Streicher, he wrote in August/September 1796:

> There is no doubt that so far as the manner of playing is concerned, the *pianoforte* is still the least studied and developed of all instruments; one often thinks that one is merely listening to a harp. And I am delighted, my dear fellow, that you are one of the few who realize and perceive that, provided one can feel the music, one can also make the pianoforte sing. I hope that the time will come when the harp and the pianoforte will be treated as two entirely different instruments.
>
> ANDERSON, Vol. I, pp. 25–26

This letter, written four years after Mozart's death, casts a clear light on Beethoven's ideals for a fortepiano sound, not at all in line with what was possible with the instrument at that moment. In this respect, too, builders were seeking a certain ideal. The one did not wish to deviate from the clear sound of the harpsichord, while the other sought a sound more in keeping with the more rounded and warm sound of string instruments. Such a deeper sound could be achieved by moving the contact point of the hammer more to the middle of the string, so that fewer overtones arose. Walter was seeking it in a different soundboard construction that led to a rounder, fuller, and also louder sound in the bass, even though the treble remained somewhat feeble in comparison with the bass.

Even so, it is not inconceivable that this development appealed to Beethoven, because in a letter written in November 1802 to his friend and amateur cellist Baron Nikolaus Paul Zmeskall he gave permission for him to buy an instrument from Walter for not more than 30 ducats,[16] suggesting that this manufacturer's instrument was an attractive proposition for him. The usual price at the time was between 40 and 100 ducats, so it seemed that Beethoven hoped for a firm discount.[17] It is not certain whether Walter accepted his proposal and the sale went through. Because Beethoven was also quite tight with money, it was fortunate that such a deal was not necessary, either, for he could make use of instruments rented or loaned to him by various manufacturers.[18]

There came an end to this for a while when in the summer of 1803 he took possession of a brand-new instrument from the Frenchman Sébastien Érard. Although until recently it was assumed that Érard had delivered this instrument to the composer as a present, more recent research has shown that the manufacturer charged him 1,500 francs, although apparently Beethoven never paid for it.[19]

Beethoven probably became acquainted with such an instrument through Haydn, who had received one as a present from Érard in 1801, and he must have been impressed by the exceptional qualities of this instrument, which he must have rated more highly than those of the Viennese instruments of the period.

Into this slender instrument, built in Empire style—Érard called it a "piano en forme de clavecin"—with the thin, column-like legs supporting a trim case 87 inches (221 cm) long, Érard built an "English action," the so-called *Stossmechanik.*

There are indications that, even before the French Revolution began in 1789, Érard had on several occasions been in London and had probably also visited John Broadwood, who had a workshop there. While Érard's brother, Jean-Baptiste, continued to run the enterprise in Paris, Sébastien opened another shop in London in 1792.

The similarities in the building methods of Érard and Broadwood are evident. Both instruments have an English action whereby the hammer is directed onto the string via a jack. This mechanism therefore deviates completely from the Viennese action (see Appendix).

In 1796, Érard had refined the English action to such a degree that he obtained a patent for his *mécanisme à échappement (simple).*[20] (In 1822 he would play an important role in the development of piano building through his revolutionary invention—the double escapement action, *mécanisme à double échappement.*) Anyway, around 1800 he also started introducing four pedals, following the English example,[21] namely from right to left:

- One pedal for the *due corde/una corda*, whereby due to the shifting of the keyboard fewer strings are hit, resulting in a softer sound—the present-day left pedal.
- A *moderator*, with which a strip of cloth is introduced between the hammers and the strings. This produces, along with a damping effect, a more muffled timbre.
- Alongside this a pedal to raise all dampers: the resonance pedal (the present-day right pedal).
- And to the left a so-called *peau de buffle*, perhaps best described as a kind of *pianissimo* pedal with which (as with the moderator) a strip of soft buffalo leather is introduced between the hammers and the strings, producing a warmer and more somber sound.

Even so, differences between the instruments of Érard and Broadwood are also noticeable. The damping mechanism in Broadwood's instruments, for example, comprises light, small wooden "clothes pegs" with strips of woven cloth on the underside. This means that the instruments—especially in the bass—always resonate a little further, in line with what the English consider to be the ideal sound. Érard built a damper system that, in contrast, is very tight and direct, for which he used relatively large dampers in the treble and all higher tones and wedge-shaped dampers for the bass, which fall precisely between the strings.

Beethoven was over the moon with his new Érard, as his friend, the diplomat Georg August Griesinger, recounted in a letter to the publisher Gottfried Christoph Härtel dated December 14, 1803:

> The Erard Brothers in Paris have given Beethoven (just as Haydn earlier) a fortepiano of mahogany as a present. He

> is so over the moon with it that he regards all local work as rubbish in comparison.
>
> KOPITZ/CADENBACH, Vol. I, p. 380

The Viennese builders were not having an easy time. Between 1780 and 1790, French, German, and Austrian magazines were already advertising English pianos, and the London builders were doing everything possible to conquer the European continent. Muzio Clementi was an example. Already established in London for many years, in 1798 he became a partner of builder James Longman, and when Longman left the firm in 1801, Clementi started building instruments in his own name with the English mechanism. Between 1802 and 1810 he made sales on concert tours in countries such as Germany, Austria, and Italy. Business was so good in Russia that he opened a branch in St. Petersburg. A visitor there would have had the good fortune to be assisted by an extremely musical salesman, for the Irish composer John Field, who from an early age was initiated into the marketing profession by Clementi in London, was in charge there for a considerable period. The Bohemian pianist and composer Jan Ladislav Dussek was also prepared to sell Clementi's instruments—with a generous commission, of course.[22] Grand pianos with an English mechanism were popular.

However, Beethoven must have quickly come to the conclusion that the Érard also failed to fulfill his wishes. Within a year of his receiving the instrument, changes were already being made, as is apparent from a letter of January 2, 1805, from Streicher to the publisher Gottfried Christoph Härtel:

> Beethoven is certainly a vigorous player, but so far he has been incapable of treating his fortepiano, which he received from Erard in Paris, with fitting respect, having had changes made to it twice already, without improving on it in the least, because the construction of the same does not permit a different action. —With several pianos I have chosen a middle course between light and heavy, but had to abandon this again, because not only local but also out-of-town amateurs protested. [. . .]
>
> LÜTGE, pp. 65–66

The middle ground between "light" and "heavy" developed by Streicher has to do with the fact that the English action, due to the heavier construction and more complicated mechanics, had a heavier touch than the Viennese *Prellzungen* action. With the English action, the hammer is mounted on a separate rail; the jack presses at the starting point of the hammer, so the moment with which the lever works is small. Therefore, as soon as the key is depressed, the pianist feels the weight of the hammer on his finger, which gives a feeling of resistance and heaviness. In addition, the "nod" at the moment the jack is released from the hammer and the hammer falls back feels like a relief to the finger because the resistance has suddenly disappeared. In contrast, the Viennese action has a very different pressure sensitivity. The hammer is on the key lever. Everything works so lightly that the percussion of the beak (referring to its special shape) against the pawl of the escapement can hardly be felt. At the moment of contact, the hammer is, as it were, launched like a catapult.

The great difference between the two actions was of course also due to the ideals the various builders had in mind for the sound. While the Viennese style of building aimed at a more intimate, clear, and light sound, the English tried to achieve a fuller and especially louder one. One of the conditions for succeeding in this was that the depression of the key (the key dip) had to be large enough to give the hammer the velocity it needed to hit the string hard. In the English fortepianos the key dip appears to be almost twice that of the Viennese instruments.

Beethoven, who did not shun a robust treatment of the piano and was, as Streicher says, a "vigorous" player, will indeed have found satisfaction in the heavier touch of his Érard, which must have given him the feeling of being able to convey his expressive musical eloquence better than he could with the Viennese grand pianos, where the action, as it were, "plays itself," but he probably did not wish to interfere with the key dip of the Viennese instruments.[23] His brief for Streicher must have been to adapt the key dip of his Érard to correspond to that of the Viennese instruments, while maintaining the greater volume and the resistance of the keys—an impossible task, as is evident in Streicher's words.

Even so, Streicher had done everything possible in his workshop to please Beethoven. Érard's keys were lengthened by 0.47 inch (12 mm) and the pivot was moved 1.78 inches (45 mm) toward the front. Because of the balance of the key lever, wood had to be removed from under the key at the back and lead was inlaid on the front to restore the balance. The result was that the original dip of about 0.34 inch (8.6 mm) could be reduced to 0.24 inch (6.1 mm)—still, however, twice that of a Walter pianoforte, the key dip of which is 0.12 inch (3 mm) in the descant and 0.16 inch (4 mm) in the bass.[24]

In addition to the differences between the English and Viennese actions, other great differences between these instruments can be observed. In the English grand pianos, for example, thicker strings were used which were stretched more tightly in order to achieve the desired volume, while the Viennese builders kept to a lighter tension. The most important difference is, however, that around 1790 the heavier soundboard in the English instruments was already twice as thick as that of the Viennese grands.

The consequences for the sound are evident: a higher volume and more length of tone in the English instruments as opposed to a softer, light, and clearly profiled, short tone in the Viennese fortepianos.

It is, however, interesting that Beethoven's instrument also possessed "Viennese" elements. Due to the precise damping system in Érard's instruments, the tone is much more clear-cut than in an English instrument such as those of Broadwood. Furthermore, in Streicher's workshop Beethoven's Érard was provided with new leather on the hammer heads, making the tone more compact.

However, with a range of five-and-a-half octaves (FF to c^4), Beethoven's Érard still did not reflect the latest developments in piano manufacture, with instruments already being built with a range of six octaves (FF to f^4), something Érard would adopt only in 1810. The French pianist and piano teacher Louis Adam described the development in his *Méthode de piano:*

> Previously the keyboards had only four octaves, it is only in the past twenty-five years that they have been extended to five. At the time these instruments were called pianoforte of extended range; but now the larger pianofortes go seven notes higher, some even an entire octave higher, amounting

> to six octaves in all. This addition offers a very big advantage, since it enables the imitation of the high-pitched sounds of the piccolo flute and to equal the whole range of the violin.
>
> ADAM, p. 3 (nouvelle édition, ca. 1805)

The next piano sonata Beethoven composed once he had his Érard was the "Waldstein," Op. 53, an extremely pianistic composition in which, with a^3 as the highest note, he did not yet take advantage of the Érard's full range.

When, however, on April 5, 1803, he gave the first performance of his Third Piano Concerto, a composition that had been completed in 1800, he saw his chance and wrote a cadenza for the first movement that did reach to c^4. That apparently pleased him, for in the Sonata Op. 57, the "Appassionata," composed in 1804–1805, this highest possible note is also to be found.

Beethoven must have used his Érard intensively in the ensuing years, for by 1810 the instrument had been rendered unplayable. It is quite possible that his Fifth Piano Concerto was one of the culprits. He composed this large-scale and pianistically challenging concerto in 1809 and it is not inconceivable that the Érard simply could not cope with it. Now that this "Emperor" Concerto was complete, it was high time for the instrument to be replaced. In a letter dated September 18, 1810, he wrote to Streicher:

> Dear Streicher!
>
> As I shall be back in Vienna by the beginning of October, let me know whether I may have another piano from you—My French piano is no longer of much use; in fact it is quite useless. Perhaps you can advise me where we can find a home for it.
>
> ANDERSON, Vol. I, p. 292

Because Streicher had apparently not reacted to this letter, Beethoven came back to the subject a few months later:

> Dear Streicher!
>
> You promised to let me have a piano by the end of October; and now we are already half through November and

> yet I haven't received one—My motto is either to play on a good instrument or not at all—As for my French piano, which is certainly quite useless now, I still have misgivings about selling it, for it is really a souvenir such as no one here has so far honored me with. [. . .]
>
> ANDERSON, Vol. I, p. 300

Whether the Érard was in a bad condition or whether the Viennese preferred a Viennese action to an "English" one, we do not know, but in any case there was no sale and the instrument remained in Beethoven's possession until 1825, when he gave it to his brother Johann.[25]

It is possible that Beethoven already had a Streicher in mind with the hoped-for proceeds of the sale, but it is not known whether he could then again—after all, in the September 18 letter he writes "wieder" (another)—own such an instrument.

The Streichers' instruments were highly sought after, especially since the couple had introduced numerous improvements from around 1805 onward, whereby they oriented themselves not only on the Viennese tradition but also on English piano building. In addition, the instruments were now provided with a check action, like those of Walter, and they could be delivered in various sizes, the largest with a keyboard range of six octaves (FF—f^4).

This enlargement did, however, result in an even greater tension on the wooden casing, meaning that the instrument had a tendency to warp. While in the instruments of Walter and other builders of that time a single metal bar in the treble still sufficed to ensure stability, as early as 1805 Streicher had to start fixing three metal bars here.

The necessity of strengthening the frame was made even more urgent by the ever-higher tuning and in addition its impact on the degree of tension on the frame. The a^1 on a Walter fortepiano, for instance, was still tuned at 415 hertz; twenty years later that had increased to 435 hertz, about half a tone higher.[26] Even so, all these problems dwindled into insignificance compared with the increasing demand for more volume. For this would go against Streicher's concept of an ideal sound. In a letter of June 22, 1805, to Gottfried Härtel, he wrote:

> I believe I can claim that my more recent instruments are not inferior to others regarding strength of tone, as well as internal and external solidity and durability. It would require small effort from us to make them even stronger, but then the flexibility of the tone would suffer.
>
> LÜTGE, p. 67

Nevertheless, it seems that only two years later Streicher had indeed managed to adapt his instruments more to the English taste. Czerny noted:

> In 1807 I made the acquaintance of Andreas Streicher, who, formerly a piano teacher, had even then dedicated himself to the manufacture of the fortepiano and who, through reflection as well as imitation of the English instruments, gave his instruments a fuller tone and a more robust treatment than was common before then.
>
> CZERNY (I), p. 24

Beethoven's possible role in this can be gathered from what the composer Johann Friedrich Reichardt wrote on February 7, 1809, in his *Vertraute Briefe:*

> Streicher has abandoned the soft, yielding, repercussive tone of the other Vienna instruments, and at Beethoven's wish and advice has given his instruments greater resonance and elasticity, so that the virtuoso who plays with strength and significance may have the instrument in better command for sustained and expressive tones. He has thereby given his instruments a larger and more varied character, so that they must give greater satisfaction than the others to all virtuosi who seek something more than mere easy brilliancy in their style of playing.
>
> THAYER/FORBES, Vol. I, p. 461

Now that Beethoven had put aside his Érard, other builders fancied their chances. Sebestyén Antal Vogel from Budapest, for instance, gave him an instrument in 1812. It is unclear whether Beethoven was displeased with this instrument or whether he found himself in dire financial straits—which happened now and then. In any event, his possession of the Vogel was short-lived, for in 1814 he sold it.[27] It was, however, not until the summer of 1817 that he turned to Nannette Streicher in a letter requesting that she ask her husband whether he could provide him with an instrument with as great a volume as possible:

> Now I have a great favor to ask of Streicher. Request him on my behalf to be so kind as to adjust one of your pianos for me to suit my impaired hearing. It should be as loud as possible. That is absolutely necessary. I have long been intending to buy one of your pianos, but at the moment that would be very difficult for me. Perhaps, however, it will be possible for me to do so later on. But until then I should like *to borrow* one of yours.
>
> ANDERSON, Vol. II, p. 686

It is totally understandable that he was at that of all times looking for a really loud instrument. For, almost completely deaf, he had started on his monumental "Hammerklavier" Sonata Op. 106.

It was not, however, Streicher, but rather the English builder Thomas Broadwood, whose acquaintance Beethoven had made in Vienna in the summer of 1817, who—encouraged in this by London pianists and friends of Beethoven—unexpectedly gave him a new instrument.[28]

A hefty argument in persuading Broadwood to make this generous gesture must have been their convincing him that if the greatest composer of that era possessed one of his instruments, then the sales figures would improve significantly. In Broadwood's workshop, the initiators, Ferdinand Ries, Friedrich Kalkbrenner, Johann Baptist Cramer, Jacopo Gotifredo Ferrari, and Charles Knyvett, added their signatures to Broadwood's nameplate on the grand they had chosen.

When Beethoven heard that he would receive the gift of a Broadwood, he wrote on February 3, 1818, a thank-you letter in French:

> My very dear friend Broadwood!
>
> Never did I experience a greater pleasure than was caused me by the announcement of the forthcoming arrival of this piano with which you honor me by making me a present: I shall regard it as an altar upon which I will place the choicest offerings of my mind to the divine Apollo. As soon as I shall have received your excellent instrument I will send you the fruits of the inspiration of the first moments I shall spend with it, as a remembrance from me to you, my very dear B., and I only wish that they be worthy of your instrument.
>
> ANDERSON, Vol. II, pp. 755-756

After the necessary preparations, the instrument was shipped immediately after Christmas 1817 via the Mediterranean Sea to Trieste, to be further transported overland by the firm Giuseppe Antonio Bridi to Vienna. In Broadwood's records is to be found the note:

> 27.12.1817. A 6 octave Grand P.F. No. 7362, tin and deal cases. Tho Broadwood Esq., marked VB care of F. E. J. Bereaux et Co. Trieste—a present to Mr. van Beethoven, Viene.
>
> BRANDENBURG, Vol. IV, p. 150

Beethoven was, however, decidedly not amused when, having heard early in 1818 that the instrument was on its way, he also learned that import duty would have to be paid. Fortunately, Count Moritz Lichnowsky came to his rescue and it was apparently possible, through his intervention, to avoid the taxes. When the Broadwood arrived half a year later, the following report appeared in the *Wiener Zeitung* of June 8, 1818:

> Herr Ludwig van Beethoven, who not only in Austria, but also other countries beyond our borders is revered in the appreciation of his great, all-encompassing musical genius, received in London from one of his admirers a very rare and valuable pianoforte as a gift which was shipped free of

> charge to Vienna. With exceptional liberality the Imperial and Royal Chamber has waived the customs duty which would otherwise have been levied on any foreign instruments, and has thus once again provided the handsome proof, so gratifying for the arts, of how much one strives to encourage with humane appreciation the merits of the genius so rare in their magnitude.
>
> BRANDENBURG, Vol. IV, p. 172

The Broadwood's quality and size did not go unnoticed, as is apparent from a report in the *Wiener Zeitschrift für Kunst, Literatur, Theater und Mode* of January 23, 1819:

> This precious and magnificent instrument has six whole octaves from the contra C to the five-line C [c^5] (sic) whose sound is throughout full, beautiful and strong, and in the contra tones majestic, in the treble *cantabile*.[29]
>
> BRANDENBURG, Vol. IV, p. 170

With these enthusiastic lines, it is no wonder that Viennese music lovers very soon found an advertisement in their daily paper:

> Anyone who wants to play Beethoven now can safely banish to the attic their old Walter or Schantz *Hammerflügel* that served the music of Haydn and Mozart so perfectly. They should order a new one, with an extended range and a more robust corpus, preferably immediately one with the fashionable French Erard action, or with the fast-repetition English Broadwood action, such as Herr van Beethoven himself now plays on.
>
> BADURA-SKODA/DEMUS, p. 124

Although Beethoven will have been happy to have at home an instrument that could be well played, the six-octave compass must also have disappointed him. Although the range of the Broadwood was a quarter lower in the bass, with CC, the descant remained the same, at c^4. In Vienna, meanwhile, six-and-a-half-octave instruments were being constructed and, inspired by this, works were being written for them. In his Sonata Op. 81a, "Les Adieux," which he had written in 1809–1810, and in his Piano Trios Op. 70 of 1808–1810, the range of the music had already been extended by a quarter to f^4.[30]

He had also probably hoped for more volume. The painter August Karl Friedrich von Kloeber, who painted his portrait a number of times in August 1818, described how he found the brand-new Broadwood provided with a *Blechkuppel*, a soundboard resembling a kind of prompter's box, with which Beethoven, by keeping his head in it, could collect more sound.

He must at that time not have been completely deaf, for when he posed for Kloeber, sitting with his back to the piano, he still noticed the mistakes that his nephew Karl was making when playing. Kloeber's description is set down in a letter he later wrote to the composer Friedrich Wilhelm Jähns:

> *Beethoven* sat down now, and the boy had to study on the grand piano which was a present from England and had a large tin canopy. This instrument stood about four to five steps behind him, and it was strange that *Beethoven*, notwithstanding his deafness, noticed every mistake the practicing boy made, let him repeat passages, etc., and made corrections.
>
> KOPITZ/CADENBACH, Vol. I, p. 515

Even so, it is not unlikely that the possession of the Broadwood stimulated him to compose his last three piano sonatas, Opp. 109, 110, and 111, in the years 1820 and 1822 and, shortly thereafter, in April 1823, to complete his *Diabelli Variations*.

One feature of Broadwood's grand is its separate right pedal. This pedal, which serves to negate the damping, is, as it were, sawn through the middle, so that a separate damper is possible for treble and bass, the division lying at c^1. Originally, Broadwood built three pedals together with the *una corda*, which was awkward because, if the whole damping had to be canceled out in combination with the *una corda*, two feet did not suffice. The separate right pedal was a practical solution to this problem.

In addition, the left pedal could be used for *una corda*, *due corde*, and *tre corde* playing, whereby a gradual decrease or increase in volume

Drawing by August von Kloeber (1818). H. C. Bodmer Collection, Beethoven-Haus, Bonn.

> *Beethoven looked very serious, his extremely lively eyes generally glowed with a somewhat dark, upward-looking expression, which I have tried to reproduce in the picture; his lips were closed, but the lines round his mouth not unfriendly. [. . .]*
>
> *He was dressed in a light-blue coat with yellow buttons, white waistcoat, and cravat as were worn at the time, all very ill-kept. His complexion was healthy and rugged, his face pitted as a result of smallpox, his hair like steel, as it had been black and was beginning to gray. His eyes blue-gray and extremely lively. [. . .]*
>
> *Kopitz/Cadenbach, Vol. I, pp. 515 and 517*

became possible, an effect that was also possible on the Érard. Beethoven takes advantage of these possibilities in several of his works. The result of this is, however, different from that experienced with modern-day grands.[31] While Broadwood in actual practice moved the action from three strings to one, these days in the triple-strung part of the grand the minimum is already reached at two strings. Furthermore, the action on the modern grand is shifted in such a way that the hammer heads touch the strings with a less frequently played, more softly intonated part of the felt, which alters the timbre.

Now that there was fierce competition between the Viennese and English manufacturers, this presented Ignaz Moscheles, living in London, with an ideal opportunity to give a concert in Vienna on December 15, 1823, with both types of grand on the podium. For this he hit on the brilliant idea of asking Beethoven whether he could borrow his Broadwood. Such a combination of two different types of instrument on the podium, not to speak of an instrument belonging to the great composer himself: that would be sure to give him extra publicity.

It can be assumed that the agreement was quickly made, for Beethoven's grand was yet again, after the completion of the last three piano sonatas, in a deplorable state. Beethoven lent his Broadwood and Moscheles had it restored by the well-known Viennese builder Conrad Graf. That was a fine deal!

> Beethoven, whom I saw frequently about this time [from October 19, 1823 to January 2, 1824], lent me the instrument in question to perform upon at a concert which I gave on December 15, 1823, at the Kärntnertor Theater, Vienna; my object being to display the difference between the effects producible on Viennese, and on English instruments, by playing on one of the former in the first, and upon Beethoven's piano in the second act. The latter was internally and externally in so bad a state, owing to frequent removals and severe treatment on the part of its owner, that I should not have been able to avail myself of it, had not M. Graf, the imperial pianoforte maker, been kind enough to put it into perfect order.
>
> KOPITZ/CADENBACH, Vol. II, p. 586

At this concert, Moscheles played his Piano Concerto Op. 56 and his *Variations on Alexander's March* for piano and orchestra Op. 32 on a grand by the Viennese manufacturer Wilhelm Leschen, and then on Beethoven's Broadwood he improvised on themes from Haydn's *Kaiserhymne*[32] and Handel's *Alexander's Feast*.

Despite all efforts, Johann Andreas Stumpff, a harp and piano manufacturer from London, who had once before, in 1818, tuned Beethoven's Broadwood, again found a ruin of broken strings and jammed keys when he visited Beethoven a year-and-a-half later, in September 1824:

> Beethoven complained about the inadequacy of the pianoforte upon which, in the present condition, one could play nothing with power and effect! "I myself own a London instrument, which does not however perform as one might expect. Come, it is here in the adjoining room in extremely miserable condition."
>
> When I opened it, what a sight met my eyes! The upper part was toneless and the broken strings were entangled in one another like a thorn bush whipped by the stormy wind!
>
> KOPITZ/CADENBACH, Vol. II, p. 974

With such a grand, Stumpff naturally could not persuade Beethoven to play something for him. When, however, some days later the latter was away from home for a while, Stumpff made the most of the opportunity and immediately had the instrument repaired by Matthäus Andreas Stein, Nannette's brother.[33] Stumpff got his way and in a footnote to a report about Beethoven's playing provided a further description of the "prompter's box" that Kloeber had seen at Beethoven's in 1818. This must have undergone some improvement, for now there was no mention of a *Blechkuppel*, a metal construction, but rather a wooden one, which probably offered better resonance.

> An unfulfilled wish became ever stronger in my mind, namely, to hear Beethoven play, and in the state his piano was in this was impossible. I instantly went to Herr Stein, piano manufacturer, and divulged my desire and bade him assist me in bringing the piano into a playable state. He promised and

> kept his word, and with a number of his workmen and some aid on my part the piano was before long once more in playable condition. Beethoven was gone for a few days, traveling with his brother on family business, and that suited us well, we could therefore achieve our aim unimpeded.—Upon his return, his nephew, who had accompanied his uncle, came to lead me to him; on the way I divulged to him that the piano had now recovered its voice and bade him place the attachment in question unnoticed on it and then surprise his uncle with what had transpired.* So as agreed Karl led his uncle to where the piano stood and removed the attachment; then Beethoven beheld with wonderment the new shape of his piano and exclaimed: "This is not the work of an enemy!" - and took my hand, which he clasped warmly. [. . .] Then he sat down under the guard in front of the keys and a web of notes with surprising transitions made the poor strings and the whole instrument quiver and a chaos of sounds developed into the most soul-stirring melodies. In short, who could depict in words what the imagination of such a mind is capable of!
>
> *[Stumpff's note] The attachment mentioned, which Beethoven had had made for himself and with which he came to the assistance of his faulty organs of hearing, consisted of a large half-circle of resonating wood, which was closed at both ends and raised itself above the keys of the piano from the bass to the treble, so that the head of the player was enveloped by the dome of the half-circle—resembling a high roof—and consequently the sonic rays had to concentrate therein and have a beneficial effect on an injured organ of hearing—which was the case with Beethoven.
>
> KOPITZ/CADENBACH, Vol. II, pp. 974-975, 978-979

But this time round, too, the repairs did not last long, for in January 1826 Graf tried to repair the Broadwood yet again.[34] On this occasion Graf lent him one of his own grands, a gesture for which Beethoven thanked him in a letter of January 24, 1826:

> My very worthy friend,
>
> I thank you for your obliging kindness toward me and am sure that through your instrument *harmonies* will emerge within me.
>
> BRANDENBURG, Vol. VI, p. 208

It was Beethoven's last grand.[35] Of course, Graf built his grand pianos with a Viennese action. In the bass the instrument was triple-strung from CC to C-sharp, and from D to f[4] even quadruple-strung. This was not especially intended for Beethoven, for Graf had used it in his instruments in the past, not to achieve more volume but to limit the breaking of strings, because the force of the impact of the hammer head was now spread over four instead of three strings. Additionally, Graf built instruments with a thin soundboard to better transmit the vibrations, and of course the "prompter's box" was also again fitted for Beethoven. None of this, however, led to new "harmonies" in Beethoven's piano works. He had already written his *Diabelli Variations* Op. 120 between 1819 and 1823, and with the Bagatelles Op. 126, which he composed in 1825, his last-ever piano work was completed.

Three years earlier he still had been bemoaning the quality of the fortepianos of that time. After he had finished his last piano sonata, Op. 111, in 1822, he said to his pupil Karl Holz:

> These solo sonatas [Opp. 109, 110, 111] are certainly the best, but also the last that I have written for the piano. It is and remains an inadequate instrument.
>
> KOPITZ/CADENBACH, Vol. I, p. 474

This raises the question of the extent to which the grands that Beethoven had known during his lifetime had fulfilled his ideal.

The instruments of Stein and Walter, for instance, are, through their light construction and measured damping, eminently suited to clear, distinct playing. The various kinds of notation, like the *non legato* and the numerous articulations that we see in, for example, the sonatas of Haydn or Mozart, really come into their own on these instruments, and Beethoven made good use of them, too (see Chapter 4).

On the other hand, it cannot be said that he handled these instruments with care. He regularly transgressed the boundaries of the possible. In those days he also found the instruments too "harp-like" and was searching for a vocal, singing, long-sounding tone—not surprising, since he was renowned for his *legato*.

The Érard grand he received in 1803, with its more extensive possibilities for sound, might have satisfied the musical expansion required in the "Waldstein" Sonata composed shortly after this or in the "Appassionata" and sonatas composed later on, but he was less happy with the "touch." The effective damping of the Érard did, in contrast, approach the Viennese sound ideal.

It was in those days that the Viennese grands, including Streicher's, were prominent. There was still, however, the demand for more volume, something the English instruments had but to which Streicher submitted only around 1808, the year in which Beethoven composed his Sonata Op. 78. Beethoven was probably satisfied with the sound of Streicher's instruments, but not with the volume, especially as the first signs of deafness had become apparent as early as 1796, the year in which his first piano sonata, Op. 2, was published. Since that time his hearing had been constantly deteriorating.

When Broadwood's grand arrived in 1819, Beethoven's life as a concert pianist was well in the past, and the last works he wrote for piano were his Sonatas Opp. 109, 110, and 111, the *Diabelli Variations* Op. 120, and the Bagatelles Op. 126. He must hardly have been able to hear the grand that Graf put at his disposal after that, in view of his deafness.

After Beethoven's death, numerous significant changes took place in piano manufacturing that eventually led to the present-day construction. The size of the piano, the slightly wider keys, the greater key dip, the ever-heavier manner of playing, the volume, the invention of the double-escapement action by Érard—all of this means that the pianistic approach to Beethoven on the modern grand must be viewed from a completely different perspective than on historical instruments or copies of these. It is a matter of course that in our time pianists have to realize that the expressiveness of the highest and lowest notes on a historical instrument represents the limit of the intensity of Beethoven's conception of sound, while the modern grand offers much more, not only in range but also in volume. Playing on a historical instrument influences the psyche of the interpreter, who is conscious of reaching to the extremes of what is possible.

For this reason, a musician playing on a modern grand piano has to find the right balance between the possibilities of the instrument and what must be expressed in musical terms. The different possibilities for sound and a totally different touch as compared with the instruments of Beethoven's time lead to a different expression—the musical outcome will, however, always need to be found in the context of the spirit of the composition.

CHAPTER FOUR

Performance Practice and Beethoven's Notation

> Keep at it, don't just practice art, but penetrate also to its inner laws; it deserves it, for only art and science raise men to the Divine.
>
> —BEETHOVEN IN A LETTER TO EMILIE M., JULY 17, 1812; THAYER/FORBES, Vol. I, p. 536

ALTHOUGH IN GENERAL THESE days our knowledge of historical performance practice is increasingly influencing interpretations, the way in which a composer handled this personally in his notation of a composition is less well researched. In Beethoven's case, for instance, there are to be found examples not only of the prevailing performance practice of the time but also of how he explored new forms of notation to communicate his musical concepts.

Different types of touch, *rubato*, the use of the beam or the pedal, or such aspects as the character of the music, the structure, the musical motion, or the tempo must be understood through his eyes to be able to express all of this in a well-considered interpretation.

In this chapter, these topics are presented in relation to his piano sonatas, each part being preceded by a short historical introduction.

Types of Touch

Legato playing of keyboard instruments became general practice only at the beginning of the nineteenth century. Until around 1800, *non legato* was counted as the normal touch. Having the notes played separately, the one following shortly on from the other, as opposed to letting them "slide" into each other, can be compared with the articulation of language. Articulation—the creation of separate units or "joints"—has in speech the function of clarifying the sound structure of words and sentences, for example by separation into syllables, by means of the greater or lesser expression of vowels and consonants.

In instrumental music, this slight separation of the notes was achieved by applying various articulations, for example, on the recorder, where the way of blowing was determined by forming various syllables such as "tidi" and "riti," so that the air flow was interrupted in a certain way, each note assuming its own specific character.

In the case of string instruments, it was common practice to give each note its own bowstroke, meaning that the change of note was not camouflaged as much as possible, as was the case from the Romantic era onward, but in contrast was distinctly audible so that each note could have its own impulse. We find descriptions of this articulated playing in the oldest keyboard methods, too, including that of Girolamo Diruta in his *Il Transilvano* from 1593, or later with Guillaume-Gabriel Nivers in his *Premier livre d'orgue* from 1665.

Around 100 years later, it appears that in many tutors for keyboard instruments three ways of playing were distinguished:

- the *non legato*, also known as *ordentliche Fortgehen*, regarded as the standard, usual, or "common" touch;
- the *legato*, indicated with a slur, whereby the notes should be tied;
- the *detached touch*, a shorter touch, represented in notation by a dot or a stroke (the stroke could also be printed as a dash or a wedge).

In most methods, the so-called *tragender Ton*, the combination of notes with dots under a slur, the present-day *portato*, is also included in the category of *Abstoßen*. However, because there is a connection between *portato* and *rubato*, we will look at this later in this chapter.

From "Common" Touch to *Legato*

The "common" or "usual" touch is described in eighteenth-century German tutors as *ordentliche Fortgehen*, a *non legato* way of playing about which we can read in Friedrich Wilhelm Marpurg's *Anleitung zum Clavierspielen*, published in 1755:

> Opposed to both the tied and the detached touch is the *ordentliche Fortgehen* (literally, regular movement), which consists in raising the finger from the previous key very shortly before touching the following note. This *ordentliche Fortgehen* is never indicated because it is always understood.
>
> MARPURG, p. 29

This way of playing was also later summarized as follows by Daniel Gottlob Türk in his *Klavierschule* of 1789:

> For tones which are to be played in customary fashion (that is, neither detached nor slurred) the finger is lifted a little earlier from the key than is required by the duration of the note. Consequently, the notes in *a* are played approximately as in *b* or *c*, depending on the circumstances. If there are some notes intermingled which should be held out for their full value, then *ten.* or *tenuto* is written over them (*d*).

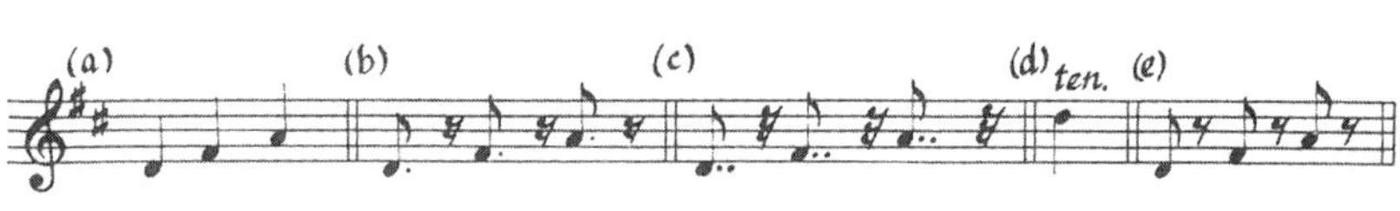

TÜRK, p. 345

In the course of time, however, there was a shift toward the gap between the separate notes becoming ever smaller and eventually disappearing, as is apparent from the description of the *gewöhnliche* (usual) or *natürliche* (natural) way of playing in the *Die wahre Art das Pianoforte zu spielen* by Johann Peter Milchmeyer from 1797:

> I will now analyze the various modes of execution, of which I presume there to be three, and explicate them in more detail. I call the first the normal, or natural, the second the tied, and the third the detached mode of execution. In pieces of good composers who write music as it should be, all notes that have no dots, dashes, or small slurs above them are of the natural mode of execution.
>
> The finger is lifted from the first key when the second has been played, from the second when the third has been played, and so on. In this usual way of playing, two fingers should never lie [on two keys] simultaneously in a simple melody.
>
> MILCHMEYER, p. 5

Legato

While there was no special notation for the common touch, in mensural (or measured) music the tying of two or more notes was indicated by various signs, the so-called ligatures. It seems, however, that around 1600—in, for example, *Syntagma Musicum* by Michael Praetorius—the ligatures were replaced by the notation of a tie or slur. Although ligatures remained in use until about 1700, especially in church music, notation with slurs quickly became the most commonly used way of indicating the tying of notes. The tying of notes by use of a slur did, however, not only indicate *legato,* but at the same time was meaningful for the technical aspect of the performance. So it was that notes gathered together under one slur also had to be played on string instruments with a single stroke of the bow. This was described by, among others, John Playford, in his *An Introduction to the Skill of Musick*. In the seventh edition of this book, published in 1674 (the first had been published in 1654), he wrote that the tie was used for two different purposes:

> A *Tye* is of two uses; first, when the Time is broken or struck in the middle of the Note, it is usual to *Tye* two *Minims*, or a *Minim* and a *Crotchet* together, as thus,

PLAYFORD, p. 35

Although here two notes of equal pitch are being tied, the sign, a slur, is also used for a *legato* performance of notes with different pitches, as in the following example:

> The second sort of the *Tye* is, when two or more Notes are to be Sung to one Syllable, or two Notes or more to be plaid with once drawing the Bow on the *Viol* or *Violin*, as thus,

PLAYFORD, p. 36

Or, as later is described by Johann Gottfried Walther in his *Lexikon* from 1732 with his description of *legato:*

> That in vocal execution only one syllable lies under such notes [i.e., connected by a slur], but in instrumental execution these are drawn and to be executed with one stroke of the bow.

WALTHER, p. 359

On keyboard instruments, tying went so far that, even with repeating notes, now and then a *legato* touch was wanted, despite the fact that here a real *legato* can merely be suggested. Such an example is to be found in J. S. Bach's Trio Sonata No. 6 in G minor, BWV 530, for organ, where three repeating notes must be performed *legato:* they are, as it were, included under one "stroke of the bow."

Bach, Trio Sonata BWV 530, 1st movement

While the *Schleifen* was regarded as an exception in Baroque music, this way of playing became more general with the rise of the *galant* style. In compositions of the First Viennese School, or Viennese Classical period, the slurs became more numerous, and it is also noticeable that the length of the slur increased, leading eventually to the indication of phrasing. Having notes merge rather than being played individually gradually became the accepted convention, making it possible to achieve a better *legato* effect on keyboard instruments by holding onto the previous key slightly longer, as described by Milchmeyer:

> The tied mode of execution, which for a few notes is indicated with a small half circle, with several measures by a line that is slightly curved at the end and at the beginning, requires a soft, melting touch. [. . .] This mode of execution now requires that one lets the fingers rest somewhat longer and on several notes.
>
> MILCHMEYER, p. 6

In the end, *legato* became the general way of playing, so much so that Muzio Clementi, in his *Introduction to the Art of Playing on the Piano Forte* from 1801, changes to advising that, if there are no indications as to the way of playing, it is best to choose *legato:*

> The notes marked thus , called LEGATO in Italian, must be played in a SMOOTH and CLOSE manner; which is done by keeping down the first key, 'till the next is struck; by which means, the strings VIBRATE SWEETLY into one another. N.B. When the composer leaves the LEGATO, and STACCATO to the performer's taste; the best rule is, to adhere chiefly to the LEGATO; reserving the STACCATO to give SPIRIT occasionally to certain passages, and to set off the HIGHER BEAUTIES of the LEGATO.
>
> CLEMENTI, pp. 8–9

Beethoven, who was well aware of these developments and was himself highly praised by his contemporaries for his *legato* playing, made a considerable effort over a period of time to obtain this translation of Clementi's method for the piano lessons of the thirteen-year-old son of his friend Stephan von Breuning.[1] In September 1826 he succeeded:

> Here is the Clementi piano method for Gerhard that I promised. If he uses it in the way I am going to show him, it will certainly give him good results.
>
> VON BREUNING, p. 76

It is not surprising that, in his piano sonatas, Beethoven takes advantage of the possibility of setting *non legato* and *legato* against each other in order to vary the expression within certain passages.

A good example is the last movement, Rondo: Allegro, of his Sonata in C minor, Op. 13, the "Pathétique," where in mm. 182–187 the triplets are constantly played *legato* in the right hand, indicated by a slur, but from m. 188 the slur is no longer present, meaning that coming from *piano* in a precisely articulated *non legato*, the long *crescendo* is built up.

Sonata Op. 13, 3rd movement

Or in the first movement, Allegro, of his Sonata Op. 14 No. 2, where the *legato* playing in the right hand changes suddenly in m. 109 into a more *jeu perlé* manner of playing, which, in contrast to the melodic left hand, prepares the way for the *decrescendo* to *pp*.

Sonata Op. 14 No. 2, 1st movement

Another example of this contrast can also be observed in the first theme of the Sonata in E-flat major, Op. 27 No. 1, where the sixteenth notes in the bass at the end of the phrase display a striking contrast in sound and expression.

Sonata Op. 27 No. 1, 1st movement

That this really is the intention of this notation is apparent with the return of the theme after the Allegro, where the same alternation, now also for the right hand, is notated:

Sonata Op. 27 No. 1, 1st movement

It seems as if in this sonata Beethoven is playing a game with these contrasts, for in the Allegro, too, there is such an alternation. It leads to an interpretation with much more color and musical expression than is the case with a uniform manner of playing.

Sonata Op. 27 No. 1, 1st movement

Or the same kind of contrast that we find in the first movement, Allegro, of the Sonata in E-flat major, Op. 81a, as can be seen by a comparison of mm. 36–40 with mm. 43–44 and mm. 62–63 with mm. 64–65. The same notation follows from m. 154 onward in the Recapitulation.

Sonata Op. 81a, 1st movement, mm. 36–44

These means of expression are also encountered in sonatas composed even later, such as the Sonata in E minor, Op. 90, where in the first movement the descending scale is played twice *non legato* and *forte,* after which the character suddenly changes through the appearance of a surprising B-flat, now notated not as an eighth but as a quarter note, and the soft scale figure played *legato.* The descending scale that at first sounded so bold and confident now sounds more like a question. The B-flat is rightly ambivalent, for as early as m. 40 it changes into an A- sharp, whereby the modulation to B minor has become a fact.

Sonata Op. 90, 1st movement

The distinction between the two ways of playing is accentuated even more strikingly in the fugue of the Sonata Op. 106, when, arising from the *crescendo*, the *forte* is reached in m. 184 and Beethoven, in contrast to the preceding *legato* groupings, specifies this moment most emphatically with the notation *non ligato* in both hands.

Sonata Op. 106, last movement

It is understandable that here, too, the instrument, the fortepiano, played a role. The instrument forced him to exploit the difference in sound creatively in the low register, where it enhances the clarity of expression, as, for instance, at the end of the last movement, Allegro, of the Sonata in D major, Op. 10 No. 3.

Sonata Op. 10 No. 3, 4th movement

Or in the first movement, Allegro, of the above-mentioned Sonata in E-flat major, Op. 81a, as can be seen in mm. 62–65 and 154–157 with the same notation.

Sonata Op. 81a, 1st movement, mm. 62–65

While Beethoven is in this case already taking care to maintain clarity in the bass register when using a fortepiano, it should most certainly be a point of attention for the present-day pianist performing on a modern grand. Here, he or she not only needs to consider the limits of tempo to ensure that clarity remains, but also ought to consider not only a *non legato* touch but even a quasi-*staccato* to be certain that the desired clarity will be maintained.

The use of the *non legato* could even play a role in the notation of the first movement, Adagio sostenuto, of the "Moonlight" Sonata, Op. 27 No. 2. It is a movement for which Beethoven was trying to find a special sound, asking the performer to play it *sempre pianissimo* and *senza sordino*, asking for a continuous resonance of the strings by lifting the damping. What a pity that the first page of the autograph is missing, but is it not remarkable that in the first edition by Cappi in Vienna the triplets of the first two measures are printed without a slur? If this is not a mistake, it could be that Beethoven had the resonating sound of a harp in mind, where the strings are plucked and damping can be attained only by hand: specifically because in the year this sonata was composed, 1801, Beethoven had a demonstrable interest in the Aeolian harp, an ancient instrument with strings softly vibrating in the wind.[2]

Sonata Op. 27 No. 2, 1st movement

A really outstanding example in which he applies the *non legato* highly expressively is the theme of the second movement, Andante con moto, of the Sonata in F minor, Op. 57, the "Appassionata." It really is a pity that his notation without slurs is totally ignored right up to the present day. The intention to play the theme *non legato*, like an oration as it were, is surely clear enough: chords, sober, expressive and stepwise. What a contrast he achieves with the flowing *legato* lines of the first variation! Beethoven affixed the theme in the manuscript over an earlier version, whereby it is less legible, but that the slurs or a *legato* indication are missing is clearly recognizable.

Sonata Op. 57, 2nd movement, autograph

Sonata Op. 57, 2nd movement, Variation I, autograph

When, after all the variations, the theme returns via thirty-second-note passages played *non legato*, its character is transformed. Especially because of the slur, which now ties the first two chords of the theme, notated by Beethoven with a bold stripe, its effect is warmer, darker than in the beginning.

Sonata Op. 57, 2nd movement, Recapitulation, autograph

Prolonged Touch

About the prolonged touch, also called super-*legato* or finger pedal, meaning holding notes for longer than is actually indicated in the notation, we also find interesting information in a large number of methods.

For example, if the harmony favors this, notes under a slur can be held for longer than the notation prescribes.

Marpurg writes in his *Die Kunst das Clavier zu spielen* from 1762:

> This half slur is also used frequently when different notes that are struck in succession and form a certain chord among themselves should rest from the first to the last (note) as in Fig. 2 in the bass. It is however better if such passages are written out properly, as in Fig. 3.

MARPURG (II), pp. 19, 20

In 1789 Türk agreed in his *Klavierschule:*

> When there is a curved line over harmonies which are to be slowly arpeggiated, as in the following examples, it is customary, especially in compositions of agreeable character, and the like, to let the fingers remain on the keys until the appearance of the next harmony. For this reason the following measures (*a*) can be played as shown in (*b*). However, I would not recommend the overly uncertain notation of (*a*) in this case.

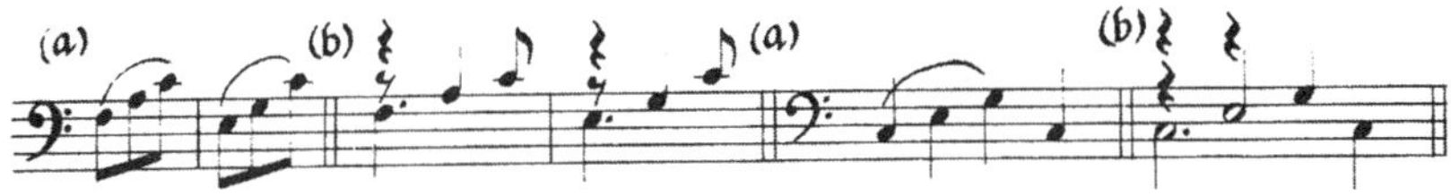

TÜRK, p. 345

While in this case this style of playing referred to the bass, in Louis Adam's *Méthode de piano* it appeared that it can also be applied to broken chords in the treble.[3] In the staves of the following example, the notation and manner of performance are combined.

> If the higher notes form a song in those passages where there is a tie and if the accompanying notes are in one chord, then one can hold all the notes as long as the chord lasts, as thus:

Quand les notes les plus hautes peuvent former un chant dans les endroits, où il y a une liaison, et que les notes, qui accompagnent ce chant, peuvent former un accord, on peut tenir alors toutes les notes sons les doigts tant que ce même accord peut durer: voyez ci aprés:

Bilden die höhern Noten einen Gesang an den Stellen, wo die Bindung steht, und sind die begleitenden Noten in einem Akkorde, so kann man die Noten alle, so lange der Akkord dauert, anhalten, wie Folgendes zeigt:

ADAM, MÉTHODE DE PIANO, p. 152

In his *Notenbüchlein* for Anna Magdalena, Johann Sebastian Bach notated a Rondo in a simple form.

Bach, Rondo

This piece appears to be François Couperin's *Les bergeries*, where the two-part texture of the bass is written out. Of course, a performance of Bach's notation will have to correspond to this.

Couperin, Les bergeries

In Beethoven's notes for Cramer's etudes, which were already referred to in Chapter 2, this manner of performance also comes to the fore. In the Fifth Etude, for example, Beethoven indicates that even if the melody were notated as a single voice, one should still illuminate it with polyphony.

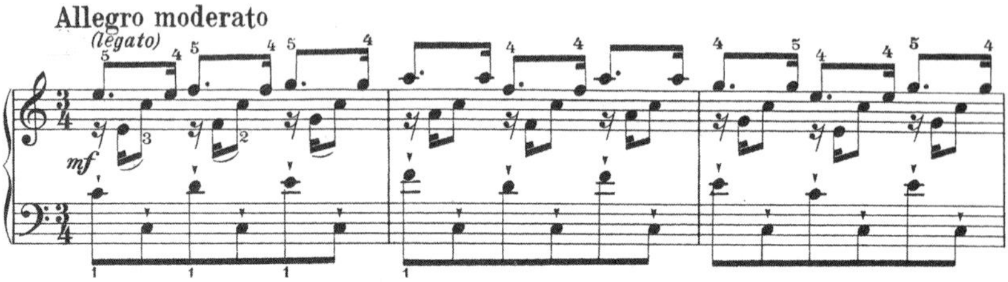

Cramer, Etude No. 5

Or in the Sixth Etude, where it appears that the left hand, too, must be played as two voices.

Cramer, Etude No. 6

Indeed, such a performance can also be used for Beethoven's piano sonatas, as in the last movement of his Sonata in A-flat major, Op. 26. Through the notation of the slur, the double voicing is realized by using the super-*legato*. In the part without the slur, mm. 3–6, this is only hinted at.

Sonata Op. 26, 4th movement

Or, in the second movement, Allegretto, of the Sonata in F major, Op. 54, where in the same way at various points a full polyphonic sound is set against a lighter *non legato* performance, whereby nevertheless sufficient attention must still be given to the hidden double voicing.

Sonata Op. 54, 2nd movement

Mm. 267–278 of the last movement, Presto con fuoco, of the Sonata in E-flat major, Op. 31 No. 3, are also illuminating.

Sonata Op. 31 No. 3, 4th movement

Finally, another example from the "Waldstein" Sonata, in which mm. 112–120 of the first movement are notated in an unusual way. The triplets that must be played *non legato* are conceived predominantly melodically, horizontally. With the triplets that are played *legato*, the harmonic aspect is also very important, while at the same time the fullness of the chords in mm. 114 and 118 in Beethoven's notation is emphasized by holding all the notes.

Sonata Op. 53, 1st movement

Detached Touch

In addition to the "common" or "usual" touch (*ordentliche Fortgehen*) and the *legato* (*Schleifen*), the "detached touch" (*Abstoßen*) is also important. This was already mentioned by Girolamo Diruta when, in his *Il Transilvano* of 1593, he differentiated organ and harpsichord playing. As far as notation is concerned, we see the shortening of a note described possibly for the first time in Jean-Henri d'Anglebert's 1689 *Pièces de clavecin*, which indicates *détacher* with a special mark. This *détacher* was also possible on string instruments, where around 1700 marks such as a stroke and a dot were of significance for the manner of bowing.

Although at first no distinction was made between the two marks, it quickly appeared that the stroke resulted in a particular form of accentuation through the manner of applying the bow. In the preface of his method published in 1739, the Italian violin virtuoso Francesco Geminiani defined both the single and the double stroke in this respect.

> This I I Mark expresses a Beat; and the following I a sudden taking off of the Bow from the strings.

In his *Versuch einer gründlichen Violinschule* (1756), Leopold Mozart presents a large number of examples of this accentuation, which can also be applied to light notes within the melodic progression, as in the following example:

L. MOZART, p. 221

The difference between this style of playing, indicated with a vertical stroke with the much less commonly used notation of dots, and the combination bow/dot was described as follows by Johann Joachim Quantz in his *Versuch einer Anweisung die Flöte traversière zu spielen* of 1752:

> If the word *staccato* appears in a piece, all the notes must be played with a short and detached bow. Since, however, an entire piece is at present rarely composed in a single species of notes, and we take care to include a good mixture of different types, little strokes are written above those notes which require the *staccato.*
>
> In notes of this kind you must be regulated by whether the tempo of the piece is very slow or very quick, and must not shorten the notes in the Adagio as much as those in the Allegro; otherwise those in the Adagio will sound all too

> dry and meager. The general rule that may be established in this regard is as follows: if little strokes stand above several notes, they must sound half as long as their true value. But if a little stroke stands above only one note, after which several of lesser value follow, it indicates not only that the note must be played half as long, but also that it must at the same time be accented with a pressure of the bow.
>
> QUANTZ, p. 232

While in the violin methods and therefore also in Quantz's case, which of course as flutist refers to this style of playing the flute, the distinction is already made between the dot and the vertical stroke, this is not the case in methods for keyboard instruments. This probably has to do with the fact that keyboard methods still concerned all "clavier" instruments, with predominantly methods for the harpsichord, except in France. The specific possibilities of the fortepiano, still in the course of development, had yet to be discovered. While Carl Philipp Emanuel Bach and, for example, Marpurg were still making no distinction between dot and vertical stroke, and restricted themselves to stating that the *Abstoßen*, depending on the context, could be longer or shorter, it appears that Türk in his 1789 *Klavierschule* indicated for the first time a difference in meaning.

> The signs at *a* and *b* have the same meaning, but some would like to indicate the stroke (*a*) that a shorter *staccato* be played than that indicated by the dot (*b*).[4]

> TÜRK, p. 342

In the case of Wolfgang Amadeus Mozart, it can be seen that he notates the stroke in his early compositions, but that in the course of time (around 1770) he also makes increasing use of dots in his works for piano. The marks became more independent: the stroke with *forte* passages and longer note values, the dot with *piano* passages and shorter notes. Later there are, however, examples where, for instance, upbeats that are by nature "light" become accentuated by the use of a stroke.[5]

The difference between the two signs in a handwritten manuscript was, however, often not reflected in the printing of that period. Apart from its being not all that easy, because there were also intermediate forms in the handwriting, such as the transition from dots to strokes or vice versa to indicate a gradual increase or decrease in accentuation, and of course because the handwriting itself could also be unclear, it seems that printers were not all that fastidious, and regularly printed a mark that happened to be to hand, meaning that in some editions the stroke was printed as a somewhat broader dash (or even heavier wedge), the shape in both these cases being more significant than the much more slender stroke.

It is not known whether Haydn and Mozart paid special attention to the differences. Beethoven, however, pointed out the difference in a letter to Karl Holz from 1825 with corrections for his String Quartet in A minor, Op. 132.

> All the notes are correct—but do read me correctly—Volti Subito. Well, now for your copy, my dear fellow. Obligatissimo—but the marks p <> etc. etc. have been horribly neglected and frequently, very frequently, inserted in the wrong place. No doubt haste is responsible for this. For God's sake please impress on Rampel to copy everything exactly as it stands. If you will just have a look now at what I have corrected, you will find everything that you have to tell him. Where a dot is above the note a dash must not be put instead and vice versa—( and  are not identical.)
>
> ANDERSON, Vol. III, pp. 1241–1242

The differences are most apparent in Beethoven's manuscripts, where the vertical strokes are sometimes 0.4 inch (1 cm) long and in print must of course be clearly represented, as in mm. 9 and 10 of the second movement, Lebhaft marschmäßig, of the Sonata Op. 101.

Sonata Op. 101, 2nd movement, autograph

Regarding clear examples of dots, meaning a lighter manner of playing, there are less of these because it appears that Beethoven mainly wrote a stroke anyway, small or longer. One convincing example of dots is, however, to be seen in mm. 221–222 of the last movement, Allegro ma non troppo, of the Sonata in F minor, Op. 57, the "Appassionata." Coming in *pianissimo* from the preceding measures, the short, light *staccati* make the *crescendo* more exciting than would have been the case with longer accentuated notes, as is reflected in the autograph as well as in the Henle urtext edition.[6]

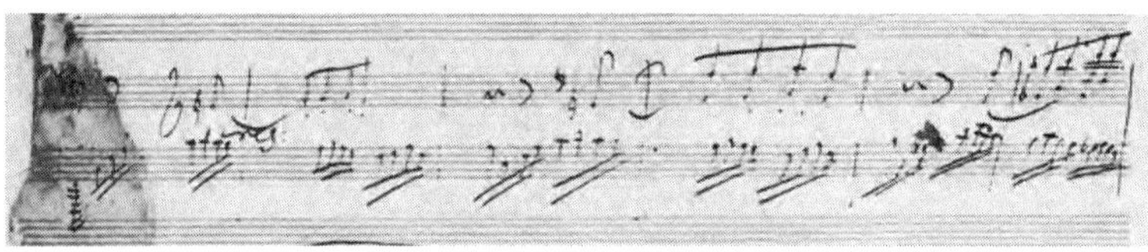

Sonata Op. 57, 3rd movement, autograph

Sonata Op. 57, 3rd movement, Henle edition

In Artaria's original printing of the first movement of the Sonata in C major, Op. 2 No. 3, where both marks are used, the examples also correspond to the character of the music. The beginning, soft and with dots, then, from m. 69 onward and the corresponding measures in the Recapitulation, with *forte* and strokes, are printed here by Artaria using their characteristic sign of a narrow dash.

Sonata Op. 2 No. 3, 1st movement, Artaria edition

Sometimes even the alternation between the notation of a stroke and its absence can be of significance. This is the case in the first movement of the Sonata in E-flat major, Op. 81a, in mm. 38–44, in which this sign on the quarter note in the right hand is sometimes absent. The Wiener Urtext presents this correctly, corresponding to the original publication by Breitkopf & Härtel:

Sonata Op. 81a, 1st movement

Beaming

Another way of introducing nuances in a phrase was to use a beam. Examples of this are also to be found in the 1674 edition of John Playford's *An Introduction to the Skill of Musick*, where the notes are so concentrated together by means of the beams that various groupings are discernible:

PLAYFORD, p. 28

It appears that Playford combines the eighth and sixteenth notes sometimes two-on-two but also in groups of four by use of the beam, thereby elucidating the melodic progression.[7] However, in the long tradition of this manner of notation, reaching far into the nineteenth century, this also gains significance for the articulation. Shorter or longer groupings characterize the manner of notation and appear to have, along with other factors, a deciding role in the music's breathing.[8]

To begin with, an example from Bach's French Suite in B minor, BWV 814, where in the Courante the 6/4 time is sometimes divided into twos (2×3) and sometimes into threes (3×2). The beginning is clearly in two.

Bach, French Suite BWV 814, Courante

In m. 14, however, the metrical division between the treble and the bass occurs in a more varied way.

Bach, French Suite BWV 814, Courante

In m. 17 the movement is again parallel in threes.

Bach, French Suite BWV 814, Courante

But in m. 22 the borders blur, while in m. 24 yet another distribution is to be seen.

Bach, French Suite BWV 814, Courante

At the beginning of the Praeambulum of the Fifth Partita in G major, BWV 829, the eighth notes in the bass and the sixteenths in the treble are connected by only one beam within the measure. But from m. 57 onward, the melodic and harmonic twists and turns of the sixteenth-note passages present a much more varied picture. It is of course clear that it is possible to hold the first notes of each group somewhat longer.

Bach, Partita BWV 829, Praeambulum

It is obvious that here it is not just about making the text clearer, but rather that the alternation is also significant for the pulse, whereby groups are longer or shorter and thereby influence the music's motion.

Such notations are also to be found in the Viennese Classical period, as in the last movement of Beethoven's Sonata in B-flat major, Op. 22, where the groupings emphasize the various courses of the harmonic progression.

Sonata Op. 22, 4th movement

In the second variation in the Sonata in A-flat major, Op. 26, a really varied image is captured by Beethoven in the notation. This, however, has suffered slovenly treatment from the very first printing up to our own time. Only in recent publications of the Wiener Urtext and the latest Henle publication, on which the pianist Murray Perahia collaborated, have the beams been adopted so as to correspond with the autograph.

Sonata Op. 26, 1st movement, autograph

These notations can also be encountered in Beethoven's later sonatas, as is apparent from the diversity of the beaming in the Fourth Variation of the Sonata in C minor, Op. 111. The lower voice constantly displays groups of three sixteenth notes, while the subtle mobility of the upper voice is evocatively expressed in groups of three, six, or nine consolidated notes.

Sonata Op. 111, 2nd movement, autograph

How Beethoven used these possibilities to make his intentions clear can also be ascertained in mm. 91–96 of the Adagio sostenuto of the "Hammerklavier," Op. 106. While at first the thirty-second notes are notated in a *legato* four-by-four, in accordance with the "rhythmic accent"—as discussed in Chapter 2—from m. 94 the movement suddenly becomes more expansive, not only through the notation of the longer slur, but also by the continuation of the beam, which now combines three groups of four thirty-second notes.

Sonata Op. 106, 3rd movement

Finally, a very personal example of this manner of expression in the autograph of the first movement of the Sonata in F minor, the "Appassionata," Op. 57. Within the 12/8 time, the beams are presented in an unusual way in several measures in the left hand—namely as a curved or straight line, with as dramatic climax mm. 215–217, where, in octaves, the theme heralds the cadence-like broken chords starting in m. 218. The enormous tension of this moment is apparent from the "impetus" of the curved beams on the first and third groups of three tied eighth notes.[9]

It is perhaps going too far to present such a notation in print, but it does emphasize the importance of, where possible, involving the original manuscript when generating an interpretation.

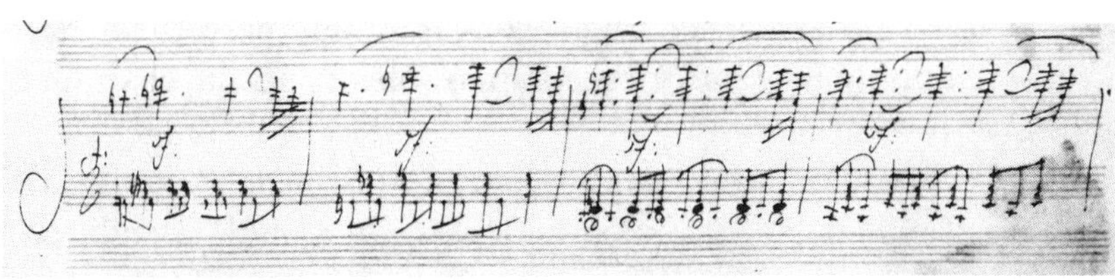

Sonata Op. 57, 1st movement, autograph

Sonata Op. 57, 1st movement

Pedaling

While the above examples can be realized on both the fortepiano and the modern grand, this is far less the case with Beethoven's pedal notations. For a performance on a present-day grand, compromises must be made while not losing sight of what Beethoven actually had in mind. From his notations it is clear that Beethoven gave pedal indications only where he had a special expression in mind—for example, to have different harmonies intermingling in very softly performed measures, resulting in an ethereal, intangible sound. We find this idea in, for instance, the *pianissimo* recitatives in the first movement of the Sonata in D minor, Op. 31 No. 2.

The connection of the musical picture of this sonata with Shakespeare's play *The Tempest* has already been mentioned in Chapter 1, and it is clear that the speaking voice in these recitatives is reaching to us from far away, lost in the mists, from heaven as it were (see also Chapter 6).

Such a color is not difficult to realize on an instrument of Beethoven's time, but it is far more difficult to achieve it with the depressed right pedal on modern grand pianos. On these, the musical outcome quickly becomes incomprehensible due to the creation of excessive resonance. Solutions can be found in not completely depressing the pedal, or by using a quick "flutter" pedal, but also, and with a much better result, silently depressing a random collection of black and white keys in the bass with the left hand, so that these notes keep resonating even with the changes in the right pedal. The result is a melting of the notes in the recitative, whereby a certain distinctness is still retained.

Sonata Op. 31 No. 2, 1st movement

Another well-known example where harmonies intermingle is to be found at the *pianissimo* beginning of the last movement of the "Waldstein" Sonata, Op. 53, where the tonic and dominant must sound through—here, too, to achieve an intangible, mysterious sound palette. The solution on a modern grand might be found in playing the sixteenth-note passages extremely softly, the low bass note a little more loudly, and, of course, with the pedal not fully depressed.

Sonata Op. 53, 3rd movement

However, such a solution is not available for the performance of the first movement, Adagio sostenuto, of the Sonata Op. 27 No. 2, the "Moonlight." Here, also in *pianissimo*, an uninterrupted use of the sustaining pedal, as is indicated by Beethoven with his inscription *senza sordino* for sixty-nine measures with a constantly changing bass, would lead to complete confusion about the harmonic progression of the music, whether one is playing a historical instrument from Beethoven's era or one from the present day. Beethoven's indication probably has to do with the exceptional structure of this movement, with successive broken chords from beginning to end. Indeed, also with some change of pedal during the movement, the specific atmosphere of continuously very softly resonating strings must have been the musical image he had in mind.

This sonata was the second of the two Sonatas Op. 27 that were published under the name "Sonata quasi una Fantasia," and what a perfect match it is to see the following words in Carl Philipp Emanuel Bach's *Essay on the True Art of Playing Keyboard Instruments*, Chapter 7, "Improvisation," under the heading "The Free Fantasia":

> The undamped register of the pianoforte is the most pleasing, and, once the performer learns to observe the necessary precautions in the face of its reverberations, the most delightful for improvisation.
>
> C.P.E. BACH, p. 431

C.P.E. Bach published this book in 1762, decades before Beethoven wrote his sonata, but apparently this performance practice was still not forgotten later on, specifically because improvising on a harmonic progression of broken triads, as is the case in the first movement of this sonata, was one of the main tools a pianist had in his reservoir of possibilities.

That Beethoven meticulously notated special effects through pedaling can also be observed in the last measures of the Coda in the first movement of the "Appassionata," Op. 57, where the doom motif at first still sounds muffled in the pedal but then in m. 237 must be performed without the pedal, thus sounding shorter and drier. There then follows an expressive *portato* blossoming into a *piano* with pedal, after which the *fortissimo* outburst of the Coda, decisive and of course without pedal, sets in.

Sonata Op. 57, 1st movement

In the Scherzo of the "Hammerklavier" Sonata, the motif, previously performed *pianissimo,* is suddenly pedaled in m. 26 (repeated in m. 42), a special variation of color before the *crescendo* sets in.

Sonata Op. 106, 2nd movement

A similar extremely soft, dwindling ending could already be heard in the last measures of the first movement of Op. 26. Beethoven's *senza sordino* notation, the lifting of the dampers, is his first pedal notation in his sonatas after having used them earlier in his First and Second Piano Concertos (Op. 15 and Op. 19) and in the Quintet for wind instruments and piano, Op. 16.

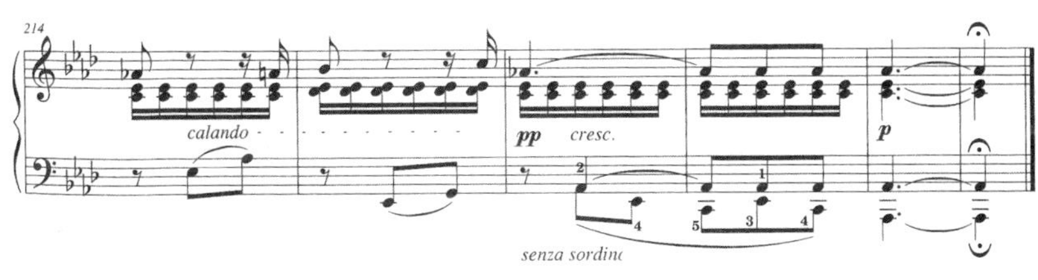

Sonata Op. 26, 1st movement

His pedal notation in the Sonata in E major, Op. 109, is also exceptional, this time employing the usual marks. There, too, the pedal is indicated in the last measure of the first movement. The last chord of this movement, conceived as soft, light, and "exalted" because it comes in the second half of the measure, explodes into the *fortissimo* chord of the next movement, Prestissimo, where at the same moment the pedal is lifted. It also means that the two movements with their huge contrasts must be linked to each other without any break.

Sonata Op. 109, transition from the 1st to the 2nd movement

Beethoven's conceptions of sound appear, however, not only in soft coloring effects or a special link, but also in massive blocks performed *forte*, which contrast with sections notated without pedal. The final measures of the Sonata in E-flat major, "Les Adieux," Op. 81a, are a good example of this.

Sonata Op. 81a, 3rd movement

In this example it is clear that the last two chords are to be played without pedal. In the next example, however, presenting the final chords of the last movement of the "Appassionata," we see a different notation. Here, the pedal is also indicated for a massive block of *fortissimo,* but in spite of the rests in the final measures, in the autograph the mark to release the pedal is missing. Therefore, the question arises, should these last chords stay in the pedal? The first printing by the Bureau des Arts et d'Industrie in Vienna also fails to offer a solution. There, even the *fermata* on the last rest, clearly noticeable in the autograph, is missing. Modern urtexts correct this mistake and follow the autograph, but the release of the pedal remains unclear.[10]

Sonata Op. 57, 3rd movement

There are also special notations where Beethoven uses the *una corda* to transmute the sound gradually, whereby on the grand pianos of his time, where the strings of the bass were polychoral, the volume could be increased string by string. A fine example of this is to be found in the third movement, Adagio ma non troppo, con affetto, of his Sonata in E major, Op. 101. For this short movement of only twenty measures, Beethoven demands that it be played completely *Sul una corda.* This means that only in the final measure should the *una corda* pedal be gradually lifted to attain the same sound as at the very beginning of this sonata.

Sonata Op. 101, 3rd movement

The refinement of the sound at the end of the Adagio in the third movement of the Sonata Op. 106 is even more special. In this Adagio, where Beethoven is already using the *una corda* pedal very often, we find in the final measures no less than three colors of sound in his notation: coming out of *pp* in m. 180, at first the *una corda* is added, this being followed by four measures with the addition of the right pedal (damper pedal), and finally the last two chords, the first one *pp* and the last one with an *arpeggio* in *ppp.* This broken chord, now with the abolition of the *una corda,* indeed returns to *tre corde.* As in a vision, all single notes of the chord shimmer in a magical incandescence.

Sonata Op. 106, 3rd movement

Although it is a well-known comment of Czerny about Beethoven's playing that he used the pedal much more frequently than he notated, the pianist performing on present-day grands must be aware that Beethoven's pedal notations still need to be recognized as being intended for special effects. After all, if one uses the pedal so much that those notations can no longer be distinguished from the rest of the music, then they become meaningless. In many cases the prolonged touch will have to be used in those parts that adjoin a pedal notation given by Beethoven, so that there is still enough contrast in timbre without the sound becoming too meager. It is, however, obvious that the musical expression intended by Beethoven can be realized more readily on instruments from his time than on the modern-day grand.

Rubato

While the word *rubato* is generally associated with a style of playing connected with the Romantic period, such as in the works of Chopin, ways of indicating a certain freedom of movement in music were known much earlier, as in the case of Girolamo Frescobaldi, who, in the preface to his 1637 *Toccate e partite*, wrote:

> This form of execution should not, as is the custom in modern madrigals, be subjected rigorously to the beat. Although these madrigals are difficult, they are made easier by conducting the beat sometimes slowly, sometimes quickly, or even holding back, depending on the expression or the meaning of the words.
>
> FRESCOBALDI (11), Introduction

A parallel can be found in a text from Beethoven's era in a description of the playing of Beethoven's pupil Dorothea von Ertmann. In this, too, there is mention of having the music within a given phrase flow along with the musical expression.

> She grasped intuitively even the most hidden subtleties of Beethoven's works with as much sureness as if they had been written out before her eyes. This sensitive musician used the same insight with respect to nuances of tempo in a way that cannot be described in words. She knew how to give each phrase the motion of its particular spirit, how to move artistically from one phrase to the next, so that the whole seemed a motivated unity. [. . .] She seemed to have an inborn instinct for playing the free tempo correctly.
>
> SCHINDLER (II), p. 210

This taking a little more time, or a little less, sometimes accelerating, always in concordance with the musical expression, is in fact a reflection of the natural course of playing, were it not that in many performances such liberties are not at all taken or are in contrast exaggerated. A balance is not easy to find, as Leopold Mozart also remarked once in his *Violinschule* of 1756:

> What this "stolen tempo" is, is more easily shown than described.
>
> L. MOZART, p. 224

Master pedagogue Carl Czerny could not be satisfied with such a comment. He made an attempt to be more concrete in the section titled "On Playing with Expression" in the third chapter of his *Complete Theoretical and Practical Piano Forte School.*

1. The first measure must be played in strict time.
2. The three last eighth notes of the 2nd measure must be *retarded* a very little; indeed almost imperceptibly so, as the next or 3rd measure is a repetition of the first measure, and therefore of the principal subject, though on other degrees of the scale.
3. The last somewhat arpeggioed chord in the 3rd measure should be played rather ritenuto.
4. The three last eighth notes in the 4th measure must be executed with somewhat more fire (and therefore almost *accelerando*), which is again relinquished in the last three eighth notes of the 5th measure.
5. In the 6th measure is one of those embellishments, consisting of many notes, which is a measure that obliges us to employ a *ritardando* in both hands, in order that the quick notes may not be hurried and confused, but that they may flow gracefully and tenderly onwards; only the last notes of this embellishment must be perceptibly retarded, and on the last note but one (the G#) a kind of short pause should be introduced. With respect to the distribution of this long embellishment, as regards the measures, we shall speak hereafter.

6. The 7th and 8th measures are in strict time.
7. The 9th measure must be played with power and spirit (consequently *almost accelerando*).
8. The 2nd half of the 10th measure somewhat tranquil.
9. The 11th measure somewhat *ritardando*, and the last dissonant chord very soft, and also something slower, because every dissonant chord (when it is marked Piano), produces the best effect, when played in this manner.
10. The three eighth notes of the 12th measure in exact time; on the contrary the last five eighth notes *ritardando*, as they form the transition into the Theme.
11. The 13th measure in Time.
12. The first quarter note in the 14th measure somewhat *ritard*, which is increased considerably in the 2nd quarter note, and in which the 8 upper notes must be marked *forte* and *cresc.* The Pause must last for almost five eighth notes, and the following run must be moderately fast, equal, tender, and *diminuendo*, till ultimately the last 8 notes must be played with a marked *ritardando*.
13. The first half of the 15th measure in strict Time; the 2nd half *ritardando*, where the close of the embellishment must fall with extreme tenderness.
14. The last measure in a tranquil degree of movement.

CZERNY (III), Vol. 3, p. 35

With this description, Czerny tried to follow an expressive presentation precisely, which if followed literally of course results in a labored, artificial performance. It is, however, more important to see that a performance does not always need to be "to the letter." An interpretation follows the musical tension; it must reflect the characteristics whereby a composition's musical picture must always retain a certain flexibility.[11]

While this freedom of movement is not notated in the note picture, in the era of Viennese Classicism there are forms of *rubato* that are linked to a certain notation. The first to be mentioned are the *anticipatio* and *retardatio*, playing the melody earlier or later in relation to the bass.[12] Türk wrote in his *Klavierschule:*

The so-called *tempo rubato* or *robato* (actually *stolen* time) I have specified in § 63 as the third resource whose application should be left to the sensitivity and insight of the player. This term appears with more than one meaning. Commonly it is understood as a kind of shortening or lengthening of notes, or the displacement (dislocation) of these. There is something taken away (stolen) from the duration of a note and for this, another note is given that much more, as in the following examples *b* and *c*.

At *a* are the basic notes, at *b* tempo rubato is put to use by means of the *anticipatio* and at *c* by means of the *retardatio*. From this it can be seen that through this kind of execution, the tempo, or even more, the meter as a whole is not displaced. Consequently, the customary but somewhat ambiguous German term *verrücktes Zeitmaß* [displaced tempo] is not very fitting, for the bass voice goes its way according to the meter (without displacement), and only the notes of the melody are moved out of place, as it were. For this reason the expression *Versetzen* or *Verziehen* [changing the place of, or dragging out] the *notes* or the *beat divisions* would be more correct. Even when more notes are added to the melody, as in examples *e* and *f*, both voices must nevertheless correctly coincide each time at the beginning of the measure. In this case, then, there results no actual displacement of the tempo.

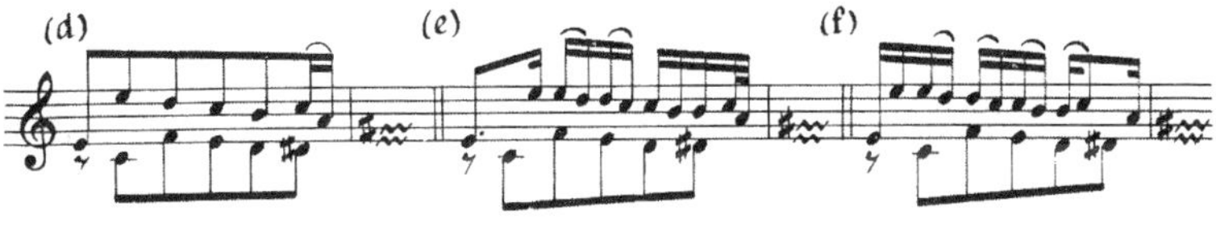

TÜRK, pp. 363, 364

The notation written by Türk is to be found in many of Haydn's sonatas. In some early sonatas, the Trios are even notated totally according to the *retardatio* principle, as in the Trio from the Minuet of the Sonata in A major, Hob. XVI:12.

TRIO

Haydn, Sonata Hob. XVI:12, 2nd movement

This notation naturally gives only a global indication of the intended effect. For the upper voice does not always need to fall precisely on the half beat, but can sometimes be played a little earlier, sometimes a little later than the bass, according to how the tension is developing, such as, for example, the playing of the b^2 in m. 2 a little on the late side. It is striking that Haydn writes this form of notation in the Trios, with their characteristic *mineur* keys, so that the contrast with the minuets—written in *majeur*, light but more strictly metrical—is increased.

A very extended example of this form of *rubato* can be found in the Andante con moto of Haydn's Sonata in C minor, Hob. XVI:20.

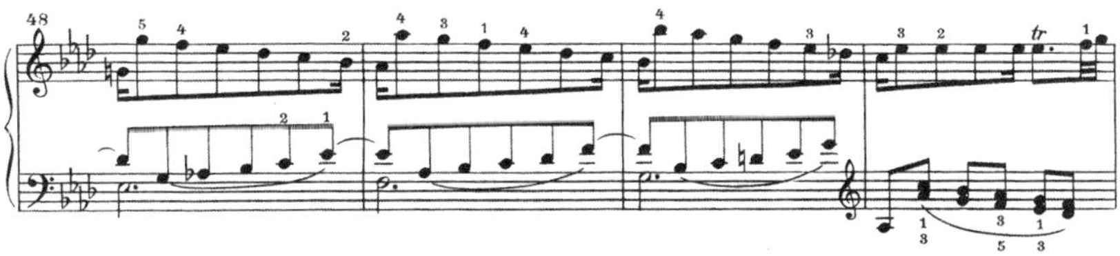

Haydn, Sonata Hob. XVI:20, 2nd movement

This form of *rubato* occurs regularly in the work of Mozart, too, such as the *retardatio* in mm. 23 and 24 of the first movement, Allegro, of his Sonata in G major, K. 283.

Mozart, Sonata K. 283, 1st movement

Or the *anticipatio* at the opening of the last movement, Allegro assai, of the Sonata in C minor, K. 457, where his addition of *agitato* reinforces the dramatic character of this theme.

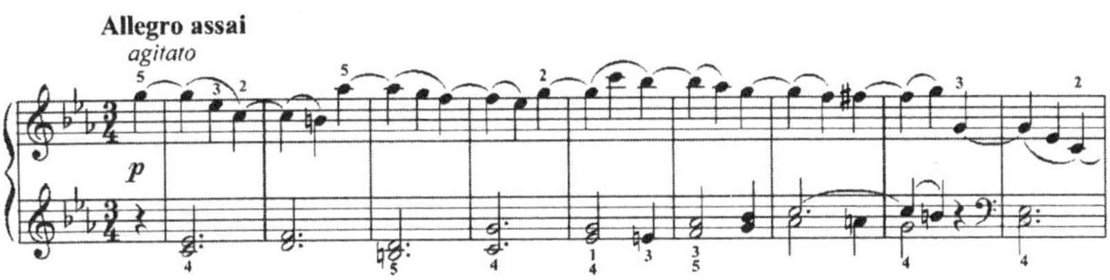

Mozart, Sonata K. 457, 3rd movement

From Beethoven's handling of the first theme in the last movement of his Sonata in E major, Op. 14 No. 1, it can be seen that he, too, made highly effective use of these possibilities.

Sonata Op. 14 No. 1, 3rd movement

Sonata Op. 14 No. 1, 3rd movement

A most eloquent example is to be found in the Adagio sostenuto of the "Hammerklavier" Sonata, Op. 106. From m. 36 onward, both the upper and middle voices come in too early relative to the accompaniment. The *anticipatio* together with the *crescendo* and the impressively ascending bass comprehensively express the agitated tension of these measures.

Sonata Op. 106, 3rd movement

As already mentioned in the introduction to this chapter, the *portato*, indicated by notes with dots under a slur, can also be connected with a kind of *rubato* playing. In keyboard works, this notation initially applied only to the clavichord. On this instrument, the so-called *portamento*, *portato*, or *tragende Ton* was achieved by depressing the key a little deeper. The tangent, positioned on the end of the key, is pressed a little more firmly on the string, leading to a tightening of this and thus a slightly higher note. This also makes the *bebung* effect possible. By varying the pressure of the finger on the key, the note becomes correspondingly higher or lower, comparable with a kind of vibrato. C.P.E. Bach and Türk mention this special effect in their methods. This way of playing was, however, later applied to piano methods, as can be seen in Louis Adam's 1804 *Méthode de piano du Conservatoire*. It is interesting to see that here the *portato* is notated by repeating notes, in contrast to the other two examples.

Adam, Méthode de piano, *p. 154*

An example from Beethoven can be found in m. 48 of the Largo e mesto of his Sonata in D minor, Op. 10 No. 3, where the freely played repeating notes prepare, almost "speaking," for the entry of the theme.

Sonata Op. 10 No. 3, 2nd movement

In the following example, Adam shows the notation of the *portato* and the manner of playing in two systems one under the other. In a comparison with the art of singing, it appears that here the *retardatio* principle is applicable, because the playing of the melody, as it is notated in the second system, does not run in parallel with the bass notes.

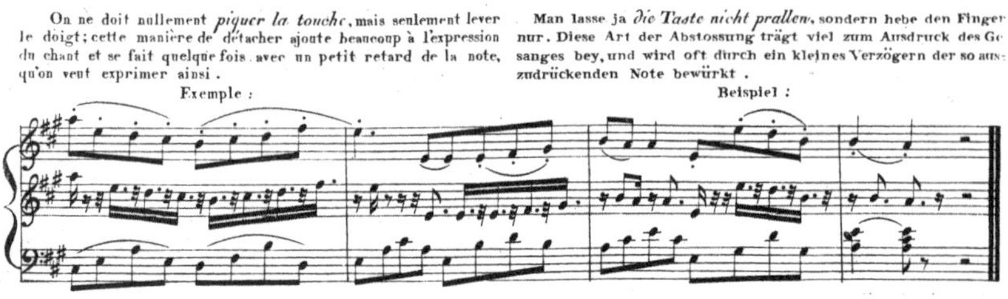

Adam, Méthode de piano, *p. 156*

> One should *under no circumstance let the key bounce*, but just lift the finger. This form of detachment contributes much to the expression of the song and is often effected by slightly delaying the note to be expressed thus.

In addition to these notations, it appears that just a word or two could also be sufficient to indicate a certain freedom of performance. Clementi writes in his method:

> CON ESPRESSIONE, or CON ANIMA, with expression; that is, with passionate feeling: where every note has its peculiar force and energy; and where even the severity of time may be relaxed for extraordinary effects.
>
> CLEMENTI, p. 14

Such a *con espressione* notation can be seen in the first movement of Beethoven's Sonata in F minor, Op. 2 No. 1, where the increasing intensity of the closing measures of the Exposition through the broadening of the tempo leads to a culmination of the musical tension in the full *fortissimo* chord.

Sonata Op. 2 No. 1, 1st movement

Beethoven understood the meaning of *espressivo* very well indeed, something which can also be gathered from the second movement, Prestissimo, of the Sonata in E major, Op. 109. His notation *un poco espressivo* in m. 29 does more justice to the more intense lyricism of this section, in a slightly gentler tempo, in comparison to what has gone before. In m. 32 he then also prescribes *a tempo*, which would have been unnecessary had this not been decreased somewhat in the preceding measures.

Sonata Op. 109, 2nd movement

Now and then Beethoven uses an even clearer indication to make his intentions plain. An example is seen in m. 34 of the first movement of the Sonata Op. 111, where he combines *espressivo* with *poco ritenente*. He already wrote *poco ritenente* in m. 23, an expression that was certainly used by him to retain the musical tension in the face of a deceleration. While there the melodic line is not supported by chords, it is apparent in m. 34 that his voice leading proceeds within a close succession of exciting harmonies that require more time to sound out.

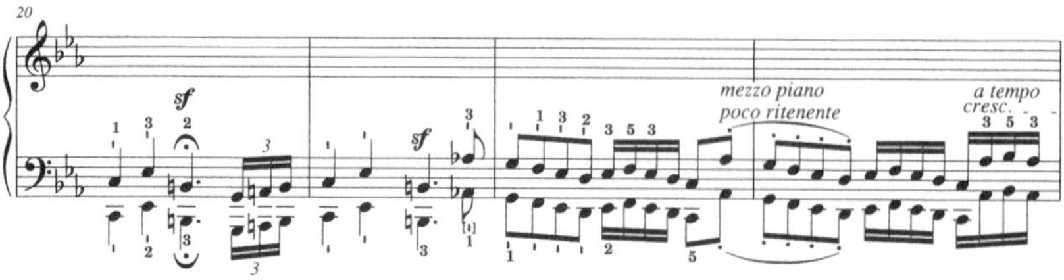

Sonata Op. 111, 1st movement

Sonata Op. 111, 1st movement

Finally, certain freedoms of movement can also be observed in Beethoven's handwriting, for he frequently wrote spatially; that is, in the spontaneous process of writing he allowed more space for measures that would take longer to play. It is probably going a little too far to have these nuances expressed in print, but in his autographs these fluctuations occur quite often.

A really evocative rendition is to be observed in m. 27 of the first movement of Op. 110, where the intensification, already prepared in the four preceding measures, is given expansively in Beethoven's manuscript.

Sonata Op. 110, 1st movement, autograph

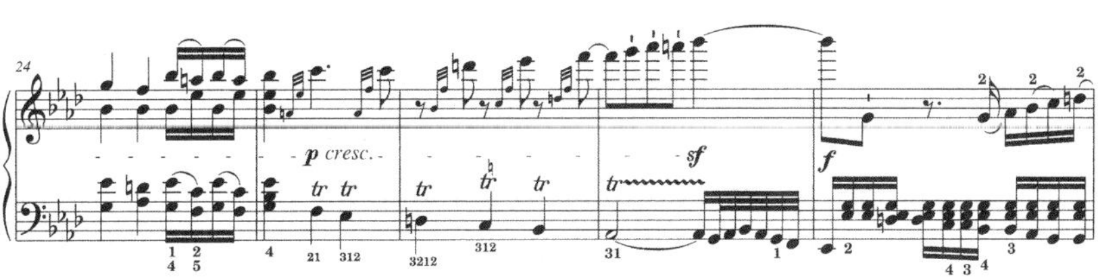

Sonata Op. 110, 1st movement

Or the way in which, in the first movement of the Sonata Op. 90, after the *fortissimo* outburst in m. 53, the space needed by the subsequent *ritardando/diminuendo* is rendered optically. It also appears from his forceful notation that Beethoven dipped his pen deeper into the inkpot to express the harrowing chord in m. 54.

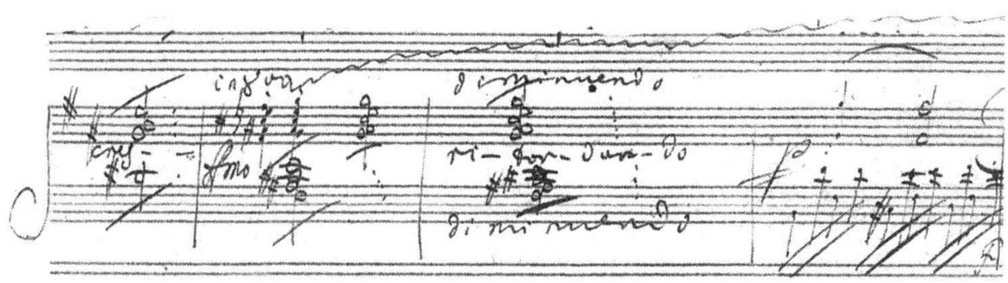

Sonata Op. 90, 1st movement, autograph

An even more impressive example of spatial notation can be found in the third movement, Adagio, ma non troppo, con affetto, of Op. 101. The profundity of this movement, with its surreal and delicate atmosphere, approaches the indescribable. The use of the *una corda* pedal throughout the movement, the amazing inception, as if Beethoven is beginning in the middle of a phrase, or the last measures (mm. 11–20), where the bass descends stepwise half a tone until the key of E major is reached, impart to this short section of just twenty measures an almost ethereal character. Then a lonely, tender voice awakens out of the last E-major chord, and the same ascending melodic line based on this chord, already so prominent in the first theme and sequel of the first movement, is featured again in the top note of each quintuplet. In this way, we are transported to the dispersed main theme of the first movement, as in a flashback.

For the melodic line of minutely notated notes in m. 20, Beethoven marks *non presto*, meaning not to play them very fast, indeed a warning against too rapid playing. This is confirmed by Beethoven's autograph, where it is crystal clear how much space he is using to spread out this passage over the page, and even the space between each quintuplet might suggest the time that is needed for the gesture of the hand to reach out for the next top note. Indeed, this wonderful transition needs time to express its musical content. Unfortunately, this is not visible in any printed score. Compare, for example, the first edition by Steiner in Vienna with Beethoven's autograph.

Sonata Op. 101, 3rd movement, Steiner

Sonata Op. 101, 3rd movement, autograph

This information gained from the autograph may lead to an interpretation completely different from one that is only based on looking at an urtext, but also here, mistakes can be easily made. For example, the typeface used for the words *non presto*: Steiner prints it in boldface and even with initial capitals. Fortunately, most urtexts, including the Wiener Urtext, are more careful.

From all of this it is clear that carefully consulting an autograph, when available, should be a task for any pianist who is trying to come closer to the intentions of the composer.

Character and "Heavy" and "Light" Execution

A significant tool that was available to a composer in the Classical period in Vienna to express the character of a composition directly in the notation was to use a specific meter related to the concept of "heavy" and "light" execution. Türk wrote in his *Klavierschule:*

> That meter has very marked influence on heavy or light execution, or certainly should have, has already been mentioned in passing in the note on p. 90 f. The following should be noted in this connection. The larger the values of the main beats of a measure, the heavier must be the execution. Therefore, a composition in 3/2, for example, is played more heavily than it would be if it were in 3/4 or even in 3/8.
>
> TÜRK, p. 349

Not only the meter but also the use of certain note values in itself was connected with this. Türk continued:

> Various species of notes require, regardless of the kind of meter, a more or less heavy execution. For example, if in a composition there occur mostly larger note values, namely whole, half, and quarter notes, then the execution must be generally heavier than if many eighth and sixteenth notes, etc., were intermingled.
>
> TÜRK, pp. 349–350

The "light" or "heavy" execution in this regard concerned not so much the dynamics, but rather whether or not the given note values were to be maintained consistently. For a heavy execution the notes were played to their full, notated value as much as possible, while for a lighter execution they were played more briefly than indicated. Türk wrote:

> For a *heavy* execution every tone must be played firmly (with emphasis) and held out until the very end of the prescribed duration of the note. *Light* execution is that in which every

> tone is played with less firmness (emphasis), and the finger lifted from the key somewhat sooner than the actual prescribed duration.
>
> TÜRK, p. 347

Johann Philipp Kirnberger illustrated the significance of this in his *Die Kunst des reinen Satzes in der Musik*, written in the years 1771/1776–1779:

> Two-four time has the movement of the *alla breve* time signature but is executed with more lightness. The difference in execution in both types of meter is too pronounced, such that one should believe it did not matter whether a piece is set in ¢ or in 2/4. See for example the following melodic passage in both types of meter:

> If this passage is correctly executed, everyone will notice that in *alla breve* time it is much more serious and emphatic than in 2/4 time, where it almost acquires something dance-like. This is the difference of types of meter of similar time, as already mentioned above.
>
> KIRNBERGER, Vol. II, Part 1, pp. 118 ff.

The extent to which such a difference in character plays a role in the notation process is also apparent from Mozart's String Quartet in B-flat major, K. 458. He notated the last movement originally in an *alla breve* time with the direction Prestissimo, whereby a few quarter notes are given dots for a light *staccato* style of playing.

Mozart, String Quartet K. 458, 4th movement, autograph

In the definitive version, however, Mozart wrote a 2/4 time with shorter note values in which the dots above the notes are missing and Allegro assai replaces Prestissimo. It is clear that in this notation the intended lightness is expressed much more effectively than in the *alla breve* notation, the Prestissimo (seldom used by him), and the *staccato* way of playing.

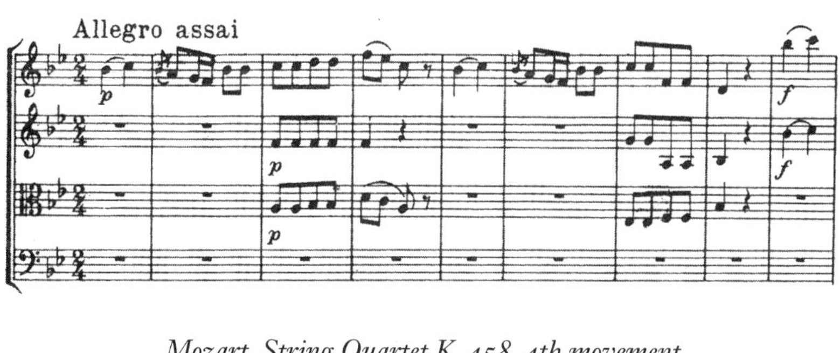

Mozart, String Quartet K. 458, 4th movement

By combining meters, note values, and tempo/character directions, the intended character of a composition could be recorded with great precision. Johann Georg Sulzer wrote in the second printing of his *Allgemeine Theorie der Schönen Künste* of 1771/1774:

> If a piece is to be executed lightly, but at the same time moving slowly, then the composer will, depending on the kind of light or lighter execution, choose a time signature of short or shorter beats, and use the words *andante*, or *largo*, or *adagio*, etc., according to which the slowness of the piece should exceed the natural movement of the meter; and conversely: if the piece is to be executed in a heavy manner and at the same time have a fast speed, then he will choose, according to the type of execution, a heavy beat and indicate it with *vivace*, *allegro*, or *presto*, etc.
>
> SULZER, Vol. 2, p. 1133

How Beethoven exploited these possibilities is seen clearly in the notation of the central movement of his Third Piano Concerto, in which he combines 3/8 time with the designation Largo, so that it is even possible to write 128th notes in this movement. Beethoven's notation, very unusual in appearance—certainly in those days[13]—was motivated by the fact that, in terms of character, this Largo must be played extremely subtly, in a flowing manner, and with hardly any emphasis or, in Czerny's poetic words: "Like a holy, distant and celestial harmony" (Czerny [II], p. 108).

Third Piano Concerto, 2nd movement

The opposite can also be found, however, such as in the theme of the last movement, Andante molto cantabile ed espressivo, of the

Sonata in E major, Op. 109. Here, the concrete, more sober, and somewhat sarabande-like character is expressed in 3/4 time in combination with only quarter and eighth notes.

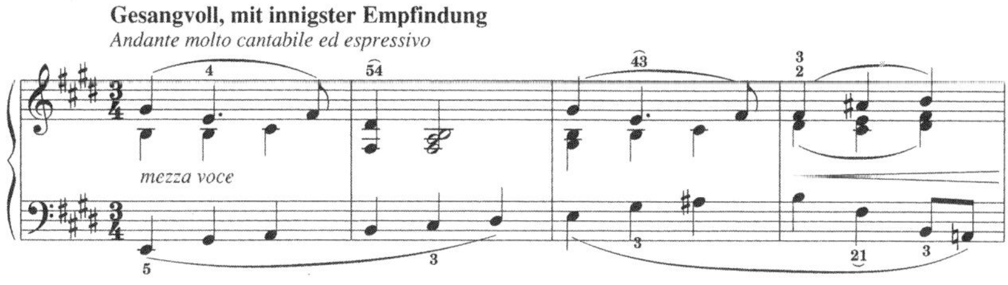

Sonata Op. 109, 3rd movement

Or in the very fast tempo of the second movement of the same sonata, in which—with the eighth as the shortest note value—despite the Prestissimo, a certain weight must still be maintained within the melodic progression, so that the polyphony in the further development of this movement can still be meaningful.

Sonata Op. 109, 2nd movement

With all these combinations, Beethoven could express exceptionally subtle differences in character in the notation, as can be observed by comparing the First Bagatelle of Op. 126 with the Third. Regarding tempo, there is probably not so much difference: an Andante con moto cantabile e compiacevole and an Andante cantabile e grazioso. The character is, however, not completely identical. In the First Bagatelle, the slightly heavier (*compiacevole*) character can be deduced from the notated 3/4 time, while the immaterial (dance-like) character of the Third Bagatelle is to be found in the 3/8 notation and the direction *cantabile e grazioso*.

Bagatelle Op. 126 No. 1

Bagatelle Op. 126 No. 3

Meter and Metrical Construction

As described in methods centered around the Viennese Classical period, a meter, or time, was associated not only with a heavier or lighter style of playing but also with the concept of the *Fuß*, or metrical foot: the heavy/light unit that must come to the fore within a chosen meter.[14]

Türk wrote:

> A foot [metrical foot] in music is approximately the same as that which is understood in prosody. Just as long and short syllables belong to a foot in poetry, so can accented and unaccented beats in music belong to a foot [measure].
>
> TÜRK, p. 446

In this way it was possible to include one or more "feet" within the measure, which determined whether a meter (time) was simple or compound. Türk wrote:

> The chief categories of meters [even and uneven] are further classified into simple and compound. The simple meters are those containing only one foot and which cannot be

divided in the middle; the compound meters, on the other hand, consist of two feet and therefore can be divided in the middle of the measure, for example:

TÜRK, p. 91

If the melody was composed such that the one meter was perceived as "heavy" and the next one as "light," then these meters were combined to form a compound meter. Kirnberger wrote in his *Die Kunst des reinen Satzes in der Musik:*

> There are both in the simple meter of two beats as well as in the triple meter melodies in which evidently entire measures are alternately of heavy and light weight, so that one perceives a whole measure as only one beat. If the melody is such that one perceives the whole measure as only one single beat, then two measures have to be taken together, to result in one, whose first part is long and the other short.

KIRNBERGER, Vol. II, Part 1, p. 131

While, according to music theory, a composer may choose a simple or compound meter depending on the melodic and harmonic course, in practice there seems to be a lot of deviation from this. We see in Bach's case, for instance, examples of this in his Rondeaux from the Second Partita in C minor, BWV 826. In the beginning, the melodic motif, with the appropriate heavy/light relations of the 3/8 notation, is clearly completed within the measure and strengthened by the imitation that follows one measure later.

Bach, Partita BWV 826, Rondeaux

From m. 81, however, it seems from the slurs in the top part that the pulsation that takes the whole measure as its point of departure is just as easily palpable as a pulsation that is based on the eighth note. In the bass, too, it seems useful to think in terms of two measures together, with the first measure feeling heavy and the second light. This is reinforced by the low bass note in mm. 81 and 83. In this way a so-called measure of higher order, or "hypermeasure," is formed whereby the heavy/light relationship is no longer found within the measure but is spread over two measures as a *due battute*.[15]

Bach, Partita BWV 826, Rondeaux

This development is continued later on in the Viennese Classical style, which means that a large number of examples are to be found that are important for the way the interpreter feels the pulsation of a work and expresses the heavy/light relationships within the motion. Take, for example, the third movement, Presto, of Mozart's Sonata in G major, K. 283. In the Coda, the successive dominant (light) and tonic (heavy) are both followed by a measure of rest. The smallest unit here must comprise two measures, or else the notation of the measures of rest would be meaningless.

Mozart, Sonata K. 283, 3rd movement

Beethoven would not have been Beethoven had he not breached the dictates of music theory on this point, too. This can be seen, for instance, in the first movement, Allegro molto e con brio, of his Sonata in E-flat, Op. 7. This movement is written in 6/8 time, but the harmonic structure and the slurs from m. 5 onward clearly show that the motion covers two measures. The melodic motif, comprising two chords in which the harmony remains the same, corresponds much more to 12/8 time than to 6/8.

Sonata Op. 7, 1st movement

It was an original thought of his to have the initial motif return at the end of this movement (m. 352 onward) with a totally different (i.e., opposite) accentuation. The character of this motif, which originally had the sound of a call, changes into something that, supported by the *crescendo*, sounds much more confirmatory and definitive. It is no surprise that at the close of this movement the last measure is notated as a rest. This measure is indeed necessary to complete the unit of motion.[16] The *forte* in m. 355 and the *fortissimi* on the dominant chords are typical Beethoven mischiefs.

Sonata Op. 7, 1st movement

In this simple way, therefore, the hypermeasure can be established in a number of sonatas, such as the *due battute* in the first movement, Allegro molto e con brio, of the Sonata in C minor, Op. 10 No. 1. The cadence over two measures continues to the end of this movement. The change of harmony occurs per measure, however: dominant-tonic (V-I), the motion being completed only by the additional rest.

Sonata Op. 10 No. 1, 1st movement

However, that it was not always so easy for Beethoven to clearly indicate a hypermeasure can be seen from the notation of the first movement, Andante con variazioni, of the Sonata Op. 26. From sketchbooks it is apparent that he wrestled to determine the time and decided on 3/8 notation only after lengthy consideration. Having originally notated the theme in 6/8 time, he later decided against this. But it can be seen from the last measures of the last variation, where he ties the chord over two measures, that there does remain something of a 6/8 motion.

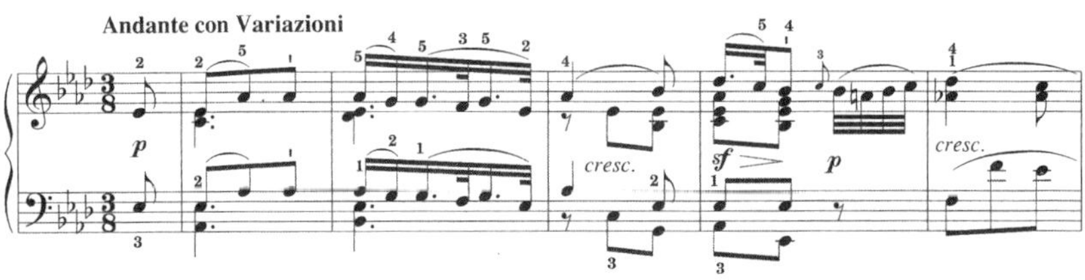

Sonata Op. 26, 1st movement, theme

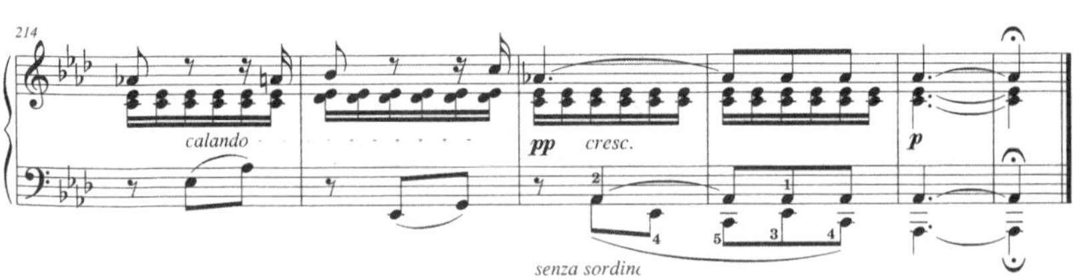

Sonata Op. 26, 1st movement, Variation V

Such a notation is also present in the first movement of the Sonata in D minor, Op. 31 No. 2, where the last chord in *alla breve* notation stretches over two measures and the sound dwindles into nothingness.

Sonata Op. 31 No. 2, 1st movement

Uneven Metrical Constructions

In addition to this *due battute* construction, it also regularly happens that grouping of measures within a movement leads to other structures. An example of this occurs in the first movement, Allegro, of the Sonata in F major, Op. 10 No. 2, where first a conjunction of two measures can be discerned, but where from m. 44 a grouping of three measures suddenly arises. This broadening works as a structural *ritenuto.* The pulsation of the motion is broadened by the lengthening of the rests, as compared with m. 44.

Sonata Op. 10 No. 2, 1st movement

A similar broadening is also found in the last movement, Allegro vivace, of the Sonata in E-flat major, Op. 27 No. 1. There, from

m. 106 a new episode seems to begin, the grouping of which comprises three measures.

Sonata Op. 27 No. 1, 4th movement

The effect of such a change of motion does not always need to be connected with the feeling of broadening or with a structural *ritenuto.* It can also be a sign of increasing musical tension, such as in the first movement, Allegro, of his Sonata in F minor, Op. 2 No. 1. Although a *due battute* forms the basis, at several points there are groups of three measures, as in mm. 30–32, where such a mounting tension is expressed.

Sonata Op. 2 No. 1, 1st movement

In addition to these expansions, the opposite is also encountered, where the groups suddenly contract. This "ejection" of a measure occurs in m. 12 of the first movement, Allegro vivace, of the Sonata in G major, Op. 31 No.1, where the entry of the new phrase in fact comes a measure too soon. In this movement, known for its humorous character, this change has an exceptionally capricious effect.

Sonata Op. 31 No. 1, 1st movement

In the third movement, Scherzo: Allegro, of the Sonata in C major, Op. 2 No. 3, up to m. 33 there is a collection of four measures, *quattro battute*. There then follows yet another group of four measures, followed by a group of three. It might therefore be imagined that the new entry in m. 40 in fact comes too soon, because the harmony has not changed, and it is also possible to regard seven measures as a unit, meaning that we are dealing with an expansion from four to seven measures. Whatever the case may be, the entry sounds surprising and humorous.

Sonata Op. 2 No. 3, 3rd movement

Just how important it is to recognize such groups in order to feel a work's correct pulsations is also apparent from the following example, where Beethoven connects two movements. In the third movement, Allegro, of the Sonata in E-flat minor, Op. 7, with a *quattro battute*, it seems as if this movement ends on a second "beat." The preceding m. 94 is clearly the last point of support in this section in that it confirms the tonic. The Minore that directly follows on from this and also comprises a *quattro battute* therefore continues on the third "beat," whereby the first two measures are relatively light, and only at m. 98 can the start of a new group of four be conceived. This process is dramatically underpinned by Beethoven's notation of *ffp*.

Sonata Op. 7, 3rd movement

It can also happen that, taking certain considerations into account, an interpretation of pulsation can vary. This is the case in, for example, the second movement, Allegro molto, of the Sonata in A-flat major, Op. 110. In a harmonic analysis it is not inconceivable to consider mm. 3 and 4 as being in C major within a *quattro battute.* In that case, m. 4 is to be conceived as the tonic (i.e., "heavy") along with m. 8, a concept that is reinforced by the *sf* notation. If, however, the theme is considered as being in F minor, which is the most obvious consequence arising from the first movement in A-flat major, then mm. 4 and 8 must be regarded as "light." Now, the *sf* in m. 8 is a typical Beethoven counter-accent. It is even more remarkable that when the theme is played in the Recapitulation, the intention of the chord in m. 8 is totally different. From the continuation it appears that Beethoven has really modulated toward C major, so that this same chord now feels like a first "beat" coming too soon, is therefore even more unruly in expression, and must accordingly be played as such.

Sonata Op. 110, 2nd movement

Such a subtle process is similarly to be discerned in the last movement of the "Waldstein" Sonata, Op. 53, where there can be considered to be various layers, each with its own cadence, tension span, and accentuation. This is the case in the first theme of this movement. On the one hand, we see from the first measure the four-measure structure grouped by the low bass note; on the other hand, the melodic aspect is seen within a motion where the second measure—preceded by an upbeat—will have to be regarded as the first "beat": two layers of tension that do not set in simultaneously, but rather one measure after the other. It is clear that this unusual construction, together with the veiled pedaling that has already been discussed, contributes to this theme's intangible, poetic character.

Sonata Op. 53, 3rd movement

It furthermore appears from all this that in order to establish the pulsation, and along with this the heavy/light relationship, all voices must be involved, which sometimes produces remarkable results. Take, for instance, the first movement, Allegro, of the Sonata in D major, Op. 28, the "Pastorale," in which in the same way various motions can be observed. It is clear that the first theme is more suggestive of a 6/4 motion than Beethoven's 3/4 notation, and also that in mm. 7–10 a *quattro battute* can be discerned. But then the situation becomes even more complicated. For from m. 11 for ten measures the tenor appears to be devoid of any accentuation whatsoever, and neither can any grouping be established within the long organ point (or pedal point) in the bass. Two layers of voices not forming any melody, to be characterized as so-called *mouvements intérieurs*, which here play a role in determining to a great extent the magnificent character of this movement.

In this case it would no longer seem useful to speak of measures of higher order, but rather about "breaths," stretching out over a much longer distance. To achieve such a "breathing span," the course of the tension must be realized over a much longer distance without breaking the line. When, during a performance, the phrasing is too short, its span will be broken and the music will be gasping for breath, while if the phrasing is even more protracted, all tension will be lost.

Sonata Op. 28, 1st movement

Meter and Subdivisions

While the above examples concern hypermeasures, whereby the number of pulsations (the sequential heavy/light) is smaller than the meter or time would indicate because they are divided over several measures, the opposite is also encountered, with the number of pulsations being higher than the time signature dictates. It thus appears in various compositions that a notated 2/4 time in fact has the motion of 4/8 time. The 4/8 had, however, fallen into disuse, as observed by Kirnberger, who published his *Die Kunst des reinen Satzes in der Musik* in 1774. He wrote:

> Four-eight time is, of the meters of four beats, the lightest with regard to expression and in movement. It differs from 2/4 time by the weight of its beats, which are all equally heavy, whereas in 2/4 time the first and third beats pronounce the weight of the meter, e.g.
>
> 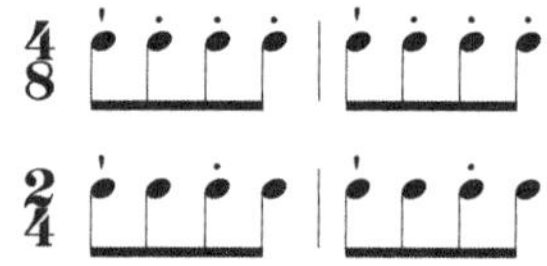
>
> and therefore have a slightly slower movement than 2/4 time. But both meters do not differ as much from one another as 4/4 time does from *alla breve* time, because of the liveliness of their movement in which the weight of the beats is not so perceptible. Additionally, today's composers will no longer mark a piece with 4/8 but instead always with 2/4.[17]
>
> KIRNBERGER, Vol. II, Part 1, p. 123

It is clear that Kirnberger shared the opinion that Leopold Mozart had already published in 1756 in his *Violinschule*. Leopold wrote:

> Let not our friends the critics be startled if I omit the times 4/8, 2/8, 9/8, 9/16, 12/16, 12/24, 12/4. In my eyes they are worthless stuff. One finds them seldom or not at all in the newer pieces; and there really are enough variations of times for expressing everything, to be able to do without these last. He who likes them, let him grasp them with might and main. Yea, I would even generously present him with 3/1 time, were it not that it still gazes defiantly at me out of a few old church pieces.
>
> L. MOZART, p. 32

Others, however, considered that through the discontinuation of time signatures, certain nuances were lost. Johann Georg Sulzer wrote in his *Allgemeine Theorie der Schönen Künste:*

> Joh. Seb. Bach and Couperin, who without doubt are masters of the most faultless performance and not without reason have written fugues and other pieces in this and other nowadays unusual time signatures, confirm that every time signature has its own execution and its own natural movement, that it is therefore by no means arbitrary in which time signature a piece is written and performed.
>
> SULZER, Vol. 2, p. 563

There are, for instance, examples to be found in the work of Haydn or Mozart where 2/4 time is notated but in which the motion in playing feels more like 4/8. This occurs, for example, in the first movement, Allegro moderato, of Mozart's Sonata in C major, K. 330, where a tempo must also be chosen that allows the many thirty-second-note groups—some even with ornamentation, as, for instance, from m. 129—still to be played meaningfully.[18]

Mozart, Sonata K. 330, 1st movement

Beethoven went much further and even notated in the Largo assai ed espressivo of his Piano Trio in D major, Op. 70 No. 1, in 2/4, eight small groups of four sixty-fourth notes. Here are mm. 135–136:

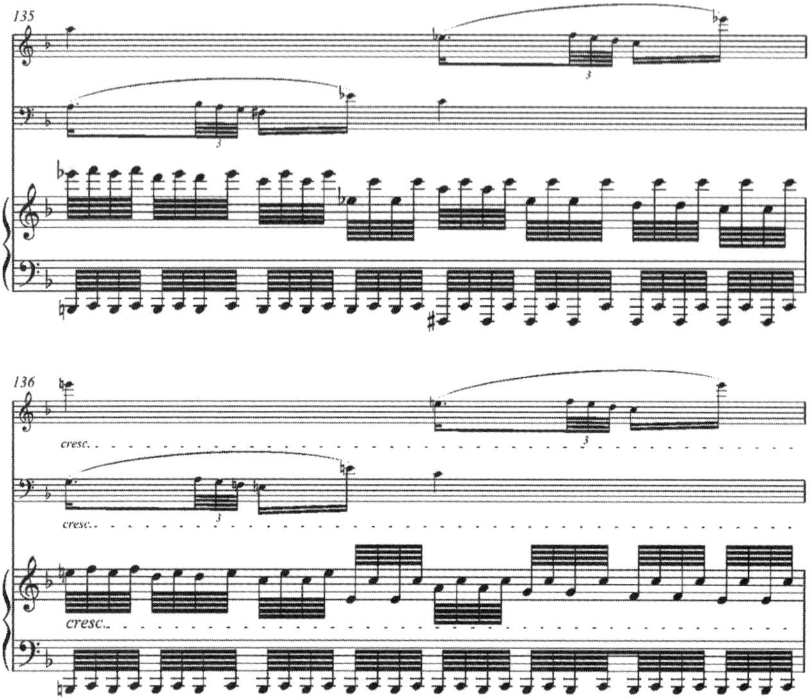

Piano Trio Op. 70 No. 1, 2nd movement

This could be imaginable in 8/16 time, but this meter was, like 4/8 time, not at all in vogue in his time. One realizes just how far Beethoven's notation is removed from normal 2/4 time by attempting to play the second half of the measure more lightly than the first: something that is totally impossible. Beethoven's notation, with its unusually light note values, expresses suggestively the intangible, mysterious, and immaterial character of this music, and renders the nickname "Geistertrio" ("Ghost Trio") most appropriate.

The same sort of mysterious atmosphere is also to be found in the second movement, Largo, of his Third Piano Concerto, already mentioned in this chapter: within the 3/8 notation, the subdivision of the beat unit (in this case the sixteenth) is so extremely important that one might wonder whether 3/8 time is in fact the correct notation. At the time that Beethoven composed this concerto (1806), he was apparently still too bound to tradition to notate a 6/16 signature instead of a 3/8 time with the unconventional 3×2 sixteenths instead of 2×3 sixteenths. Later, in 1822, he would indeed progress to this in the second variation of the last movement of his Sonata in C minor, Op. 111.

He did in his later works have a clear view of this problem, as is apparent from his text accompanying the fourth movement, Largo, of his Sonata Op. 106, the "Hammerklavier," where he states that one always counts four sixteenth notes.

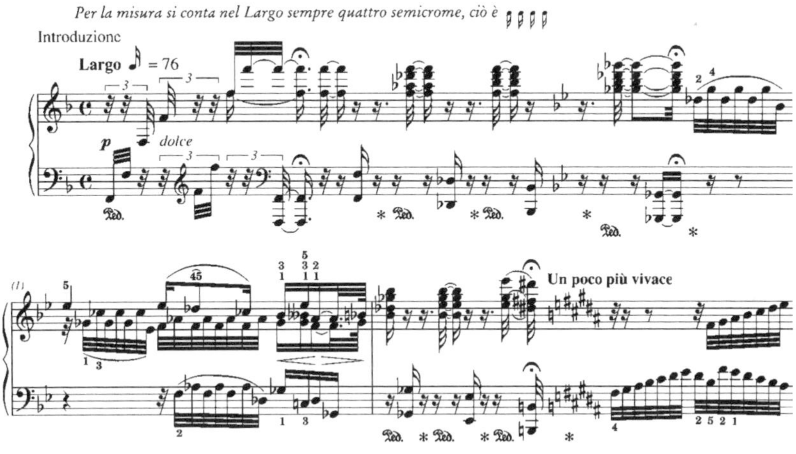

Sonata Op. 106, 3rd movement

This highly exceptional, sumptuous notation expresses strikingly the exploratory, almost fumbling character of this quasi-improvisational introduction to the fugue. This character is amplified further by Beethoven's irregular notation of the bar lines. The notation of a **c** that is omitted from some editions lends a certain expansiveness to the music, even though in fact no trace whatsoever is left of the somewhat normal accentuation of 4/4 time.

Tempo

It will come as no surprise that the meter constructions discussed thus far also bear consequences for the determination of the tempo.

The central movements of the Sonatas Op. 10 No. 2 and Op. 14 No. 1 are good examples to illustrate this. These Allegrettos are notated in 3/4 time. The normal accentuation of a 3/4 measure would be that the first beat is regarded as "heavy" and the other two as "light." However, the length of the musical sentences (sixteen measures), in fact four hypermeasures, and the notation of the last measure as a measure's rest indicate a motion with much more fluid accentuation than a normal 3/4 time would suggest.

This spread-out motion, where within the *quattro battute* each measure can, as it were, be regarded as a "beat," of which the first "beat" is heavy, the second light, the third relatively heavy, and the fourth light again, leads automatically to an increase in tempo, because the cadence is now spread out over more than one measure. Beethoven's *sforzato* on the relatively heavy "third" measure "colors" the *quattro battute* motion somewhat.

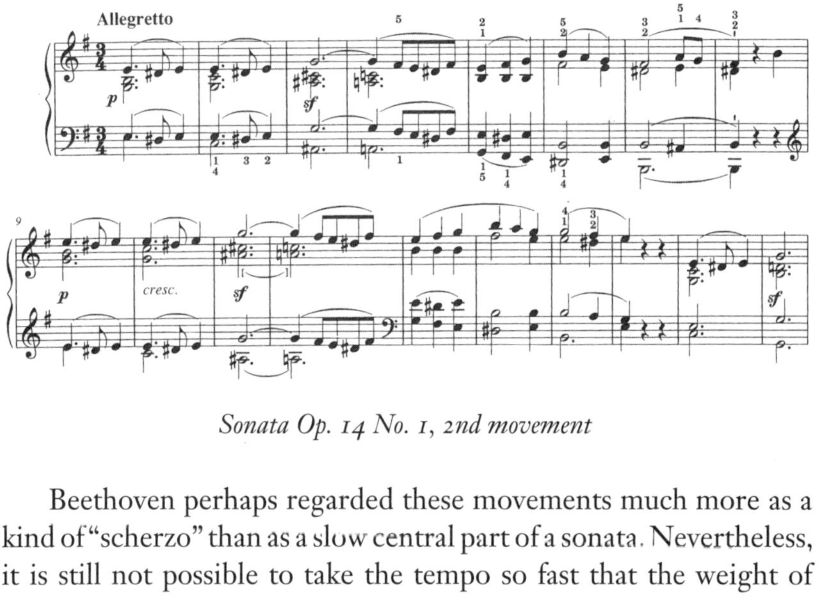

Sonata Op. 14 No. 1, 2nd movement

Beethoven perhaps regarded these movements much more as a kind of "scherzo" than as a slow central part of a sonata. Nevertheless, it is still not possible to take the tempo so fast that the weight of the quarter and eighth notes is lost. That is perhaps why Beethoven chose the designation Allegretto.[19]

How different is the last movement of the Sonata in A major, Op. 2 No. 2. Here, the motion does follow Beethoven's notation in a c measure. The slurs per measure and the spreading of the harmonic process also fit his notation. Instead of a tempo designation, here it suffices to simply indicate the character: *grazioso*.

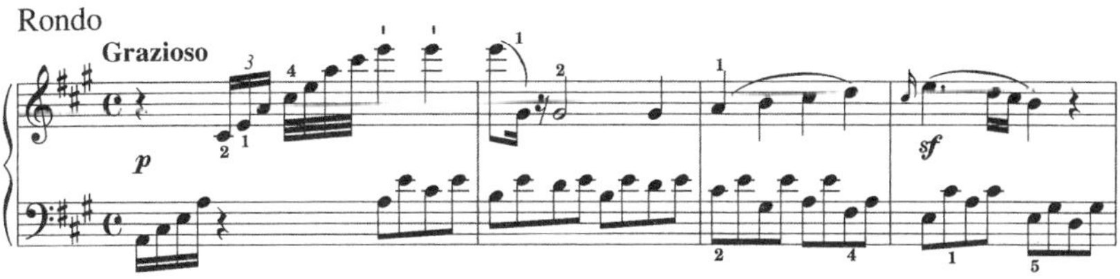

Sonata Op. 2 No. 2, 4th movement

Then the finale, Prestissimo, of his Sonata in F minor, Op. 2 No. 1, which is characterized by Czerny as follows: "Impetuously excited, almost dramatic, like the description of a serious event" (Czerny [II], p. 34).

Here, Beethoven's *prestissimo* tempo is clearly more complicated. Out of all his sonatas, he uses this tempo again only in Op. 10 No. 1 and Op. 109. In Op. 2 No. 1 and Op. 10 No. 1, both movements are notated in combination with an *alla breve* measure type, which produces a motion just slightly faster than that for which the pulsing is based on the quarter note. In this Op. 2 No. 1 Prestissimo, too, it is possible to involve a motion based on the half note, but in mm. 5, 6, and 7, for example, it seems even more obvious to take only one single pulse per measure and to combine two measures to form a *due battute*. This unit is reinforced because the melodic motif comprising three chords is spread across the bar line. All this leads to a tempo at its limits.

Sonata Op. 2 No. 1, 4th movement

In the "alternative," beginning in m. 59, the diffusion of the melody over several measures is clear to see. Of course, not every measure has the same weight and every "second" measure of this *due battute* must be absorbed unaccentuated into a flowing motion. The fusion of measures in this Prestissimo, with accentuation spread over the measures, will naturally be easier to create than with a tempo that is far slower.

Nevertheless, too fast a tempo will not have been Beethoven's intention, either. Whereas this movement features eighth-note triplets throughout as the fastest note values, without changing the tempo, the long values of the notes in the middle section, with the eighth notes as the fastest ones, ensure a certain resistance for the whole movement, and a certain weight must be maintained despite the *prestissimo* marking and hypermeasure.

Sonata Op. 2 No. 1, 4th movement

The same kind of balance between particular elements that make up a composition can often be observed to play a significant role in determining the tempo. Take, for example, the first movement, Allegro con brio, of the Sonata in C minor, Op. 13, the "Pathétique," where the smallest note value is also an eighth. Here, too, each note of the melody is harmonized independently: the antecedent and consequent phrases in fact form two complete cadences. This harmonic process takes place, however, above a *tremolo* in the bass which for four measures can be interpreted as an organ point on C with a tonic function. When this theme appears for the last time, it is apparent that from m. 303 the latent hypermeasure assumes the initiative and maintains this right to the end, where it is not for nothing that the last "light" measure is notated as a rest to conclude the heavy/light motion. The two layers determining the course of the musical tension here must be balanced out in an interpretation. The tempo may not be so fast that the changes of harmony on each note of the melody are not audible and lose their significance, but also not so slow that they become too independent of each other, whereby the broader motion in the bass, which runs in parallel with the harmonic functions, is lost.

Sonata Op. 13, 1st movement

Taking one thing with another, it means that an effective reconciliation of various musical ingredients is necessary to establish a tempo. Indeed, should this fail, audibly incorrect tempi can arise.

We constantly hear, for instance, interpretations of the Scherzo: Allegretto vivace from the Sonata in E-flat minor, Op. 31 No. 3, that are too fast for the heavy/light relationship within these 2/4 measures to be felt. Although for the listener such an extremely fast tempo is certainly effective, it is then sounding just like a *quattro battute,* while in fact each measure here, accentuated with the contrasting *sf,* clearly forms an independent unit. Beethoven's real intention in designating the movement *allegretto* is in fact clear enough, and of course *vivace* has more to do with the light character of this movement than with the tempo.

Scherzo

Sonata Op. 31 No. 3, 2nd movement

Too slow a tempo can also come about if, for example, a prescribed slow tempo in 6/8 time is played so slowly that the second half of the measure is no longer regarded as "light" but, instead, two "3/4 measures" are formed within one single 6/8 measure. This danger exists in the Largo e mesto from the Sonata in D major, Op. 10 No. 3. Due to its tragic character, many pianists take this movement so slowly that there is no longer any question of 6/8 motion.

Sonata Op. 10 No. 3, 3rd movement

It is interesting to see that Clementi, in his *Introduction to the Art of Playing on the Piano Forte* of 1801, a method much valued by Beethoven, mentions in his tempo table the *largo* as slow, but not as the slowest.

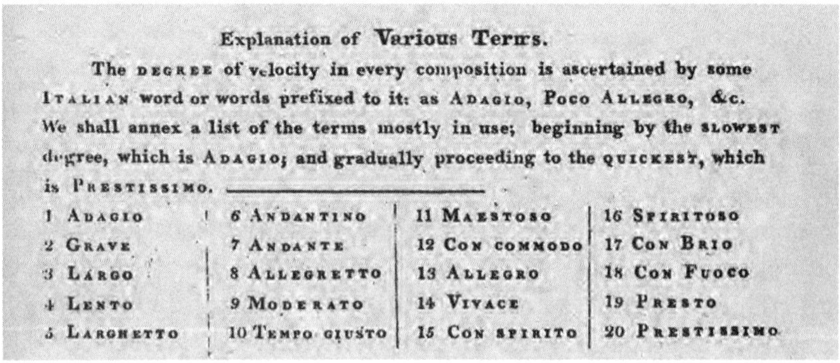

Explanation of Various Terms.

The DEGREE of velocity in every composition is ascertained by some ITALIAN word or words prefixed to it: as ADAGIO, Poco ALLEGRO, &c. We shall annex a list of the terms mostly in use; beginning by the SLOWEST degree, which is ADAGIO; and gradually proceeding to the QUICKEST, which is PRESTISSIMO.

1 ADAGIO	6 ANDANTINO	11 MAESTOSO	16 SPIRITOSO
2 GRAVE	7 ANDANTE	12 CON COMMODO	17 CON BRIO
3 LARGO	8 ALLEGRETTO	13 ALLEGRO	18 CON FUOCO
4 LENTO	9 MODERATO	14 VIVACE	19 PRESTO
5 LARGHETTO	10 TEMPO GIUSTO	15 CON SPIRITO	20 PRESTISSIMO

CLEMENTI, p. 13

Also noticeable is the positioning of *tempo giusto*, just in the middle of the table and around which all other tempi are grouped. In Georg Simon Löhlein's *Klavierschule*, published in 1804, is written:

> Tempo giusto: In tempo approximating to Moderato, in expression usually lighter.
>
> LÖHLEIN, p. 298

Expressions like *grave, largo, maestoso, vivace, con spirito,* or *con fuoco* serve to indicate not only a character, but also a tempo.

Although nothing must ever be based on just one source, and the tables in the various methods from that era do not all agree, it is surely surprising to find in Clementi's method a table in which many expressions differ so much from the associations we often have today. For example, that *maestoso* is regarded as much faster than *allegretto*.

Such an observation must be a warning for the pianist who is led astray by the *maestoso* indication at the beginning of the first movement of Beethoven's Sonata Op. 111, a movement where performance at a really slow tempo is almost a tradition.

Fortunately, Beethoven extends a helping hand in the way he puts the transition from m. 16 to m. 17 on paper. The long trill in thirty-second notes in the last measure of the Maestoso is connected with the sixteenth notes of the Allegro con brio ed appassionato. It is clear that this bridge means that the Allegro con brio ed appassionato should be played twice as fast as the Maestoso to avoid any break in tempo of the trill, something that can be achieved only when the tempo of the Maestoso is not too slow. Only in such a way can an interpretation contribute substantially to the most piercing expression of the immense impact of this music.

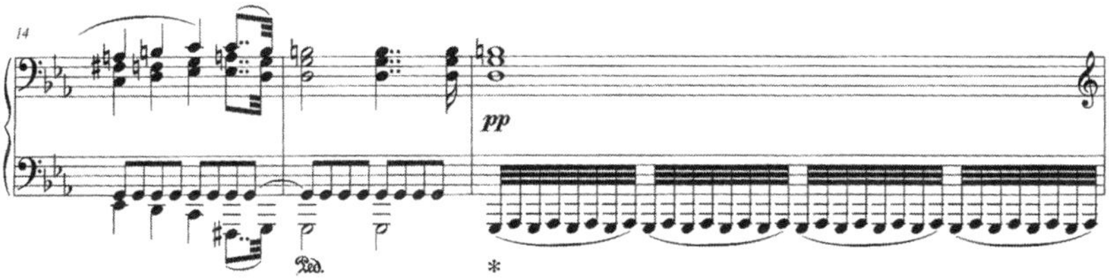

Sonata Op. 111, 1st movement

This is, however, by no means the only case.

Looking for connections to find convincing tempi is always very interesting: for example, where Beethoven writes variations, as in the Sonatas Opp. 14, 26, 57, 109, and 111. Of course, small differences depending on the character of each variation are always possible, but in principle, maintaining the underlying pulse in successive variations comes from a long tradition and is encountered, for example, in many compositions of Haydn and Mozart. In the first movement of Mozart's Sonata in A major, K. 331, it is very natural to keep the pulse of the eighth note as a guide for the whole movement: in Variations I—IV the same eighth-note pulse as in the theme; in Variation V, with Mozart's indication *adagio*, twice as slow; and to conclude this movement in Variation VI, with the indication *allegro*, twice as fast.

The same approach is very convincing for the second movement of Beethoven's Sonata Op. 14 No. 2, where the pulse of the *alla breve* can be continued in all variations, or in the Sonata Op. 26, where the pulse of the eighth note from the theme works as the connecting element for all variations, besides also preventing Variation II from being played all too fast, something we unfortunately notice far too often.

For the variations of the last movement in Op. 109 it is really convincing to retain the pulse of the quarter note of the theme for Variation II (compare, for example, the theme with m. 41).

Sonata Op. 109, 3rd movement

Sonata Op. 109, 3rd movement, Var. II

After which, for Variation III, as a result of Beethoven's indication *allegro vivace*, this pulse becomes twice as fast. In Variation IV he writes, "A little slower than the theme," leading us back in the direction of the pulse of the quarter note from the beginning. In Variation V the pulse of the half note takes the tempo of the pulse of the quarter note again, but now, as a consequence of the *alla breve* notation, with a weightier character. Here, the firmly pronounced half notes of the opening theme and the polyphonic writing with the continuous addition of voices are reminiscent of the Credo from his *Missa Solemnis*, a work on which Beethoven was working at the same time. Even the tempo, *Allegro ma non troppo*, is the same in both compositions. With a choir in mind, the text "Credo in unum Deum" (I believe in one God) for the beginning of this variation is not too difficult to imagine.

Sonata Op. 109, 3rd movement

The broad character in *forte*, confirmed twice by *sempre forte*, abruptly changes in m. 145. In *piano*, the final eight measures form a bridge to Variation VI, where Beethoven returns to the pulse of the beginning with the indication *Tempo I del thema*. From then on, he brings everything home by leading this variation to the theme itself and to the conclusion of this movement.

Is it not striking that, being consequent in this approach, the thirty-second notes in this last variation, beginning at m. 169, will have the same tempo as the sixteenth notes of Variation III?

Looking at the variations of the second movement of the "Appassionata" Sonata, Op. 57, and its connection with the final one, it is not surprising that the outcome is precisely the same. In this sonata, too, this movement is directly connected with the final one, this time by a single chord, and here as well, the tempo of the thirty-second notes of the last variation is the same as that of the sixteenth notes in the Allegro ma non troppo that follows. Of course, this can only be successful when the tempo of the second movement is not too slow, indeed a tempo where the *con moto*, which Beethoven has added to the *Andante*, should be carefully observed, otherwise such a tempo relation between the two movements will fail.

Another example of such a unification of motion can be achieved in the second movement of the Sonata Op. 111. Although the different successive time signatures, beginning with 9/16, followed by 6/16, 12/32, and 9/16 to finish this movement, look rather complicated, the underlying pulsation remains the same, based on the value of the sixteenth note. The impression that the music is speeding up each time comes only from the increase of the number of notes covered by the same pulse. For an interpretation, it would be advisable to keep the underlying harmonic progression also firmly in mind, a kind of counterpoise to the acceleration of the melodic progression. In Variation III, for example, the broad harmonic rhythm helps the performer to render the top line still with a felicity of melodic expression. Unfortunately, we often hear this variation with the performer not only playing *fortissimo* and very fast, ignoring Beethoven's indications *forte* and *L'istesso tempo*, but also adding a lot of accents, trying to convince us with a kind of "jazzy" approach. However, the melodic line, based on the theme (notice the top notes c^2, g^1, g^1, f^1 of each group), does not point to any specific accentuation different than that from the theme itself. Because these groups are slurred and must be played *legato*, any additional accentuations would disturb the melodic line.

Sonata Op. 111, 2nd movement

Different accentuation occurs only in mm. 53–55, where all the *sforzati* are on weak beats and slurs are missing. Here, the *sforzati* syncopate the melodic line, avoiding specific accents on the first beat, which is only supported by the chromatically ascending line in the bass.

Sonata Op. 111, 2nd movement

Indeed, with this variation it is a real challenge for the performer to find a tempo in which it is possible to realize all these details within the specific rhythm Beethoven is asking for. To achieve a complete perception of this subject, one should even look at the possibility of connecting the tempi of all movements within a sonata. Perhaps surprisingly, perhaps not, this approach, too, can produce interesting results. The observation, for example, that in Op. 109, where the first and second movements are already connected by Beethoven's special pedal indication, the pulse of the quarter note that is used for the first movement is also very natural as a continuation for a full measure in the second movement, and then again for the quarter note in the theme of the third movement. Even if such an approach is not relevant for every sonata, it will always be challenging to seek it out.

It is also interesting to observe how Beethoven is providing standard tempi like *adagio* and *allegro* with additional information in trying to indicate his intentions more precisely. Here, it is regularly seen that he combines certain expressions to break through the limits within which a tempo should be played, such as:

- *Adagio grazioso* (Op. 31 No. 1): slow, but not so slow as to become heavy
- *Adagio sostenuto, appassionato e con molto sentimento* (Op. 106): a solemn, stately, slow tempo that must, however, sound passionate and therefore not drag
- *Allegro risoluto* (Op. 106): indeed fast, but not so fast that the resolute character is lost

These indications play an immediate role in the formation of a musical image of a composition. Other indications, such as the shifts in meter mentioned above, the hypermeasure, and so forth, and their influence on the way in which a tempo comes about, must be gathered from the notation. In addition, it is important how the themes are constructed, more rhythmic or melodic. After all, in the case of any melodic line, it is necessary to envisage its "profile": not only its rhythmic profile, but also how the structure of the intervals progresses. Larger and/or dissonant intervals within a theme create more tension, "move" more intensely, than do smaller and/or consonant intervals. Characteristic intervals can in this way, along with other factors, be important in the achievement of a conscious choice of tempo, because the declamatory significance of this must not be lost through a tempo that is too fast or too slow.

For such an observation that can be gathered from the notation, it is interesting to return once more to the theme of the last movement of the Sonata Op. 109. The upper voice of this sarabande-like theme, with its characteristic second beat, is an expression of heartfelt sentiment, the subjective—*innigster Empfindung*. In contrast, the bass line, along with the middle voice, is more objective in character, seeking to achieve a flowing line. Paying attention to the continuous line in the bass helps to prevent the tempo from being too slow. Attention to the expression in the upper voice discourages an approach that is too fast. It is therefore about the blend of expression and continuity. In general, it can be said that the interaction between melody and bass line, their alignment, can indeed render a significant indication of tempo. (See also Chapter 1 concerning Beethoven's *gesangvoll* indication.)

Sonata Op. 109, 3rd movement

Such considerations of working out details and at the same time paying attention to a longer line also play a role in the concept of articulation. Composers like Haydn or Mozart were brought up in a tradition where articulation was one of the main means of expression, and emphasizing details in a score by means of articulation was completely natural to them. For Beethoven, who, since his youth, was acquainted with compositions by Bach for the keyboard, the application of articulation was taken for granted when performing his preludes and fugues on the instruments of his younger years, a harpsichord, organ, or even clavichord, a practice that as a matter of course was perpetuated on the upcoming fortepiano, the popularity of which was increasing by the day.

In the first movement, Allegro assai, of the "Kurfürsten" Sonata in F minor, already mentioned in Chapter 1, this well-known performance practice of articulation comes clearly to the fore in mm. 28–30.

Sonata WoO 47 No. 2, 1st movement

Or in a passage like mm. 20–24 in the first movement, Allegro cantabile, from the E-flat-major Sonata.

Sonata WoO 47 No. 1, 1st movement

Of course, it is well known that Beethoven was copiously praised by his peers in his generation for the way he played *legato* on this instrument, but even in his case, decades after he composed his "Kurfürsten" Sonatas, specific articulation marks can still be found in his writing.

One characteristic example is to be seen in mm. 57–58 of the first movement, Allegro, of his Sonata Op. 31 No. 3. If the performance is too fast, much of the intended expression is lost; if it is too slow, the longer line of the phrase will be disturbed.

Sonata Op. 31 No. 3, 1st movement

However, not only in fast tempi, but also in much slower ones, this manner of articulation can play a significant role in endorsing the musical meaning. Take, for example, the declamatory expression Beethoven is asking for in mm. 28–31 of the first movement, Moderato cantabile molto espressivo, of his Sonata Op. 110.

Sonata Op. 110, 1st movement

In the first movement of the Sonata Op. 101 there are even two slurs notated above each other. The smaller refers to the articulation, the slightly larger one clarifies the cohesion of the motif. In this movement, this notation is found in several measures, with the indication *Etwas lebhaft und mit der innigsten Empfindung* (quite lively and with the deepest feeling). An example of such a notation is in m. 14, where its expressive significance is increased by the simultaneously notated *crescendi*, followed immediately by a *diminuendo*, but indeed, Beethoven's *Etwas lebhaft* for this movement is a warning against breaking the longer line of the phrase.

Sonata Op. 101, 1st movement

But in addition to all these specific articulations, what is really amazing is the way in which the very young Beethoven explores the dynamic discourse in his early "Kurfürsten" Sonatas. Of course, on the harpsichord and organ, changing dynamics could be done by the registration, but now, with the keyboard of a fortepiano under his fingers, the contact was much more direct, and all contrasts in sound could immediately be realized.[20] It must have been a real joy for him to exploit these possibilities. See, for example, the beginning of the E-flat Sonata:

Sonata WoO 47 No. 1, 1st movement

And how daring are the final measures from the Exposition of the first movement, Allegro, of the third "Kurfürsten" Sonata in D major.

Sonata WoO 47 No. 3, 1st movement

Finally, what a wonderful example it is that Beethoven also exploits all of this so effectively in his very last sonata, Op. 111. See the two-by-two articulations in mm. 55–57 and mm. 132–133 of the first movement, Allegro con brio ed appassionato, where Beethoven suddenly interrupts the very dramatic *fortissimo* outbursts by *piano*, followed in less than one measure by a *non ligato* and *crescendo* before another *fortissimo* is reached. It must be clear that all these sudden changes in expression demand sufficient time for a convincing realization.

Sonata Op. 111, 1st movement, mm. 55–57

Another important subject with regard to tempo is the kind of instrument that will be used (a historic instrument or a modern one) and its influence on playing and interpretation. For a musician who begins to perform on a fortepiano and is coming from a background as harpsichordist, the manner of playing is more natural than it is for the pianist who is used to performing on a modern piano. After all, the path from the harpsichord to the fortepiano runs parallel to the historical development of the instrument and to knowledge of the historical performance practice. This is different for the pianist who is used to a modern instrument and has to find his way back to the fortepiano.

Playing on a historical instrument with present-day virtuoso technique as a basis is no easy task, not only from a technical point of view, but also to do justice with regard to the repertoire, in which attention is often focused less on historical performance practice than on the possibilities for expression offered by the modern concert grand.

The plethora of possibilities on this instrument as regards tone, the range of possibilities for dynamics, evenness of sound over the whole keyboard, and the length of the tone furnish a whole range of expressions that cannot simply be transferred to a fortepiano.

A fortepiano possesses other qualities. Due to the very light action, the shorter tone, and the clarity of the different registers, fast tempi can be simply realized without erosion of clarity and texture. In this respect, a modern concert grand does have its limitations. Especially in the bass register, it is more difficult to maintain clarity in fast tempi. However, the fortepianist is also not invited to play fast tempi so fast that expression is lost. One must conclude that Beethoven's words to Václav Jan Tomášek, already quoted in Chapter 2, are still very valuable for every musician to this very day, whichever instrument is to be used:

> [. . .] pianists of to-day, who prance up and down the keyboard with passages which they have practiced—*putsch, putsch, putsch;*—what does that mean? Nothing!

These words also shed light on the fast sixteenth-note passages in Beethoven's piano sonatas. Beethoven wanted to introduce a distinct perspective into these passages; just playing fast must at all costs be avoided.

Even these days, 250 years after his birth, his words are still very meaningful. Introducing perspective into fast passages avoids tempi that are too fast and fosters musical expression. A possibility to apply such an approach in practice was already discussed in Chapter 2, explaining the *Längen* and *Kürzen* and the feasibility of using this knowledge from m. 23 onward in the first movement, Allegro con brio, of the "Waldstein" Sonata, Op. 53. Delineating the many turning points within the sixteenths' movement in this way makes it impossible for any pianist to take the tempo too fast.

Sonata Op. 53, 1st movement

Hence, how valuable the following statement by the important German philosopher, sociologist, composer, and music critic Theodor W. Adorno (1903–1969) still is. In his notes concerning Beethoven, he writes:

> One of the main problems in interpreting Beethoven: playing very fast phrases (sixteenth notes) as *melodies* without slackening the tempo. "Passage-work" hardly exists in Beethoven; *everything* is melodic and has to be played as such—that is, with an immanent moment of *resistance*.
>
> ADORNO, p. 55

The Metronome

An article in the *Wiener vaterländische Blätter* of October 13, 1813, entitled "Maelzel's Musical Chronometer" must have caught the attention of Viennese music-lovers, especially because Beethoven, regarded as the greatest composer of his era, appeared to have considerable interest in this invention, as is to be gathered from the following words:

> Herr Beethoven looks upon this invention as a welcome means to secure the performance of his highly original compositions in all places in the tempos intended for them, which he regrets is so frequently lacking.

It is understandable that Beethoven was worried about the effectiveness of the indications he was using for his intended tempi. After all, he himself was highly liberal in his treatment of the standard tempi. His handling of the traditional Italian concepts, the values of the notes within a given meter, his way of pulsing across the bar line, the progression of the harmonies' rhythm, the hypermeasure, the *ritmo di due*, *tre*, and *quattro battute*, and, in some later works, his extensive descriptions to achieve the motion and character he intended: all of this made life very difficult indeed for the performing musician, something Beethoven wholeheartedly admitted. In a letter of November 1817 to the composer and conductor Ignaz Franz Edler von Mosel, he wrote:

> I am heartily delighted to know that you hold the same view as I do about our tempo indications which originated in the barbarous ages of music. For, to take one example, what can be more absurd than Allegro, which really signifies *merry*, and how very far removed we often are from the idea of that tempo. So much so that the piece itself means the *very opposite of the indication*—As for those four chief movements, which, however, are far from embodying the truth or the accuracy of the four chief winds, we would gladly *do without them*. [. . .] As for me, I have long been thinking of abandoning those absurd descriptive terms, Allegro, Andante, Adagio, Presto; and Mälzel's metronome affords us the best opportunity of doing so.
>
> ANDERSON, Vol. II, p. 727

Within two years of the above-mentioned report in the *Wiener vaterländische Blätter*, Maelzel had developed this chronometer into his metronome, for which he acquired a patent in 1815. A year later, this inventor, engineer, artist, and especially very gifted entrepreneur started to produce this instrument in Paris and London.[21]

Beethoven appeared pleased with Maelzel's invention, not only through his assumption that, by coupling a given note value on the metronome scale with the same note value in one of his compositions, the intended tempo could be clearly indicated, but also because from then on, everywhere his compositions were performed, there could be no misunderstandings as to the intended tempi.

This had, of course, to be widely publicized, and in 1817 and 1819, Steiner & Co. published two pamphlets containing the metronome indications for his Symphonies Nos. 1 to 8, a number of smaller works, and his very popular Septet Op. 20, followed by similar indications for all of his string quartets, up to Op. 95.

However, it quickly became clear that many of the tempi given by these metronome numbers were regarded as too fast, and doubts arose, not only in the case of several movements of his symphonies and string quartets, but also regarding the only piano sonata for which Beethoven provided metronome indications, the Sonata Op. 106, the "Hammerklavier." Here, the numbers appeared to be especially problematic for the two outer movements: 𝅗𝅥 = 138 for the first movement, Allegro, and for the Fugue: Allegro risoluto, where the indication ♩ = 144 was considered to be on the fast side for such a complicated, polyphonically constructed composition.

This gave rise to numerous questions, including whether Beethoven had based the metronome number on the note value given by the denominator of the meter, such as the quarter note in a 4/4 meter and the half note in an *alla breve*, or rather on the "motion," the pulsation, of the music, which could be achieved in another way, such as with the constructions of merged measures such as the *due*, *tre*, or *quattro battute*.

The discussion about this flared up especially in the mid-1900s, when the Viennese violinist Rudolph Kolisch, leader of, among other ensembles, the Kolisch and the Pro Arte String Quartets, published an extensive study of Beethoven's metronome numberings and the consequences of this for tempi in his 1943 article "Tempo and Character in Beethoven's Music."[22]

One decade later, this subject was also addressed by the German musicologist Herman Beck. Although Beck was probably unaware of Kolisch's general assertations, both men reached the same conclusion: Beethoven's metronome indications are correct, but in many cases must be interpreted on the basis of the "motion," the pulsation, of a work. Kolisch, for instance, correctly observed that in the case of many of these, and especially fast scherzi, the whole measure was intended by Beethoven's metronome indication and not the quarter note of the 3/4 meter.[23]

In the editions of the thirty-two piano sonatas that were published after Beethoven's death and that are provided with metronome numbers by Czerny and Moscheles, it appears that many of their numbers differ, but not those of the "Hammerklavier."[24] Of course, with this sonata there could not be any doubt, since Beethoven himself had written these numbers down in a letter of April 16, 1819, to his pupil Ferdinand Ries in London. This did not, however, mean that there were no further questions.

In the English edition of Beethoven's biography by Schindler, on which Moscheles collaborated as editor and perhaps also as translator, Beethoven's letter to Ries is discussed. A remarkable letter, not only because of the metronome numbers, but especially due to Beethoven's instruction to Ries to append a new first measure to the Adagio, and to scrap the *assai* of the original designation *Allegro assai* for the first movement, thereby making the tempo slower than originally notated.[25] In a footnote to Beethoven's letter, Moscheles wrote the following:

> I have, in my edition of this Sonata, marked the time of the first movement 138 of Maelzel's metronome because Beethoven himself had fixed that number, He [. . .] gives it with a minim—I with a crotchet, but neither of these can, to my mind, be made to suit the character of the movement. The minim increases it to so fearful a prestissimo as Beethoven could never have intended, since he desired the *assai*, originally prefixed to the *Allegro*, to be omitted. The crotchet slackens the movement all too much; and although I have, in my edition, allowed Beethoven's numbers to remain, in

> deference to the great man, yet I would advise the player to hold a middle course to the following mark 𝅗𝅥 = 116.[26]

These words indeed encourage the interpreter to look once again at the whole musical concept of this movement and not just at the metronome numbers, especially since a tempo or character designation is not introduced in the initial stages of a composition, but usually as a final step, with any metronome numbers following even later. That is the case with Beethoven, too. In m. 7 of the first movement of the Sonata Op. 109, for instance, he wrote the words *adagio espressivo* in small letters in pencil above the notes already written down firmly in ink, as is also the case with the penciled words *tempo primo* in m. 16.

For today's interpreter, the process is usually the reverse. The features noticed first are the Italian terms, possibly augmented by a metronome number. Then follows the notation in the score. Viewed psychologically, this is a totally different approach. Although obviously the composer has a certain musical motion in mind when creating the music, and this has had a role in the process, the most important question is not whether the work is to be approached from a tempo/character indication, but what in fact can be concluded from the notation itself.

Concerning this approach, it is noticeable that for the first movement of Op. 106 a "heavy" execution is indeed indicated—an *alla breve* with the eighth as the fastest note value. It is also striking that, in his letter to Ries, Beethoven asks for the Allegro assai to be changed to Allegro, indeed still one of those standard tempi which, in his letter to von Mosel one and a half years earlier, he had firmly declared that he wanted to dispense with. To do justice to the aforementioned musical image of a "heavy " and "light" execution, the fastest note value, and only the indication Allegro, it seems difficult to perform this movement in a very fast tempo without losing the character indicated by the notation. In fact, Moscheles' 𝅗𝅥 = 116 seems to fit perfectly both aspects of a *heavy* execution in *alla breve* in combination with Allegro: all the more so because from the musical image, the *alla breve* notation can also be called into question. Of course, this notation, based on the half note, absolutely fits the four opening measures, where the harmony stays the same, but in the further course of this movement there are many moments where the harmonic progression is far more suitable for a C notation, for example mm. 295–306.

It is remarkable that Czerny, in the English edition of the sonatas (Czerny [II] in the Bibliography), gives a C designation for the first measures as a music example, and thereby deviates from his own *alla breve* notation in his Viennese edition. At the same time, he still does apply Beethoven's 𝅗𝅥 = 138 metronome indication, thereby not taking into consideration that a C designation leads to a slower performance than is the case with *alla breve*. That Beethoven was conscious of a difference in tempo can be seen from a letter of July 17, 1812, to his publisher Breitkopf & Härtel:

> You will have received the proofs of the Mass [Op. 86]. At the beginning of the Gloria I have altered C to ¢ time signature, thus altering the tempo; and that is the way the time was indicated at first.
>
> ANDERSON, Vol. I, p. 378

For the performer, all this is rather confusing, and a solid solution is not to hand; however, it is certain that the notation of this music leads to an outcome different from that required by Beethoven's metronome number.

Sonata Op. 106, 1st movement

In the last movement, the fugue is notated in a 3/4 measure in combination with *Allegro risoluto* and sixteenths as the fastest note values. For this music, too, with its high polyphonic complexity, playing a somewhat slower tempo than Beethoven's ♩ = 144 would be welcome. Along with this argument, the term *risoluto* points to a performance where the music should stand firm, which does exclude any running.

This avoidance of running is specifically clear where the theme appears in augmentation from m. 94 on. While the time remains unaltered as 3/4 and with the notes twice as slow, the many accents and *sforzati* that support this emotional outburst are so outspoken that they need sufficient space to fulfill their musical impact.

Sonata Op. 106, last movement

A completely different musical image that could also be helpful in finding a convincing tempo for this fugue is to take into consideration mm. 250–278 in D major, with the expression *una corda—sempre dolce cantabile*. Beethoven does not change the tempo marking for these measures, but with the quarter as the fastest note value and the very special musical image of these wonderful measures, it seems that a somewhat slower tempo for the last movement as a whole should better fit its overall character.

Of course, quite apart from these diverse principles, the influence of the qualities of the specific instrument and the size and acoustics of the hall will also play a role, not to mention the fact that composers often failed (and still fail) to observe their own metronome designations when performing their works themselves. Béla Bartók, for example, played his *Allegro barbaro* faster than 𝅗𝅥 = 100, while the score gives 𝅗𝅥 = 76–84. Richard Wagner gave metronome indications for his early operas until he heard *Tannhäuser* performed at a stupid tempo and it became apparent that the conductor had kept precisely to the prescribed tempi. After that, Wagner notated only general character indications. When Johannes Brahms received a request to send a card with the metronome indication for his first *Rhapsodie*, he replied that this was impossible, as each day he would have to send a new card with a different tempo.

All of this emphasizes yet again the complexity of the subject "tempo." However, simpler means can also make a valuable contribution to the achievement of a particular tempo. In the first place must be mentioned the principle that a tempo must never be selected in such a way that there is no room left for tempi that at the time were also very well known and that are even faster (or slower) than the tempo indicated. To give an example of a fast tempo: if a sixteenth-note passage in a work with the designation *allegro* is played so quickly that there is no room left for an *allegro con brio*, an *allegro assai*, a *presto*, or a *prestissimo*, because the sixteenths can no longer be played without it all ending in disaster, then such a tempo is obviously too fast. And second, by singing the music, the "motion" of a phrase can often be felt most naturally. In the case of the tempi of the first and last movements of Beethoven's "Hammerklavier," this could even provide a possible solution.[27] After all, the first movement opens with the exclamation, "Vivat, vivat Rudolphus!" When shouting out these words, so full of energy, in the rhythm Beethoven is asking for, a tempo that corresponds to a range between 𝅗𝅥 = 108 and 𝅗𝅥 = 132 on the metronome will not be surprising.

For the last movement, singing Handel's music from the "Hallelujah" chorus—" . . . and He shall reign forever and ever"—will equally provide a possible outcome. A metronome numbering between ♩ = 126 and ♩ = 132 then seems at least plausible.

Beethoven: Fugue, theme, mm. 16–19; Handel: Theme from the "Hallelujah" chorus in Messiah, *transposed from D major to B-flat major.*

However, although this argument is quite convincing, no proof can be provided here either, and it is therefore perhaps more relevant to focus on the fact that the metronome was not immediately the perfect instrument we are using today. The first model Maelzel marketed in 1815 was a pyramid twelve inches (30 cm) high, with an inverted pendulum rod bearing the numbers 50 to 160. The price of three louis d'or was rather high, and according to Schindler, as early as the 1820s Maelzel, who was then living in Paris, asked his brother in Vienna to market a smaller model, to be manufactured in Germany. This metronome, in obelisk form, was about eight inches high and had a pendulum rod of 40 to 208; the price was now one louis d'or.[28]

According to Schindler, Beethoven used the first model for the metronomization of his Sonata Op. 106, a logical remark, because he composed this sonata in 1818. From letters from Maelzel to the publisher Gottfried Christoph Härtel, it appears that the construction of the pyramid type of metronome was substantially improved in 1821, so that it could better withstand traveling or being dropped. It is apparent that in the previous years not everything was always trustworthy. Indeed, Beethoven himself had problems with the apparatus, because he complained in a letter to Ries in London dated March 20, 1819, that he could not yet send the tempi for his "Hammerklavier" Sonata because his metronome was broken.[29]

With all these developments, one cannot exclude the possibility that not all metronomes ticked the time at the same speed for a given number, and that small deviations could be possible and indeed could differ from the speed intended.[30] Therefore, a small reduction or expansion of Beethoven's numbers is not out of the question. Here, a sincere argument in favor of a small reduction of the numbers is a very musical one, and must be mentioned.

Beethoven delivered his metronome marks for his symphonies, string quartets, and the "Hammerklavier" precisely in the period that his brand-new Broadwood grand piano arrived from London.[31] It is possible that he played parts of his works on this new instrument and notated the metronome numbers, but, because of his very serious deafness, Beethoven's inner perception of the music must also have played a distinct role in the process of finding a suitable number. It is well known that the tempo is always faster according to one's internal perception than when the music is actually performed. Not only will the mechanics of the instrument and the physical conditions of the pianist drag the tempo somewhat, but what also counts is that in the process of playing, a musician is doing two things: first, thinking ahead to what is to come in the music; and second, monitoring what he has just heard. The constant interaction between these two elements during playing does not take place with "inner" perception. Here, the controlling element does not enter into this process and concentration is focused only on what is coming. This leads to faster tempi and, as a result, higher metronome numbers than for actual playing.

But even all these arguments and deliberations unfortunately do not provide an absolute solution. Hence, to conclude, perhaps the best advice is to return to the way Johann Philipp Kirnberger put it in an article about "Bewegung" that he wrote for a chapter about music in *Allgemeine Theorie der Schönen Künste*, a book that was published in 1771 by Johann Georg Sulzer. Beethoven knew this book very well, because he had studied it as a youngster with Neefe during his years in Bonn. Long before Maelzel invented the metronome, Kirnberger came to the following conclusion regarding tempo:

> No one other than he who has composed a piece himself is able to indicate the correct degree of its pace. A small degree above or below can inflict much damage to the piece's effect.

> No matter how many words one may have devised for this, they remain nevertheless inadequate. The pace could, however, be precisely indicated through the actual fixation of the time in which the whole piece should be played. Whoever avails himself of the commendable task of perfectly performing a piece by a great master would do well to play it at the prescribed pace very often, sometimes a little faster, sometimes a little slower, every time paying close attention to the effect it engenders, so that he may afterwards maintain the most advantageous degree.
>
> SULZER, Vol. 2, p. 157

Indeed a really practical solution that for sure will be heartily endorsed by many musicians of all times.

CHAPTER FIVE

The Editions

> My sonata [Op. 22] is beautifully engraved—but it took a nice long time.
>
> —BEETHOVEN IN A LETTER TO HOFFMEISTER, APRIL 8, 1802; ANDERSON, Vol. I, p. 73

THESE DAYS, IT IS exceptional for anyone studying Beethoven's piano sonatas not to have an urtext on the music stand—an edition taking advantage of all available original sources and with the editor explaining which choices have been made to arrive at the score in question. Past editions from great Beethoven interpreters such as Franz Liszt, Hans von Bülow, Karl Klindworth, Eugen d'Albert, Frederic Lamond, or Claudio Arrau have gradually receded into the background and no longer play such an important role in our approach to an interpretation, not to mention a controversial yet well-known edition from a music theorist like Hugo Riemann, who provides Beethoven's text with "scientifically" supported phrasings, and which is just as completely out of the picture.

Today, not only is knowledge of historical performance practice increasingly coming into play, but additionally, interest in the sound potential of the fortepiano is mounting and is even influencing our approach to playing a modern grand. All of this represents developments which mean that using an urtext, whether playing on a fortepiano or a modern grand, is almost taken for granted in our effort to match as closely as possible the musical picture the composer had in mind. Even so, there are some aspects of present-day urtext publications that are given insufficient attention or are even completely ignored, just as in many "old" publications notes and recommendations can be found which, even when not contradicting an urtext, can make a valuable contribution to a convincing interpretation.

In this chapter, a number of editions will be discussed, paying attention to the original first printings as well as some influential later publications and of course to the use of urtext publications such as those of Henle and the Wiener Urtext.

Even during Beethoven's lifetime there were plans for a complete edition of all works published to date, because without the composer's prior knowledge there were various pirate editions on the market about which he complained. Then it would be better to gain personal control: not such an easy job, as can be read in his letter of February 15, 1817, to the publisher Simrock in which he points out that all kinds of mistakes have been overlooked in the original printings.

> As soon as you can, do send me your views on the publication of my collected works, beginning with my compositions for pianoforte. It would be a profitable undertaking, since so many inaccurate editions of my works are prancing about in the world.
>
> ANDERSON, Vol. II, p. 669

However, this project never came to fruition and the first republication of all the piano sonatas came only after his death. It marked the beginning of dozens of editions, in which over the years various pianists and theoreticians have created scores from ever more varied points of view. In doing this, directly after Beethoven's death it seemed obvious to base any new edition on the original printings,[1] even though, as is apparent from Beethoven's letter, there were enough doubts in this respect.[2] Research into manuscripts, sketches, or printers' proofs simply did not occur to anyone, and any new work was based on what was still known about Beethoven's playing or what his pupils could report, in addition to the original printings, where just obvious mistakes were corrected, such as the omission of an accidental.

In addition to Czerny's publication of the complete piano sonatas with Haslinger, which was announced as early as December 1828, and the slightly later publication of Ignaz Moscheles by Messrs. Cramer & Co. in London, in which information from Beethoven's favorite pupil, Dorothea von Ertmann, was incorporated,[3] it appears that Franz Liszt was also involved in one of these earliest publications of the piano sonatas, namely the first French edition from the Parisian publisher Maurice Schlesinger.

The contribution of the young Liszt is mentioned in the 1830 volume of the *Revue musicale*, a well-respected music journal that had been established in 1827 by the Belgian composer, musicologist, and critic François-Joseph Fétis. In Part VI there appears under the heading "Publications classiques":

> [. . .] All the works were collated on earlier editions of which we have scrupulously corrected the printing or engraving errors. [. . .] After a first correction of proofs, M. M. Payer and Listz [sic] have taken it on themselves to review every delivery and to set out to purge them of every error; in such a way that one has the certitude to find in the complete edition of M. Schlesinger all possible corrections. [. . .][4]

Because of his lessons with Czerny, who had been Beethoven's pupil, Liszt perhaps felt that he was the only true successor to the greatest composer of that era. Furthermore, as a boy he had actually received Beethoven's personal blessing (a *Weihekuss*)—possibly just apocryphal, though confirmed by Liszt himself. All of this brought with it certain obligations, of course.

Comparison of the Haslinger publication in Vienna on which Czerny had worked, Cramer's Moscheles publication in London, and that of Schlesinger in Paris reveals that, as Fétis remarks, this last one remains closest to the original first editions. While in the Haslinger and Moscheles editions there are numerous changes with regard to, for instance, phrasing and dynamics, and both are provided with metronome indications, Liszt's contribution, working on the Schlesinger edition along with the Austrian pianist Hieronymus

Payer, is modest, only very occasionally departing from the original publications.[5]

In 1857, however, there appeared from L. Holle in Wolfenbüttel an edition for which Liszt bore full responsibility.[6] Around 1848 he had abandoned his life as an itinerant piano virtuoso when he settled in Weimar as court Kapellmeister, and it might therefore be expected that in this edition he would clearly reflect his personal experiences with the repertoire. This is, however, only partially the case. Beethoven's fingering is used, for example, and not that of Liszt himself. It is, however, an original idea of his to indicate the structure of the movements of all the sonatas through the use of capital letters, clarifying the compositions' construction. Just now and then a footnote would be added, as in the case of the Sonata Op. 110, where he added the following note at the beginning of the second fugue: "The theme in countermovement"; and at mm. 151–152 for the bass notes: "The theme in diminution," followed immediately by: "Abridgment and double diminution of the themes."

That said, the Holle publication does depart much more from the original printings than did that of Schlesinger. That is apparent, for example, in a comparison of the pedal indications in the recitatives from the first movement of the Sonata Op. 31 No. 2. While in the Schlesinger edition Liszt retains Beethoven's original indications with, from m. 143, the long pedal over six measures that also appears in Nägeli's original printing, in the Holle edition this is canceled by keeping only the A-major chord in the pedal. It appears that Liszt found that Beethoven's original indications were no longer feasible on the grand pianos of his era.

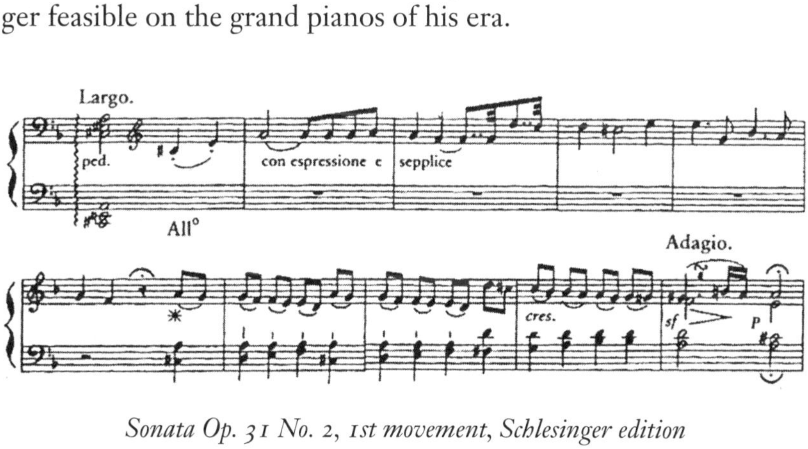

Sonata Op. 31 No. 2, 1st movement, Schlesinger edition

Sonata Op. 31 No. 2, 1st movement, Holle edition

It is also noticeable that he had made use of the Haslinger edition[7] in Vienna on which Carl Czerny had collaborated. The small accents in the last movement of Op. 26 and in the Trio of Op. 28, which appear in that edition, are, for example, adopted in the Holle edition, even though they are missing from the original publications and Beethoven's manuscript.

Sonata Op. 26, 4th movement, Holle edition

Sonata Op. 28, 3rd movement, Holle edition

In the Holle edition there are also examples to be found of similarities with Moscheles' London edition by Cramer, which also departs from the original publications. This is, for example, the case in the closing measures of the Adagio of the "Hammerklavier," Op. 106, a sonata of which Beethoven's manuscript is missing. Liszt's phrasing is the same as that of Moscheles.

Sonata Op. 106, 3rd movement, Holle edition

Sonata Op. 106, 3rd movement, Cramer edition

The original Artaria edition has a very different phrasing. That the chord in the bass one measure before the end is not tied is most probably due to a mistake in the printing, for one measure earlier, an octave higher, it is indeed given.

Sonata Op. 106, 3rd movement, Artaria edition

An example where taking something from an edition after Beethoven's death can be risky is to be seen in the Adagio molto of the Sonata Op. 10 No. 1. Here Liszt adopts the *arpeggio* mark as included by Haslinger at the *fortissimo* chord in m. 45. This notation is missing from Joseph Eder's original Viennese printing. To print an *arpeggio* here is unfortunate, because the chord is notated as an "eighth," and thus should be played short, and of course such a "secco" *fortissimo* performance has a much more dramatic impact.

Even in the case of recent urtexts, such as the 2007 publication by the Associated Board of the Royal Schools of Music (ABRSM) by Barry Cooper, as well as with the Henle and Wiener Urtext editions, it seems that a particular performance can become a tradition. There, too, this chord is still given as an *arpeggio*, despite this mark's absence from the original printing and the fact that Beethoven's original manuscript for this sonata is unknown.

Sonata Op. 10 No. 1, 2nd movement, Eder edition

Sonata Op. 10 No. 1, 2nd movement, Wiener Urtext edition

Although breaking chords was a standard performance practice and was, for instance, mentioned by Czerny for the opening chord of the Fourth Piano Concerto,[8] it is not inconceivable that Beethoven used it more subtly than is often assumed. It is noticeable, for instance, that in the original editions of the Sonata Op. 31 No. 3 by both Nägeli and Simrock, in the last movement, Presto con fuoco, the *fortissimo* chord in m. 307 is broken and the one in m. 17 is not. In the first case this is set "broadly," with the expression of an urgent question; in the second case it has the expression of a compelling command. Here Liszt did not change Beethoven's notation, and it is adopted in this form in modern urtexts, too.

Sonata Op. 31 No. 3, 4th movement, Nägeli edition

A view that has much more influence on interpretation is, however, the changing of a large number of *alla breve* notations appearing in the original printings into a common-time measure. This is the case in the third movement of Op. 10 No. 1, the first movement of Op. 10 No. 3, the second movement of Op. 14 No. 2, the first movement of Op. 27 No. 1, the first movement of Op. 27 No. 2, the first movement of Op. 31 No. 2, the first movement of Op. 106, and the Fifth Variation in Op. 109. Because these changes occur too frequently for them to be printing errors, there must be a reason for them.

In this case, too, Liszt may have taken a few examples from editions that appeared shortly after Beethoven's death. In the Haslinger edition, for instance, the *alla breve* notation is changed to common time not only in the first movement of Op. 31 No. 2, but also in the

Fifth Variation in Op. 109, and in the Cramer edition the original *alla breve* notation in the Andante from Op. 14 No. 2 appears to have been altered to common time.[9] For the variation in Op. 109 and this Andante, the reasoning must have been that this notation would do these "marches" more justice. Beethoven's choice of *alla breve* confirms, however, that there must be nothing "military" in the performance. In Op. 14 No. 2, the *alla breve* notation points more in the direction of a humorous parody of a march, and in Op. 109 the musical picture can be linked to an animated idealization of a march, where some firm stamping of feet on the ground is absolutely not done. All this is canceled out by the introduction of the common-time notation.

Concerning the other examples in the Holle edition of changing the time signature, Liszt must also have had a certain motivation—for example, in the first movement of the "Moonlight" Sonata.[10] His pupil August Stradal wrote that Liszt heard this movement in a performance by Anton Rubinstein and found the tempo much too fast. He himself played it in a much slower tempo.

> Afterwards we paid a visit to Batka's sister, who had prepared a frugal lunch. Here Liszt broached the subject of Rubinstein's concert, admired the performance of the Septet and of Chopin's works, but did not agree with Rubinstein's reading of the C-sharp-minor Sonata. After lunch Liszt sat down at the piano and played the Adagio and the second movement of Beethoven's C-sharp-minor Sonata. While Rubinstein had played the Adagio too fast, Liszt executed it almost in tempo Larghetto (♩ = 58); the triplets in the right hand completely even, without *crescendo* and toneless. [. . .]
>
> STRADAL, p. 87

Although Liszt's tempo is not particularly slow, he must have played this movement not in "twos," as in the original printing, but, in line with his Holle edition, in "fours"—an interpretation with a long tradition, as the famous English pianist Harold Bauer discovered when Victor Company asked him to record this movement in 1926.

I received a telegram from the Victor Company enquiring if I would make a phonographic record of the Moonlight Sonata on my return to New York. My first impulse was to accept immediately, but a second thought made me hesitate. Was the first movement not too long and too slow to be recorded on a twelve-inch disk (the largest size)? I played it through and it took just over five minutes. The limit was four minutes and forty seconds. I tried it faster and did not like it. I thought of making a cut . . . horrible! I thought of playing it in two sections . . . equally horrible! I did not reply to the telegram, and wandered disconsolately into the Public Library (not having the Sonata with me), in order to see if the sight of the page would offer any kind of solution. The edition was an unfamiliar one, and the time signature–two-two–was so unusual that it caught my eye at once. I had never seen anything but the ordinary common-time signature, and I had never played it or heard it played otherwise than with four distinct pulsations to the measure. The unfamiliar time notation intrigued me, and I returned to ask the librarian if he had another edition. He found two, one of which was similar to what I had studied from, and the other marked "alla breve." I made further inquiries and discovered an old edition at home of my friend Oscar Weil, which gave a time notation that I had never before seen, namely: four-four. By this time I was thoroughly perplexed. What had Beethoven written, and why these differences? In the meanwhile, I tried the effect of the first movement with two instead of four pulsations to the measure. This obliged me to play it faster, although the rhythmical effect, on the contrary, was slower, and the more I played it the better I liked it this way. I could not decide what to do, but I remembered that I had, in my library at home, a facsimile of the composer's manuscript (which I had never examined carefully), and also a copy of the first edition. Since neither of these was available in San Francisco, I determined to wait until I returned to New York, and telegraphed the Victor Company to that effect.

When I reached home, I could hardly wait to consult these authentic sources. I dashed to my bookcase and pulled out the first edition and the facsimile of the manuscript. The time signature was "alla breve" in the printed first edition, but the manuscript! . . . *There was no first page!* The original from which the facsimile was taken is carefully preserved at the Beethoven Museum in Bonn, and nobody knows how or when the first page was lost or stolen. The result is that all editors, ignoring the evidence of the first engraved edition, have considered themselves justified, ever since, in making any time notation they choose. This is a great pity, for no musician who has once been released from traditional and unreasoning obedience to the printed page can possibly doubt that Beethoven knew exactly what he wanted when he indicated two beats to the measure in the first movement of the Moonlight Sonata. And Beethoven was right of course.

I made the phonograph record in four minutes and thirty-seven seconds, and have never since reverted to the slow tempo, which today seems an absurdity to me.[11]

BAUER, pp. 268–269

As Bauer had already established, after Beethoven's death a great number of other editions had been marketed. In the meantime, virtuosity, initiated by Liszt, had grabbed the attention of the mass audience, and the best pianists of the time competed for honor and success. This presented excellent opportunities for them to include personal insights, not only in their playing but also in the text and footnotes of special editions they published, known as "critical" editions. It is no surprise that Liszt's pupils were in the forefront. Hans von Bülow, Karl Klindworth, Eugen d'Albert, and Frederic Lamond—all counting among the greatest Beethoven interpreters of their time—had editions published making their personal contribution and coloring Beethoven's text in a multiplicity of ways. Von Bülow, for example, collaborated on a series of publications with works of several composers under the editorship of Dr. Sigismund Lebert. The first of the five volumes of these

Instruktiven Ausgabe klassischer Klavierwerke of Beethoven's piano sonatas was published in 1871 by Cotta in Stuttgart. They were completed in 1875.[12]

On the title page we find the following dedication:

> This interpretation request is dedicated to Maestro Franz Liszt as the fruits of his teaching.
>
> His grateful pupil Hans von Bülow.

The famous pianist Clara Schumann-Wieck was far from pleased with the idea that these opinions of Liszt shone through in this edition. She most severely forbade her pupils to make use of it. In those days Clara did not count among Liszt's admirers, and to allow her pupils to play from an edition in which his opinions were advanced was going too far. Liszt himself, however, was extremely pleased with von Bülow's edition. In a letter of September 26, 1872, he wrote to Otto Lessmann:

> Bülow's Beethoven edition provides more instruction than a thousand conservatories.
>
> LA MARA, Vol. II, p. 176

It appears that von Bülow provides not only examples that refer back to Liszt's Holle edition, with, among other things, the introduction of the 4/4 measures for the Andante in Op. 14 No. 2 and the first movement of the "Moonlight" Sonata, but also examples of how Liszt sometimes played these works. Such an example is the descending scale and the trills at the end of the fugue in the "Hammerklavier," which he included in a footnote in his edition.

Sonata Op. 106, 4th movement, Wiener Urtext edition

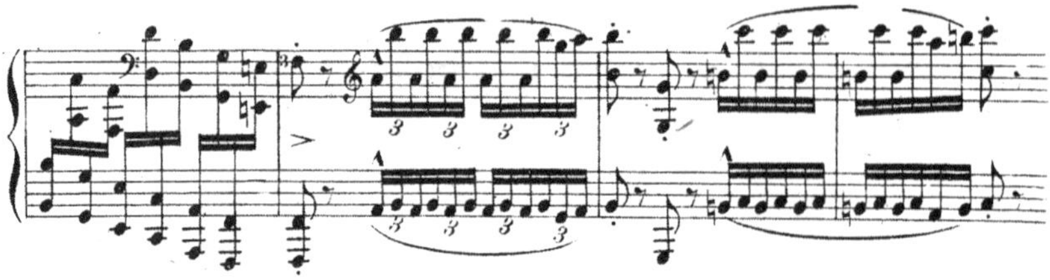

Sonata Op. 106, 4th movement, Bote & Bock edition (Klindworth), interpretation by Liszt

Such a pianistic approach was going too far for Clara, even though she did not shy away from considerable interference when publishing the works of her husband Robert.[13]

Von Bülow, too, sometimes thought that he had discovered a more effective solution for Beethoven's notes—for instance, in the last movement of the Sonata Op. 101. There, at a really specific point, where Beethoven pays extra attention to his notation by adding Contra E in m. 224 and writes out the passage yet again in pencil at the bottom of the page, von Bülow changes Beethoven's notes.[14]

Sonata Op. 101, 4th movement, autograph

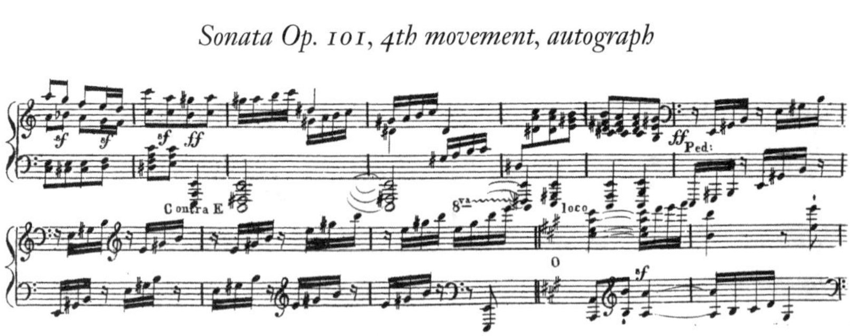

Sonata Op. 101, 4th movement, Steiner & Co. (first edition)

Sonata Op. 101, 4th movement, Bote & Bock edition (Klindworth)

This view is still reflected in a later Breitkopf & Härtel edition by the Scottish pianist Frederic Lamond, also a pupil of Liszt.

However, the reason for von Bülow to put such a proposal on paper may be clear. In his version, the head of the theme, appearing in augmentation between the tied octaves in the bass, can in this way be heard much better.[15] While this is a remarkable suggestion, there are also numerous other, more acceptable proposals—for example, his very helpful fingering, in which we recognize the experienced pianist. Other indications, like specific dynamics or Italian expressions such as *marcato*, *leggiero*, *tranquillo*, or *animato*, also enliven the note picture. He also provides metronome indications for all movements, whereby it is noticeable that these indications can alter within a movement if the interpretation gives due cause for this.[16]

Von Bülow's edition was in great demand, as evidenced by its being published as early as 1876 by Oliver Ditson & Co. in Boston for which the American composer J.C.D. Parker provided the English translation. This edition gained even more prominence when, after von Bülow's death in 1894, the New York publisher Schirmer gained the copyright. In this, von Bülow's contribution for the Sonatas Opp. 13, 26, and 27 and Op. 31 No. 3 could be included, while for the remaining sonatas the previous editing of Sigismund Lebert was used.

A further interesting edition, published by Bote & Bock in Berlin, is that of another of Liszt's pupils, the German pianist Karl Klindworth. This edition, based on that of von Bülow, was considered so good that von Bülow preferred it to his own.[17] The Portuguese pianist José Vianna da Motta, also one of Liszt's pupils, remarked on this. When Vianna da Motta, after his lessons with Liszt in 1887, went to study with von Bülow and a pupil appeared with von Bülow's edition, the latter reacted as follows:

> It is very flattering to me that you bring my edition, but I advise you, however, to take Klindworth's edition; there you will find all that is good in my edition, the superfluous excluded and the erroneous corrected.
>
> PFEIFFER (SUPPLEMENT J. VIANNA DA MOTTA), p. 98

With respect to von Bülow's metronome indications, the writing out of embellishments, and some pedaling indications, it is especially an edition in which Klindworth's fingering for difficult passages are striking, such as in mm. 137–141 of the Allegro in Op. 101:

Sonata Op. 101, 4th movement, Bote & Bock edition (Klindworth)

or in the fourth variation in the second movement of Op. 111:

Sonata Op, 111, 2nd movement, Bote & Bock edition (Klindworth); (*) the lower fingering, when both final notes are taken over by the right hand.

In 1902, Forberg in Leipzig published yet another edition by one of Liszt's pupils, that of Eugen d'Albert. D'Albert, once nicknamed by Liszt—partly in jest, partly in admiration—"Van II" because of his fame as a great Beethoven interpreter at a very young age, also based his edition on that of von Bülow. Even so, here, too, we see a personal approach. In addition to indications for interpretation, d'Albert gives advice regarding pianistics in which not only his fingering but also the way of playing is included. The hand posture in the Allegro molto e vivace from the Sonata Op. 27 No. 1 is an example of this, as is that for the dramatic introduction to the last movement of the "Appassionata":

a) Das staccato in der Linken aus dem Handgelenk, das legato in der Rechten mit flachgehaltener Hand.

a) The staccato in the left hand must come from the wrist; the legato in the right hand to be played with the hand held in a flat position.

a) Le staccato à la gauche se joue du poignet, le legato à la droite la main étendue.

Sonata Op. 27 No. 1, 2nd movement, Forberg edition (d'Albert)

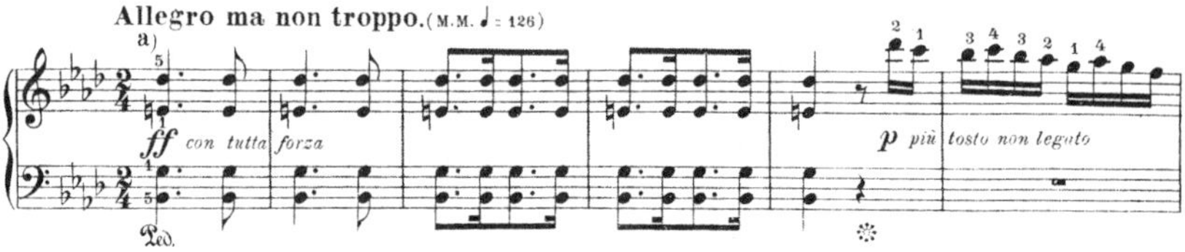

a) Mit straff-gekrümmter Hand, die nichtthätigen Finger eingezogen.

a) With firmly rounded hand, the unemployed fingers being drawn in.

a) La main arrondie et raide; les doigts qui n'ont pas à jouer doivent être repliés.

Sonata Op. 57, 3rd movement, Forberg edition (d'Albert)

His solution for the octaves to be played quickly, softly, and lightly in the "Waldstein" Sonata is also interesting. Where Beethoven probably intended a *glissando,* d'Albert provides a solution for the left hand that was indeed applied more frequently in his time, "blind" octaves:

a) Für fortgeschrittene Spieler empfiehlt es sich die Oktaven der rechten Hand wie vorgeschrieben zu spielen, die Figur in der linken Hand hingegen wie folgt:
a) The indicated performance of the right hand octaves is recommended to advanced players, but the figure in the left hand, on the contrary, should be played as follows:
a) Pour des élèves avancés, il est recommandable de jouer les octaves à la main droite comme ils sont indiqués; par contre la main gauche jouera de la façon suivante:

Sonata Op. 53, 3rd movement, Forberg edition (d'Albert)

In addition, there are some alterations which produce an interesting effect, such as the broken octaves at the end of the first movement of Op. 2 No. 3, which d'Albert even finds more easily played as rapidly alternating ordinary octaves, an adaptation that is applied to this very day at the conclusion of the Third Piano Concerto, where this manner of playing is more forceful against the orchestra.

Sonata Op. 2 No. 3, 1st movement, Forberg edition (d'Albert)

In the meantime, Breitkopf & Härtel had started in 1862 with the publication of the original editions of all of Beethoven's works in a Collected (or Complete) Edition (*Gesamtausgabe*). In this extensive project comprising twenty-nine volumes and completed only in 1888, we find in Series XVI the piano sonatas as republications of Artaria, Haslinger, Nägeli, Peters, Schlesinger, C. A. Spina, Witzendorf, and also of Breitkopf & Härtel itself.[18] Even though all original editions were now included in one single republication, this was far from satisfying, because, as Beethoven himself had once remarked, they included many mistakes. Because the personal critical instructive editions of the great interpreters had also gained in significance, there came about a reaction that led to an edition, also published by Breitkopf & Härtel, aimed at creating a first "urtext."

In the preface to this *Urtext classischer Musikwerke* published in 1898 with Carl Krebs as editor, we read:

> A work that presents the form in which the Master originally had it appear for the world.

This edition, too, returns to the original printings, but for the first time also makes use of Beethoven's original manuscripts, even though this remains limited to the Sonatas Opp. 78, 81a (first movement), and 101. This publication did, however, break new ground, resulting in a number of editions in which for the first time a personal contribution was combined with greater historical insight and understanding.

One of the most important editions following on from this and in which this outlook is to be found is that of the famous pianist and influential Beethoven interpreter Artur Schnabel.[19] Schnabel based his work on Breitkopf & Härtel's 1898 urtext, but also, as he said, on manuscripts from the Viennese archives.[20] Unfortunately, he was not consistent in this, as is apparent from his preface. He departed from the original publications with regard to slurs, accents, and performance indications because in his opinion they contained too many careless mistakes:

> The legato slurs as well as the accents and indications relative to touch were occasionally marked by the composer with such obvious, such confusing carelessness and negligence—particularly in the early works—that the editor felt himself not only musically justified, but in duty bound to change them now and then according to his best judgement, sense and taste: to abbreviate, to lengthen, to supplement, to interpret. Changes of this kind are not especially marked.

The Schnabel edition was published by Ullstein in Berlin between 1924 and 1927 and appeared in a reprint by Simon & Schuster in New York in 1935, and later also in a Russian translation. Schnabel's edition, regarded by many as holy, is especially interesting as regards notes concerning interpretation, presented in a smaller typeface.[21] These involve not only metronome indications, which, as in von Bülow's case, can vary within a movement, but also numerous dynamic markings, indications of groupings using Roman numerals, Italian performance indications, pedaling notations, and extensive footnotes. He also pays considerable attention to the subject of the *fermata*, the length of which is expressed in note values, an idea he borrowed from Lamond, who, like Schnabel, based his publication on the 1898 urtext edition.[22]

Schnabel also pays special attention to ingenious fingerings aimed at expressing his phrasing by means of an exemplary *legato* in such a way that the pedal does not have to be used. Even so, he uses it sparingly and once remarked that one plays the piano with both the hands and the feet and that the pedal is inextricably bound to the music itself.

Schnabel's edition appeared a few years after an influential edition by the English pianist, composer, music commentator, and theorist Donald Francis Tovey (1875–1940), which was published in 1931 in London by Harold Craxton in a series for the Associated Board of the Royal Schools of Music.[23] This edition became well known specifically because of Tovey's extensive commentary in the footnotes. For each sonata he goes into aspects that are important for interpretation. In the edition itself he uses instructions much more sparingly than did Schnabel, and there are for instance no metronome indications, although he did adapt the phrasing and add pedaling and fingering indications.

However, the edition that has had the most influence on how the present-day urtext has come into being is that of the Austrian music theorist Heinrich Schenker. This was published by Universal Edition in Vienna/Leipzig in four volumes that appeared between 1921 and 1923, and it was reprinted in a revised version around 1946/1947 as part of the Wiener Urtext Ausgabe, appearing in a reprint in 1975 by Dover Publications.[24]

Schenker, who even before 1920 caused quite a stir with his "Erläuterungs-Ausgaben" (explanatory editions) of Beethoven's piano sonatas Opp. 101, 109, 110, and 111, published by Universal Edition, due to the extensive, detailed analyses and great attention to Beethoven's manuscripts, also achieves a remarkably precise presentation of Beethoven's notation in his edition of the thirty-two piano sonatas.[25] With no adapted phrasings, no pedal additions, the use of the "wedge" alongside the dot as a style of playing, and with a score in which the division over the two staves corresponds to the manuscript or first original printing, this is an edition in which Schenker limits his own contribution to the fingering alone. It is interesting to present in one example for comparison a number of measures from the editions of Schnabel, Tovey, and Schenker, such as at the beginning of the Largo appassionato from Beethoven's Sonata Op. 2 No. 2, where there are remarkable differences as regards phrasing, dynamics, pedaling, and fingering. In all of this, Schenker remains very true to the original Artaria edition.

Sonata Op. 2 No. 2, 2nd movement, Ullstein edition (Schnabel)

Sonata Op. 2 No. 2, 2nd movement, Craxton edition (Tovey)

1) For the sake of "languid expression" (C. P. E. Bach), the turn may be played already on the second 8th-beat.

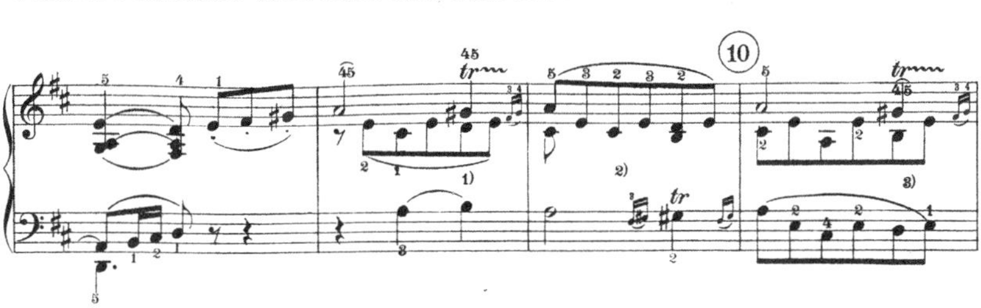

Sonata Op. 2 No. 2, 2nd movement, Universal Edition (Schenker)

Sonata Op. 2 No. 2, 2nd movement, Artaria edition

It is, however, the urtext edition published in 1952/1953 by Dr. Günther Henle in Munich, for which musicologist Bertha Antonia Wallner was responsible, that determines the view that many post-war pianists, especially in western Europe, have of Beethoven's piano sonatas. In this edition, republished in 1980, Wallner compares the available manuscripts, the transcriptions, and the original printings. The austere text that results from this is printed in a very orderly manner on off-white paper, so that the music itself also reads well.

While the von Bülow and Schnabel editions have remained ever-popular in the United States, in the same period in Russia there appeared an edition that has had—and to some extent still does have—great influence on the way pianists of the Russian school make their acquaintance with Beethoven's piano sonatas.

Along with the prevailing old German editions that were much used in Russia, there appeared from the State Music Publishers in Moscow a new edition by Alexander Goldenweiser: Part I in 1955, Part II in 1958, and Parts III and IV posthumously in 1963/1964. It is apparent that Goldenweiser was aware of the latest developments in this area, for in this case we also have an urtext, even though here, too, extensive fingering and well-considered pedaling are added. It is, however, especially Goldenweiser's appendix dealing with interpretation, in which hardly a measure is left unmentioned, that makes this edition so exceptional. It is a pity that no translation has yet appeared.

After this there appeared various interesting urtext editions, including that of the famous Chilean pianist Claudio Arrau, who collaborated with the musicologist Lothar Hoffmann-Erbrecht. The two volumes appeared with Arrau's fingering in 1973 and 1978, published by Edition Peters. In an appendix, the elaborated embellishments as well as an overview of the metronome indications from various historical editions are presented. Other editions that must be mentioned here are one by the English pianist Kendall Taylor, published by Allans Music in Australia in 1989; and a highly significant one by Barry Cooper, after that of Tovey, a new edition with the Associated Board of the Royal Schools of Music (ABRSM) in London, published in 2007, with an extensive separate commentary and an introductory CD.

One of the best-known more recent editions is, however, the Wiener Urtext, which appeared in 1999 and is the work of Peter Hauschild. Hauschild used information from sketches insofar as these exist, the various stages of the manuscript in a first version or also in fair copy, transcripts of Beethoven himself or of a copyist, the printers' so-called *Stichvorlage* (engraver's copies) and the original publication, the reprintings with any corrections or even alterations, and the accompanying correspondence with possible corrections. It is, however, apparent that choices still had to be made; this can be seen from the fact that the Henle edition uses only dots as *staccato* marks, while Hauschild uses only wedges; the difference has already been discussed in Chapter 4.

While Conrad Hansen supplied the fingerings in the complete Henle edition, in the Wiener Urtext, a number of pianists did this for particular sonatas, of course in both editions such that they could be clearly distinguished from Beethoven's own fingerings. In this edition, a critical commentary is added in which the choices made are discussed and the possibilities from other sources are mentioned.

Another, also very distinguished urtext edition in three volumes by Bärenreiter, completed and edited by Jonathan Del Mar, was published at the end of 2019 just before the Beethoven year in 2020. In this edition, printed on a cream-tinted background, very pleasant to read, the "Kurfürsten" Sonatas, composed in 1783, are also included. However, these volumes do not include a critical commentary for each sonata. It is a pity that this important information must be purchased separately.

In the very clean text of this edition, fingerings other than those by Beethoven himself are missing. This can be considered an advantage for the scholar, but at the same time a disadvantage for young pianists who are interested in practical suggestions, not only for solving technical difficulties, but even more so for fingerings that support the musical outcome such as specific articulations and expressions, as we can conclude from, for example, interesting fingerings by von Bülow, Arrau, or Schnabel.

Another important recent development in this area that has not yet been concluded has been initiated by Henle, on which Norbert Gertsch began in 2004 in collaboration with pianist Murray Perahia. In this publication, individual editions of a number of sonatas have so far been published, but with the intention that finally all sonatas will be available in three collected volumes.[26] Here, each sonata is accompanied by a critical commentary in which alternatives from other editions are mentioned. There is also sometimes a brief analysis in which Perahia's knowledge of Schenker's methods becomes clear and, beside Beethoven's own fingerings, there are very interesting fingerings from Perahia, indeed welcome suggestions for any pianist.

Additionally, in the music itself, not only are wedges and dots differentiated, but also, where these marks are missing from the sources, they are not uniformly inserted. Rather, in order to keep seemingly identical passages open as far as sound color is concerned, such possibilities are not encompassed. Beethoven's manuscript is given priority over the original printing in this edition, as is evident from the representation of the distribution of the sixteenth notes by the beam in the left hand in the Fifth Variation of Op. 26. Although it is not inconceivable that Cappi's printing includes corrections by Beethoven, this Henle edition adopts the manuscript distributions, with the exception of m. 195, where it follows the two preceding measures with the same *sforzato* indication.

Sonata Op. 26, 1st movement, autograph

Sonata Op. 26, 1st movement, Cappi edition

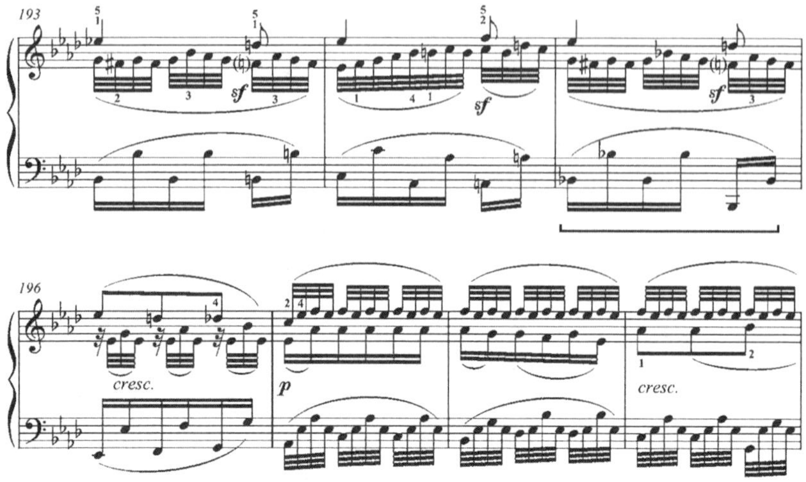

Sonata Op. 26, 1st movement, Henle edition (Gertsch/Perahia)

It is, however, by no means certain that the last word has been said with this Henle edition. It can be expected that the coming decades will see further editions appearing with perhaps further new insights.

In any event, there is one aspect to which not a single urtext edition has paid any attention, and that is the format of the original printings appearing during Beethoven's lifetime. With the exception of Opp. 106, 110, and 111, these are printed oblong (landscape), fitting precisely on the music stands of historical instruments. Although it cannot be said that there is a general tendency to print music in this format in all countries, it was frequently employed by German and Austrian publishers.

Although these days we are used to the upright (portrait) format, landscape printing offers distinct advantages, namely that the reading of the music corresponds more to the direction of motion of the music and thus has more "flow" than the shorter lines of the format that is familiar to us.[27]

On landscape pages there are more measures on one line, which reads more easily, quite apart from the fact that the measures are often spaced out more in the original printings and that the ease of turning pages is taken into account. For in those days it was not the custom to play music by heart. The consequence is that the notation has more breathing space, which in turn has a subliminal influence on the psyche of the player, who has more time to follow the music and absorb himself in it.

With so much information available, it is not easy for the present-day pianist to choose between the various editions. Of course, a recent urtext must be used, but having an original printing alongside this, or being able to consult a facsimile of the manuscript or the editions influenced by pupils of Beethoven such as Czerny and Dorothea von Ertmann, provides even more insight into Beethoven's intentions. To be able to consult, in addition to all this, the suggestions of great pianists of the past and present with their commentary, fingering, pedaling, or metronome indications is equally stimulating and amazingly informative, but something that must always be seen in the perspective of the modern urtext.

CHAPTER SIX

Style and Interpretation

> As for me, why, good heavens, my kingdom is in the air. As the wind often does, so do harmonies whirl around me, and so do things often whirl about too in my soul.
>
> —BEETHOVEN IN A LETTER TO COUNT FRANZ VON BRUNSVIK, FEBRUARY 13, 1814; ANDERSON, Vol. I, p. 445

SINCE HANS VON BÜLOW'S well-known remark that Bach's *Well-Tempered Clavier* counts as the Old Testament while Beethoven's thirty-two sonatas represent the New Testament, you can imagine that by studying and playing these works and opening your soul to them, you can learn from them and gain in inner richness. Even after so many years, this image remains unchanged in that for both listeners and performers the musical content of these masterpieces reaches far beyond a musical impression alone. For those wishing to master a very demanding work, such as a Beethoven sonata, it is therefore clear that it is a matter of course to gain an overview of the complete work, thus over the full dimensions and structure of all movements taken together.

It is remarkable to see from Beethoven's sketchbooks that such simultaneous planning is regularly encountered. For him, movements—with only rare exceptions—were not regarded as independent entities but rather belonged to a previously conceived idea for the whole work.[1] It was Franz Schubert who stated early on that for Beethoven a composition in its inception could indeed be created in such a way.

The author Karl Johann von Braunthal recorded the following conversation about this subject with Schubert.

> In a small Vienna inn, I saw Beethoven in the last years of his life on many a winter evening. [. . .] Sometimes he drew a second, firmer notebook from his heart pocket (I mean the left breast pocket of his simple gray overcoat) and wrote with half-closed eyes. I wonder what he's writing?—one evening I asked my neighbor, the unrivaled song composer Schubert, who died far too young. He's composing, he replied.—But he's writing words, not notes?—That's his way; he usually indicates with words the progression of ideas for this or that piece of music and puts at the most a few notes in between.
>
> KOPITZ/CADENBACH, Vol. I, pp. 91–92

Such a "progression of ideas" we also notice in a letter Beethoven wrote to Archduke Rudolph from July 29, 1819.

In this letter Beethoven not only praises the genius of Bach and Handel, but also aims at an artistic synthesis, a so-called *Kunstvereinigung*, indeed an idea to connect music from the past with the present. Is it not striking that, inspired by both composers, we see so many examples of this idea in his polyphonic writing and, at the same time, of his developing new forms in his music?[2]

The conversation between Schubert and von Braunthal could have taken place in Leonhard Wanner's beerhouse "Zur Eiche," a place where both composers were happy to stay.[3] An eyewitness described a Saturday evening:

> In the last years of his life there was an opportunity to see Beethoven regularly every Saturday evening in the inn "Zur Eiche" on the Brandstatt. Beethoven came there to partake of his favorite dish: black pudding with potatoes, drink some Regensburger beer, and then smoke a pipe of tobacco. He had his little table there in the corner where no one else sat out of respect. [. . .]
>
> KERST, Vol. I, p. 294

"Beethoven in a Café." Drawing by Eduard Klosson (1823).
Beethoven-Haus, Bonn.

Discovering how such ideas for constructing a composition take shape is also a popular subject for the analysis with which a large number of music theorists have occupied themselves over the decades, with perhaps Heinrich Schenker as the main proponent. Schenker's analyses are, by means of the so-called *Urlinie* and through the *Fernhören*, aimed mainly at clarifying the direction and goal of the musical process in order to achieve the spread of tension in the music over longer periods. Additionally, thematic links within a movement or between various movements of a composition, as analyzed by, among others, Rudolf Reti,[4] or the process of "foreshortening," applied inventively by Alfred Brendel, serve to prevent the performing musician from deviating from the musical path, but instead to have him focus on the creation of an all-embracing span of tension.[5] Alongside such forms of analysis, even in Beethoven's time a process had been set in motion of not just attending to the notes and structure of a composition, but more especially of attempting to look "behind" the notes and so to be able to delve more deeply into the soul of the composition.

In many of their literary works, authors such as Jean Paul and E.T.A. Hoffmann sought the music's substance in this direction, attempting thereby to expose its true significance. In his famous article "Beethoven's Instrumental Music" (1813), for example, Hoffmann created a graphic literary commentary in this manner about, among other works, the Fifth Symphony.[6]

All of this later led to the doctrine of "musical hermeneutics," of which Hermann Kretzschmar and Arnold Schering were the foremost proponents.[7] To composers such as Liszt and Wagner, for whom literature and music were closely intertwined, a certain form of musical hermeneutics was obvious. It was from this background that new musical forms also could be developed: the symphonic poem and the musical-dramatic all-embracing art form, the "Gesamtkunstwerk," uniting all forms of art via the theater.

Interpretations by performing musicians were also influenced by this idea, by which one tries to look further than the notes to explain the deeper significance of the music. It was Carl Czerny, for example, who had already found the following poetic words regarding the last movement of Beethoven's "Appassionata":

> Perhaps Beethoven (who was ever fond of representing natural scenes) imagined to himself the waves of the sea in a stormy night, while cries of distress are heard from afar:— such an image may always furnish the player with a suitable idea for the proper performance of this great musical picture. It is certain that, in many of his finest works, Beethoven was inspired by similar visions and images, either drawn from reading or created by his own excited imagination, and that we should obtain the real key to his compositions and to their performance. [. . .]
>
> CZERNY (II), Chap. 2, p. 60

The Swiss-born pianist Alfred Cortot, living in France, also immersed himself profoundly in Beethoven's sonatas.[8] Cortot discovered that he still needed to learn the art of "looking further than the notes" when, as a pupil of Diémer, he played the first movement of the "Appassionata" in the presence of one of the greatest pianists of that time, the Russian Anton Rubinstein. The situation is recounted in detail by Bernard Gavoty.[9]

> The old lion was sprawled in an armchair, warming up a glass of cognac in the hollow of his left hand, a cigar, at which he pulled in small, desultory puffs, dangling from his other hand. The illustrious virtuoso looked the boy up and down, unblinkingly; the latter sat down at the piano and, trembling with pride and emotion, played with painstaking earnestness the first movement of Beethoven's *Appassionata.* The sublime theme died down in a pregnant silence. The youth, very moved, stood up and with downcast eyes went up to Rubinstein who merely muttered: 'That cognac of yours is very good, Diémer, I'd gladly have another glass!' Not a look or a word for the young man. Cortot crimsoned and breathed faster. An ill-boding fever ran through his veins. What, not a single word? Diémer broke the tension: he signaled to his pupil that he might now withdraw. Cortot was about to obey after a respectful bow towards the silent man in his armchair; then just as he was walking out, Rubinstein changed his mind, called him back, stared at him with his golden eyes and said:
>
> 'My boy, don't you ever forget what I'm going to tell you: Beethoven's music must not be studied, it must be reinvented.'
>
> GAVOTY, p. 25

Reinventing! Later on, Cortot had no problem doing this. When, during his *cours d'interprétation*, the music of the "Appassionata" was on the music stand, he immediately found the words for the trill just before the dramatic outburst of the Presto in the last movement:

> The trill formulations that precede the "presto" must be satanic. If, instead of terrifying us with the horror of this demonic cackle, you simply play a trill, all is lost. [. . .]
>
> CORTOT, p. 112

Sonata Op. 57, 3rd movement

Such an image went right to the heart of the French writer and winner of the Nobel Prize for literature Romain Rolland.[10] He, too, could draw on rich powers of imagination, as is evident from his text for the beginning of the first movement:

> AND NOW let us contemplate the monster!
>
> The main theme, which dominates the whole movement, is constituted of two elements so closely joined to each other that at first sight they seem to be only one: the first three measures the first, measures 4 and 5 the second:

> Their duality only becomes apparent in the furious, tornado-like repetition of them that follows m. 17. Two in one: two Selves in opposition: a wild Self-force, a trembling Self-weakness. At the commencement they come clamped together in the wind that drives them along, *allegro assai*, but *pianissimo*. Then a kettledrum triplet—as so often in Beethoven; the almost immutable signification of it is the implacable decree of Destiny: "*Thus it is. Obey!*"—gives an impassive threefold answer to the moaning question:—

Then the squall bursts, and the all-powerful force surges forward again *fortissimo*, in massive columns, in three crashing accents. The Self-weakness, in agitation and anguish, supplicates despairingly; we can almost see the clenched hands and the contractions of the heart:—

ROLLAND (II), pp. 152, 153

Such a commentary was not unusual, as can also be gathered from the words of the famous Beethoven interpreter Wilhelm Backhaus, who wrote an extensive analysis of the first movement of the "Pathétique" in which there is also room for his poetic commentary. The American journal *The Etude* published this in 1926:[11]

I would like to add a few words suggesting a poetical analysis of this movement, as it has forced itself on my mind.

The opening theme (m. 1) divides in two sections, namely the *forte* chord and the pleading motive.

Let me suggest the name "opposition" for the *forte* chord, and it will then appear that the hero finds opposition in his way right at the start, and he tries to conquer it by pleading. This repeats three times, the pleading the third time being the most intense by the virtue of dynamics, tonal height and repetition.

We will notice the number three playing quite an important part as we go on. In mm. 5–7, we find the pleading theme again, three times with increasing intensity interrupted by opposing forces (to the rhythm  thrice repeated). This is the last time the opposition speaks in *fortissimo* and it seems to retire exhausted for the time being.

The hero sets to work right away (Allegro di molto e con brio) with the theme of attack (mm. 11–15) which means unceasing toil, and already in mm. 38 and 42, we seem to hear parts of some Chinese wall falling down, and more so in mm. 45–48.

This is where the hero relaxes in his work, given to more tender reflections. The phrase

appears three times up to m. 71 and then is followed by the phrase

in three repetitions, intensified each time by the change in key. Still the rest can be only temporary and work begins again in b. 89, at first *piano* and carefully, but working to a climax in mm. 99–100.

A new start is made and a higher climax reached in 111–112. Having achieved that much, the hero has a few moments of real joy and the mm. 113–120, have certainly some likeness to a little boy rolling himself down a hill on a fine summer's day. [. . .]

BACKHAUS, p. 9

This kind of comment can also be found in *Von der Poesie des Klavierspiels*, a booklet that was published in 1911 by Joseph Pembaur, in which this Austrian pianist drew a parallel with the opening theme of the Sonata in A major, Op. 2 No. 2:

> Amusing and easy, like a happy fawn springing over a boulder.

PEMBAUR, p. 8

And what inspiring words for Beethoven's Sonata Op. 28, the "Pastorale," were put on paper by the Swiss pianist Edwin Fischer!

> This work was given the sobriquet "Pastoral," and justly so. There is in this piece a connectedness to nature, the feeling of a Pan, as is expressed otherwise only in the eponymous symphony. There, however, it is thematically more distinctly profiled. In the piano sonata everything wafts and weaves, is full of quivering air, humming of bees and a fragrance such that you imagine feeling the warmth of the sun on your skin, and all our natural forces awaken, and, dazed, the old Adam in us reaches out to eternal Mother Earth.
>
> FISCHER (II), p. 71

It is, however, especially Beethoven's "Moonlight" Sonata that was from the start a popular subject for imaginative thoughts. Over the centuries numerous publications have arisen about this masterpiece, among them not only one by Edwin Fischer,[12] but also the following humorous exchange between the Russian pianist and official Wilhelm von Lenz and one of Liszt's best-known pupils, Carl Tausig:

> "Did you know that that should only be played in a room draped in black?" "No, I did not know that at all"—Holz

> wrote me about it. He knows. Beethoven told him that he improvised the adagio while sitting beside the corpse of a friend in a room hung in black.—"That is lovely!" laughed Tausig, in his humorous manner. "If a pupil ever comes to torment me with it again, I shall say: 'Is your room hung with black? If not don't play it.'"
>
> LENZ (IV), p. 64

More serious is a publication by the then well-known music writer and poet Ludwig Rellstab, who published his novel *Theodor. Eine musikalische Skizze* in 1824 in the *Berliner allgemeine musikalische Zeitung*. In this, Rellstab, whose father was a music publisher and composer, presents a discussion among three friends about Haydn, Mozart, and Beethoven that concludes with the following words:

> But stop! I must say something more! It would not be a false fifth if I were to forget the Adagio from the Fantasia in C-sharp minor. The lake rests quietly under the light of the moon at twilight; the wave thuds against the dark bank; gloomy wooded mountains rise up and divide this sacred region from the world; swans move through the water with whispering rustle, like spirits, and an Aeolian harp makes its complaints of longing, lonely love mysteriously from the ruin. Silence; good night!
>
> *BamZ* (1824), p. 274

Moon at twilight, an Aeolian harp, lonely love—all themes that in 1801, the year in which Beethoven composed his sonata, had received attention due to the publication of *Die Aeolsharfe. Ein allegorischer Traum* (The Aeolian Harp: An Allegorical Dream), a novel by pianist, composer, writer, and theologian Johann Friedrich Hugo von Dalberg. A review of this novel, set in the Bay of Naples, appeared in April 1801 in the *Allgemeine musikalische Zeitung*.

When comparing the text, it is apparent that Rellstab must have based his work on von Dalberg's novel. After a few introductory words, he quotes von Dalberg's text:

"The poet is lulled to sleep by the heavenly tones of the Aeolian harp, which, however, he does not yet know, and in dreams is enlightened as to the origin of its sweet sounds.

"In the blue, ever-cheerful air on which no mortal eye can intrude, floats an isle of clouds [. . .] inhabited by ethereal spirits. No burning ray of sunshine pierces its hazy circle; only the moon's pale silvery rays illuminate it. [. . .]

"Rocked there in sweet dreams are the souls of men who were torn away from life too soon, their earthly desires unfulfilled: innocent children, star-crossed lovers, friends too early separated; youth, men, elders. [. . .] Wistfully they look back on the earth too early left behind, and yearningly toward the moon, their native land, where choirs of their early-departed sister-souls wait for completion of the orbit of their purification-year. Only the memory of enjoyable earthy springs is left to them, yet not the gift of sharing them with each other. Veiled in twilight mists they slumber. [. . .]

"The goddess of harmony once spied this island, and was stirred by the sight of its sleepers; she freed them from their banishment and roused them from their dreams; Aeolus released their pinions, and ever since they have animated the strings of the harp that bears his name, and find pleasure in the joy of communicating with like-minded spirits."

AmZ (APRIL 1801), pp. 473–474

It is established that Beethoven read this review, for he made a note alongside von Dalberg's introductory text, concerning the construction of this instrument and how this could be accomplished.[13] The first movement of his sonata seems to be inspired by this novel, not only because of the melancholic, dark atmosphere but especially from Beethoven's instruction to have the complete movement performed *pianissimo* and *senza sordino*, bringing the musical outcome, *verhüllt in dämmernden Nebel schlummern sie* (as in the citation "veiled in twilight mist they slumber"), very close. Furthermore, it is striking that von Dalberg provides an epigraph for his novel:

> Where should this music be? In th' air or th' earth . . .
> That strain again, it had a dying fall.
> Oh, it came o'er my ear again, like the sweet sound
> That breathes upon a bank of violets,
> Stealing and giving odour . . .
>
> Shakespeare

Indeed a strange quotation, because the text comes not from one, but from two plays by Shakespeare. The first line refers to *The Tempest*, the other four lines come from Act I, Scene 1, of *Twelfth Night*. Both are plays in which a number of the same themes as in von Dalberg's novel play a role, such as the location, the Mediterranean Sea at Naples, an island and spirits (*The Tempest*), and even harp music, as in *Twelfth Night*.

Plays by Shakespeare were presented regularly at several courts in Germany at the time—among them the court in Bonn—and not only von Dalberg, but Beethoven too was a great Shakespeare admirer. Not only did he have several plays of this dramatist in his bookcase in a German translation by August Wilhelm Schlegel, but moreover he names *The Tempest* as the play that inspired him to compose his Sonata Op. 31 No. 2. In this sonata, too, the recitatives of the first movement must sound *pianissimo*, under one pedal—the spirit's voice shrouded in mist. The appellation "Moonlight" Sonata does not, however, originate with Beethoven, but rather with Wilhelm von Lenz. He took the name from the pen of the aforementioned Ludwig Rellstab. Von Lenz wrote in his study of Beethoven, appearing in French in 1852, with an elaborated version appearing in German in 1860:

> It must be further mentioned that the sonata in C-sharp minor is known by the name "Moonlight Sonata." It received this name from Rellstab, who compared the Adagio with Lake Lucerne in the moonlight . . . in which there is some truth.

The road from von Dalberg to von Lenz is a long one, and so we see that the original location, set by von Dalberg in the Bay of Naples, now has been moved a little closer to home, to Lake Lucerne. Very interesting is that von Lenz, who as a talented pianist had lessons from, among others, Tausig, Chopin, and Liszt in Paris, also gives in his book a report of the way Liszt once played the first movement of the "Moonlight," going so far with his ideas of interpretation that even the notes could be altered. Jacques-Gabriel Prod'homme summarized Lenz's words as follows:

> One day, seven or eight years ago, when Liszt played this Adagio in front of a small circle to which I belonged, he took it into his head to distort the piece, following the habit to garner applause from fashionable audiences, instead of the long sustained bass notes, instead of the severe uniformity of rhythm and tempo which I mentioned above, he applied trills and *tremolos*, sometimes speeding up the tempo, sometimes slowing down, and with passionate chords disrupting the calm of this sadness, and letting the thunder roll in this cloudless sky, which is darkened by nothing else but the disappearance of the sun. [. . .]
>
> PROD'HOMME (1), p. 126

But the circumstances could also be different, as on an exceptional evening:

> Liszt arrived in the evening and, finding us engaged in a debate about the worth of a piece by Weber which the audience had given a rather cool reception in a concert, he sat down at the piano to reply in his way to Weber's antagonists. [. . .] After finishing, the lamp that illuminated the room seemed on the verge of going out, when one of us went to revive it. "Leave it," I said to him. "If he wishes to play Beethoven's Adagio in C-sharp minor then this semidarkness will do no harm."—"With pleasure," replied Liszt, "but extinguish the light entirely and cover the fire, so that the darkness be complete." And then, in the midst of this obscurity, after a moment of collection, this noble elegy, the same that he had formerly so strangely disfigured, ascended in all its sublime simplicity: not one note, not one accent was added to the composer's notes and accents. It was the shadow of Beethoven, evoked by this virtuoso, whose magnificent voice we were hearing. Every one of us trembled in silence, crushed

> by reverence, by sacred dread, by admiration, by poetic pain, and without those benign tears that came to our rescue, we would, I believe, have suffocated. [. . .]
>
> PROD'HOMME (1), pp. 126–127

A comment from Carl Friedrich Glasenapp about a reaction of Richard Wagner is a further reminder that Beethoven's music could arouse hefty emotions. When Anton Rubinstein played Beethoven's last sonata, Op. 111, for Wagner in April 1880, the latter cried out euphorically:

> "That is divine!" and at the end he said: "That is all my teaching! The first movement is the will in its pain and heroic desire; the other is the soothed will as man will have when he has acquired reason." "Vegetarians," he exclaimed in addition, and showed in mentioning this word in this context everything that was concentrated therein: the whole train of thought of "religion and art" still lying dormant within him, a distant ideal of human development, worlds apart from what today people imagine under the term "vegetarianism" as a healthy diet.
>
> GLASENAPP, Vol. VI, p. 328

It is clear that the purity of the work had moved Wagner, and not only because he was a convinced vegetarian. The most beautiful words, however, were written by the German author Thomas Mann. In his 1947 novel *Doctor Faustus* we find his wonderful language for a description of the young Wendell Kretzschmar,[14] who plays Beethoven's Op. 111 for a small audience with great enthusiasm and a spoken introduction:

> And then he sat down at the upright and played the whole composition from memory, both the first and the stupendous second movement, but in such a manner that he shouted out his commentary while he played, and to call our attention to a lead theme he would enthusiastically sing along by way of demonstration—all of which, taken together, resulted in a partly enthralling, partly comical spectacle, repeatedly

greeted with amusement by the little audience. Since he had a very heavy touch and served up a powerful *forte*, he had to yell extra loudly just to make himself halfway understood and to sing at the top of his voice whenever he vocally underscored what he was playing. His mouth imitated what his hands were doing. *Boom, boom—voom, voom—throom, throom*—he struck the grimly vehement opening accents of the first movement, and in a high falsetto he sang along with passages of melodic sweetness, which, like delicate glimpses of light, now and then illuminate the storm-tossed skies of the piece. Finally he laid his hands in his lap, rested for a moment and said, "Here it comes." He began the variations movement, the *adagio molto semplice e cantabile*.[15]

The arietta theme, destined for adventures and vicissitudes for which, in its idyllic innocence, it seems never to have been born, is immediately called up and for sixteen measures says its piece, reducible to a motif that emerges toward the end of its first half, like a short, soulful cry—just three notes, an eighth, a sixteenth, and a dotted quarter, that can only be scanned as something like: "sky of blue" or "lover's pain" or "fare-thee-well" or "come a day" or "meadow-land"—and that is all. But what now becomes of this gentle statement, this pensively tranquil figure, in terms of rhythm, harmony, counterpoint, what blessings its master bestows upon it, what curses he heaps upon it, into what darknesses and superilluminations, where cold and heat, serenity and ecstasy are one and the same, he hurls and elevates it—one may well call it elaborate, miraculous, strange, and excessively grand without thereby giving it a name, because in actuality it is nameless; and Kretzschmar played all these stupendous transformations for us with hard-working hands, singing along very fiercely: "*Dimdada*," and shouting loudly over it all. "Chain of trills!" he yelled. "*Fioriture* and cadenzas! Do you hear convention abandoned? Here—language—is—no longer—purged of flourishes—rather flourishes—of the appearance—of their subjective—self-composure—the appearance—of art is thrown off—for ultimately—art is always thrown off—the appearance of art. *Dim—dada!* Just listen, please, how here—the melody is overwhelmed—by the weight of the chords' joints! It becomes static, monotone—two Ds, three Ds, one after the other—the chords do that—*dim—dada!* And now pay close attention to what happens here—"

It was extraordinarily difficult to listen simultaneously to his shouts and to the highly complex music they punctuated. But we tried, bent forward, straining, hands between the knees, shifting our gaze alternately between his hands and mouth. The hallmark of the movement is, in fact, the wide separation between bass and treble, between the right and left hands, and a moment arrives, a situation of extremes, where the poor theme seems to hover lonely and forlorn above a dizzyingly gaping abyss—an event of pallid grandeur, and hard on its heels comes an anxious shrinking-to-almost-nothing, a moment of startled fear, as it were, that such a thing could happen. And a great deal more happens yet before it comes to an end. But when it does end, and in the very act of ending, there comes—after all this fury, tenacity, obsessiveness, and extravagance—something fully unexpected and touching in its very mildness and kindness. After all its ordeals, the motif, this D—G—G, undergoes a gentle transformation. As it takes its farewell and becomes in and of itself a farewell, a call and a wave of goodbye, it experiences a little melodic enhancement. After an initial C, it takes on a C-sharp before the D, so that it now no longer scans as "sky of blue" or "meadow-land," but as "O—thou sky of blue," "green-est meadowland," "fare-thee-well, for good"; and this added C-sharp is the most touching, comforting, poignantly forgiving act in the world. It is like a painfully loving caress of the hair, the cheek—a silent, deep gaze into the eyes for one last time. It blesses its object, its dreadful journeys now past, with overwhelming humanization, lays it on the hearer's heart as a farewell, forever, lays it so gently that tears well up. "Now forget the pain!" it says. "God was—great in us." "All was—but a dream." "Hold my—memory dear." Then it breaks off. Fast, hard triplets scurry toward a convenient final phrase that could easily conclude many another piece.

MANN (1), pp. 58–59

It was Hans von Bülow, however, who needed fewer words to achieve deeper insight. When he was not impressed with the performance of the second movement, "Abwesenheit" (Absence) of the Sonata Op. 81a, "Les Adieux," by a pupil, he reacted as follows:

> Play the second measure more vigorously than the first time; the abandoned one sighs, and the second time with even more yearning. If you play the second measure exactly the same as the first one, the audience will say: "Good God, she's practicing!"
>
> PFEIFFER, p. 55

Sonata Op. 81a, 2nd movement

We do, however, already see practical instructions in combination with expressions of feeling and emotion as early as the historical methods from Beethoven's time. These include, for example, dynamic markings that were at the time certainly not intended purely as indications of degrees of volume. In his *Theoretical and Practical Piano Forte School*, Op. 500, Czerny writes:

> We may lay it down as an axiom, that each of these 5 principal species of Forte and Piano, expresses some determinate character, and consequently that each is capable of producing a peculiar effect. Namely.

a. The Pianissimo (*pp*) which indicates the gentlest touching of the keys, so however, as not to become indistinct or inaudible. It bears the character of secrecy, mystery, and when executed with the utmost perfection, it is capable of producing on the hearer the pleasing effect of music at a great distance, or of an echo.

b. The Piano (*p*) Loveliness, Softness, tranquil equanimity, or quiet sorrow, manifest themselves by the still soft and tender, though yet somewhat firm and expressive mode of touch with which the keys are to be struck.

c. The Mezza voce (*m.v.*) This degree lies exactly in the middle between soft and loud, and may be compared to the tranquil speaking tone used in narration; and without descending into a whisper or declaiming in a loud tone, it will interest us more by the matter to be played, than by the style of the performance.

d. The Forte (*f*) denotes the expression of self-sufficing firmness and power, without excess or presumption; Passion within the limits of proper dignity; as also, according to rule, whatever is brilliant and showy, may be executed with this degree of power.

e. The Fortissimo (*ff*) That even the highest degree of force must always rest within the limits of what is *beautiful*, and never be allowed to degenerate in a coarse thumping, or ill treatment of the instrument, has already been said. Within these bounds, it expresses the exaltation of joy to ecstasy, of grief to rage; just as it also elevates what is brilliant to absolute splendor and *Bravura*.

CZERNY (III), Vol. 3, p. 5

In his 1797 *Die wahre Art das Pianoforte zu spielen*, Milchmeyer is even more expressive:

Pianissimo (*pp*) is executed in such a way that the listener thinks he is hearing at a distance of around 100 feet two people conversing with each other in the evening under a calm serene sky. [. . .]

> With *piano* (*p*), the same manner of execution as in *pianissimo* must be observed, but the expression should already be a little stronger, as if the conversation was fifty feet closer. [. . .]
>
> *Dolce* (*d*) announces a conversation whose feature is softness, tenderness and serves for the expression of sweet melancholia, of love and fervor. [. . .]
>
> *Mezzo forte* (*mf*) requires the expression of an animated conversation, where one expresses one's words with somewhat more emphasis than normal. [. . .]
>
> *Forte* (*f*) does not express gentle feelings, but strong passions, defiance and suchlike; you could also describe the joy of the populace in this way. [. . .]
>
> *Fortissimo* (*ff*) designates intense passions, for instance anger or disturbed emotions, the din of weapons, the clamor of a crowd or of an army. [. . .]
>
> MILCHMEYER, pp. 48–50

This all means that these concepts had far wider and more imaginative connotations than is the case these days. In addition, Beethoven used in his sonatas a much more extensive palette for expressing emotion than did his predecessors such as Mozart.

Mozart:

ff (fortissimo);[16] f (forte), p (piano), pp (pianissimo), fp (fortepiano), sf (sforzato), sfp (sforzatopiano), crescendo, decrescendo, agitato, dolce, sotto voce, mancando, a piacere, calando, rallentando, ad libitum.

Beethoven:

ff (fortissimo); sempre ff, sempre fortissimo, il più forte, sempre forte e staccato, mf (mezzo forte), mezzo forte, p (piano), più piano, sempre p (sempre piano), sempre più p, sempre pp (sempre pianissimo), pp (pianissimo); ppp (pianississimo); ffp, fp, sf, sfp, sfpp, rf, rfz, <>, >, crescendo, ben marcato, sempre ben marcato, rinforzando, decrescendo, diminuendo, meno allegro, in tempo, a tempo, accelerando,

> non presto, calando, mancando, zurückhaltend, più crescendo, ritardando, poco ritardando, rallentando, poco ritenuto, poco ritenente, tenute, sempre tenuto, ligato, molto legato, staccato, staccato sempre, mezzo voce, dolce, dolce e molto ligato, teneramente, leggieremente, cantabile, cantabile e ligato, piacevole, espressivo, molto espressivo, espressivo e semplice, dolce poco espressivo, con espressione, con grande espressione, con espressione e semplice, con amabilità.

Alongside all these expressions there were also musical opportunities that Beethoven did not notate, such as playing a *crescendo* in combination with a *ritenuto,* a performance noticed by his pupil Ferdinand Ries:

> In general he played his own compositions most capriciously, though he usually kept a very steady rhythm and only occasionally, indeed, very rarely, speeded up the tempo somewhat. At times he restrained the tempo in his *crescendo* with a *ritardando*, which had a beautiful and most striking effect.
>
> WEGELER/RIES, p. 94

Joseph Pembaur, mentioned earlier, was especially taken with this example, even though it is not to be found in any publication:

> The highest summits are attained only through struggle—he who does not grapple with the retarding might of painful destiny will never experience the necessary degree of upward-thrusting yearning, the prerequisite for reaching the supreme strength of supreme victory.

Sonate op. 27 No. 1, 3de Satz.

PEMBAUR, p. 26

We find no such description from Artur Schnabel, but in his publication, too, it is clear that these measures cry out for unprecedented eloquence.

Sonata Op. 27 No. 1, 3rd movement, Ullstein edition (Schnabel)

In such ways, a work's musical picture is colored by the interpreter's personal empathy, whereby a deviation from the actual text is not uncommon. An example of this is a *crescendo* that can remain within a certain volume without progressing to a higher volume not indicated by Beethoven but that is often subject to some exaggeration by the performer. This happens, for example, at the close of the Andante grazioso in the Sonata Op. 31 No. 1, where Beethoven's *crescendo* notation begins *pianissimo* and the Chilean pianist Claudio Arrau suggests a progression to *forte* within just one measure, while Beethoven's notation goes no further than *sf*. Although Arrau's suggestion is easily distinguished from Beethoven's text by the introduction of hairpins and is certainly exciting, Beethoven's intention seems to have been a subtle undulation in the sound, leading only to a declamatory *sforzando* with thereafter a gentle close.

Sonata Op. 31 No. 1, 2nd movement, Edition Peters (Arrau)

From all of this, it is apparent that these concepts have little to do with analysis, but a lot with imagination. This conclusion even has its impact on sound—for example, the different meaning of the same dynamic indication. Each dynamic marking has its own emotional meaning, which one has to discover from the context of the music. For example, the final pages of the Sonata Op. 110, where at the *tempo primo* in m. 174, coming out of the *una corda pianissimo* of the inversion of the fugue, the theme arises again in octaves in *forte*. These measures are often played extremely loudly, but why? It should be a very intense *forte* indeed, but still reached by someone who has almost lost his life and is now trying to rediscover new strength. However, resurrection is only to be found in the very last measures of this movement in *fortissimo*.

These nuances in an interpretation should always play a role, such as a *pianissimo* that is never merely very soft. The question should be: is it coming from a distance, is it mysterious, surreal, tender, innocent or elusive? Also, it is very well known that a *forte* must produce a very different sound when playing Mozart, Beethoven, Chopin, or Tchaikovsky, and how many hours do pianists spend in finding the right expression for it in French or Russian music!

But not only that: when playing a sonata where the first theme is introduced in *forte*, and, after a long journey through the Exposition and Development, this theme returns with the same *forte* indication in the Recapitulation, this second *forte* should evoke a different impression, which must come to the fore in timing and sound. All these considerations about sound will have influence on an interpretation. As the legendary pianist Alfred Cortot once said, explaining in an almost philosophical manner Schumann's *Kinderszenen* in a master class:

> These wonders are not described by a child, but by a grown-up man, a poet who remembers his childhood. Bear that in mind and it will totally transform your touch.
>
> GAVOTY, p. 27

For Beethoven, it is the Swiss pianist Edwin Fischer, renowned Beethoven interpreter, who brings it all together in the following words:

> Forget piano, style, education, knowledge and experience Beethoven; play the organ, the violin, the flute, the drum; sing again on the piano; bring the whole world back from the shadowy kingdom of the note marks up into the vibrant light; play the "Moonlight" Sonata, if you will, as a faltering dirge and score the funeral march of Op. 26 in the most modern way; conjure up today an idyll of nature from the "Waldstein" Sonata, making it tomorrow a battle between yourself and the world—play it the day after tomorrow perfectly, as pure music, if you are so even-tempered that you delight in formal playing; everything is in there after all; then you will grow wings that will carry you and the others into the true realm of imagination, which will make you cast your eyes there where Beethoven's spirit hovered. You will again take pleasure in this wonderful piano, which today has all the colors of the orchestra and tomorrow produces sounds that hark from other worlds!
>
> FISCHER (1), p. 64

CHAPTER SEVEN

The Recordings

> More concentrated, more energetic and more intimate I have never yet seen an artist.
>
> —JOHANN WOLFGANG VON GOETHE, LETTER TO HIS WIFE CHRISTIANE, JULY 19, 1812; SONNECK (ED.), p. 88

WITH A DURATION OF more than eleven hours of music, playing all thirty-two of Beethoven's sonatas is one of the greatest challenges a pianist can give himself. Quite apart from the interpretive and technical abilities required, the mental burden of such a project makes it a task that demands the utmost of a musician. It is thus not surprising that most pianists spread the recording of all the sonatas over a number of years. What also plays a role is that it is no longer all that usual to play all the sonatas on consecutive evenings, meaning that Beethoven's sonata oeuvre has to be combined with works of other composers. In past generations this was indeed different. Bach's *Well-Tempered Clavier* and Beethoven's sonatas were the foundation on which a pianist would build his repertoire and which demanded an early start if one wished to master them while still at a relatively young age.

The first pianist to record all the sonatas was Artur Schnabel, in the years 1932–1937. Other interpreters had preceded him in the recording of a number of sonatas, as Frederic Lamond had done as early as 1920 and Eugen d'Albert, who recorded some movements from sonatas.[1]

While Lamond, in his sixties, seemed to play more as a matter of routine than with real inspiration, in Schnabel's recordings the pleasure of playing in combination with intellectual mastery, freedom, and spontaneity is striking—as the American pianist Richard Goode, who also recorded all the sonatas himself, once remarked regarding Schnabel's recordings. That naturally was also a consequence of Schnabel's just walking into the studio and giving, as it were, a live concert: an attitude far removed from today's methods, which concentrate much more than in the past on achieving perfection.[2]

After Schnabel came well-known names such as Wilhelm Backhaus, Wilhelm Kempff, Claudio Arrau, Annie Fischer, Ives Nat, Daniel Barenboim, Alfred Brendel, Steven Kovacevich, Richard Goode, András Schiff, Jonathan Biss, Paul Lewis, and many others, as can be seen in the discography below. It will be clear that it is simply impossible to name in addition all those pianists who have not recorded all of the sonatas but have even so made their names with their splendid interpretations. Nevertheless, a number of these cannot be left unmentioned. And so we have pianists such as Elly Ney, Myra Hess, Maria Yudina, Solomon, and Rudolf Serkin closely associated with high-profile Beethoven interpretations, while almost-forgotten names such as Hans Richter-Haaser, Andor Foldes, and Eduardo del Pueyo deserve our attention more often.[3]

Even pianists who in the first instance built their careers on interpretations of other composers turned out to be impressive Beethoven interpreters in later life. Maurizio Pollini, winner of the International Chopin Piano Competition in Warsaw in 1960, or the Russian pianists Emil Gilels and Sviatoslav Richter, both of whom began as interpreters of the Russian repertoire but found their way to Beethoven, are only a few of the many possible names. The influential music critic and author Joachim Kaiser discusses a great number of these Beethoven interpreters in his book *Beethovens 32 Klaviersonaten und ihre Interpreten* and looks at the various interpretations. What is immediately obvious from listening to several recordings is that, as Kaiser points out, it is in fact impossible to interpret all the sonatas to the same high standard. Of course, one performance can be more convincing than another, but the fact that the sonatas were composed over a period of more than twenty-five years means that the performing pianist has to be able to find the right "tone" for early, middle, and late Beethoven, all different worlds of musical empathy.

There are, for instance, pianists who are better at feeling the spontaneity and freshness of the early sonatas than the world behind the notes of the later ones, while the dramatic forthrightness of a number of sonatas from the middle period can be brought sharply into focus by others. It is also clear that the pianist's own personality plays a role in this. Listen, for example, to Sviatoslav Richter's dramatic, inner tension in his interpretation of the "Appassionata," or how Serkin's detailed knowledge of the text and his intellectual capacity come to the fore in his rhythmical and "firm" interpretations, engraved transparently in sound with graphic interpretations of especially the later sonatas. Wilhelm Kempff's lyricism shines through in the rather sunnier sonatas such as Op. 14 or Op. 28, while his compatriot Wilhelm Backhaus excels in finding just the right character and construction in many of his interpretations. What a pleasure it is to hear how the mastery of the Dutch pianist Egon Petri (who himself was a student of the famous Ferruccio Busoni) is reflected in his superb interpretation of Op. 106, although Solomon's performance of the same work seems to be matched only by an incredible interpretation of Murray Perahia, who recorded the work together with an outstanding interpretation of the "Moonlight."[4]

In other sonatas, however, character traits of pianists can unexpectedly cast light on a work, the expression of which it was assumed would take a different turn. Friedrich Gulda's fresh spontaneity marks all his recordings, and the individuality of Glenn Gould in his recordings of a number of sonatas, especially with regard to his choice of tempi, will rub many people up the wrong way but are nevertheless remarkable.[5]

The choice is made even more intriguing when recordings on historical instruments in recent decades are added to the long list. Various instruments suited to the period of Beethoven's sonata compositions give us the feeling of getting closer to the original musical picture. Think, for example, of Peter Serkin, who recorded the last six sonatas on an instrument by Conrad Graf; or of Ronald Brautigam, with the use of four different instruments captured with so much character; or of Malcolm Bilson achieving that with his earlier pupils.[6] Other fortepianists, too, achieve astounding results on instruments from Beethoven's era or on copies thereof. But it is of course not just the choice of instrument that counts: the interpretations must be convincing, and in this the "older" generations matter. Here, we are sometimes happy to welcome important discoveries, such as recordings of the almost forgotten American master pianist Sidney Foster, a real pianist from the "Golden Age of the piano," with live performances of the "Waldstein" and Op. 110.[7]

It is thus clear that each of us can compile his or her own list of favorite recordings, a remarkable privilege whereby the DVDs that are regularly appearing can also be taken into account, as well as the great number of performances that can be marveled at on YouTube. Today, even additional information is available, for example from the pianist Igor Levit on his playing and talking podcast "32xBeethoven," or from Boris Giltburg, who launched his own website at Beethoven32.com, where you can follow his study process. The latter is remarkable, because Giltburg's study takes place even before some new sonatas in his repertoire are performed onstage. Indeed, times are changing, but all of this provides a great deal of listening and visual pleasure, even though it must be crystal clear that nothing surpasses an inspired Beethoven interpretation in the concert hall.

The Thirty-Two Piano Sonatas of Beethoven

Recordings of Complete Cycles

Claudio Arrau	Philips	1962–1966
Claudio Arrau	Philips*	1984–1990
Vladimir Ashkenazy	Decca	1971–1981
Wilhelm Backhaus	POCL	1950–1954
Wilhelm Backhaus	Decca**	1958–1969
Paul Badura-Skoda	Gramola	1969–1970
Paul Badura-Skoda	Auvidis Astrée (fortepiano)***	1979–1989
Daniel Barenboim	EMI	1965–1969
Daniel Barenboim	DG	1981–1984
Daniel Barenboim	EMI (DVD)	2005
Daniel Barenboim	Deutsche Grammofon	2020
Jean-Efflam Bavouzet	Chandos	2016
Robert Benz	Thorofon	1988–1995

Malcolm Bilson and others	Claves	1996
Malcolm Binns	L'Oiseau Lyre (fortepiano) (LP)	1977
Idil Biret	IBA	2002–2006
Jonathan Biss	Orchid Classics	2011–2019
Ronald Brautigam	BIS (fortepiano)	2002–2010
Alfred Brendel	Vox	1958–1964
Alfred Brendel	Decca	1970–1977
Alfred Brendel	Decca	1993–1996
Rudolf Buchbinder	Teldec	1977–1982
Rudolf Buchbinder	Sony/RCA	2010–2011 (live)
Dino Ciani	Dynamic	1970 (live)
Dino Ciani	Dynamic	2004 (reissue)
Aldo Ciccolini	Cascavelle	1995–1999
Sequeira Costa	Claudio	2019
Timothy Ehlen	Azica	2011
Abdel Rahman El Bacha	Mirare	1984–1993
Annie Fischer	Hungaroton	1976–1978
Claude Frank	Music & Arts	1971
Richard Goode	Nonesuch	1989–1993
Stewart Goodyear	Marquis	2012
Maria Grinberg	Melodiya	1964–1967
André de Groote	Solal	2015
Friedrich Gulda	Orfeo	1953–1957
Friedrich Gulda	Decca	1950–1958
Friedrich Gulda	Amadeo/Decca	1968
François-Frédéric Guy	Zig-Zag Territoires	2013
Eric Heidsieck	EMI	1967–1973
Dirk Herten	White	2019
Ian Hobson	Zephyr	2014
Michael Houstoun	Morrison Music Trust	1994–1996
Jenö Jandó	Naxos	1987–1989
Paavali Jumppanen	Ondine	2014–2017
John Kane	Keynote Records	2017
Wilhelm Kempff	DG	1951–1956
Wilhelm Kempff	DG	1964–1965
Gotthard Kladetzky	Koch Schwann	ca. 1998
Mari Kodama	Pentatone	2014
Michael Korstick	Oehms Classics	2012
Stephen Kovacevich	EMI	1992–2003
Anton Kuerti	Analekta	1974—1975
Christian Leotta	ATMA Classique	2008–2014
Michaël Levinas	Accord	1984–1991
Igor Levit	Sony Classical	2013–2019

Paul Lewis	Harmonia Mundi	2004–2007
Konstantin Lifschitz	Alpha	2020
John Lill	ASV Quicksilva+	1975–1980
H. J. Lim	Warner Classics	2012
Seymour Lipkin	Newport Classics	2002–2004
Louis Lortie	Chandos	2010
Andrea Lucchesini	Stradivarius	2004 (live)
Steven Masi	Albany Records	2017
Jean Muller	Bella Musica	2010 (live)
Ikuyo Nakamichi	BMG (Japan)	2003–2007
Yves Nat	EMI Pathé Marconi (mono)	1953–1955
Tatiana Nikoleyeva	Melodiya (Olympia UK)	1984 (live)
John O'Conor	Telarc	1989–1993
Garrick Ohlsson	Bridge	2006–2010
Anne Øland	T.I.M.	1995–2002?
Gerhard Oppitz	Hänssler	2004–2006
Kun-Woo Paik	Decca (South Korea)	2005–2007
Alfredo Perl	Oehms Classics	1992–1996
Daniel-Ben Pienaar	Avie	2015
Georges Pludermacher	Transart	1998 (live)
Maurizio Pollini	DG	2015
Jean-Bernard Pommier	Warner Classics	2006
Eduardo del Pueyo	Pavane	2017
Martin Rasch	Audite	2018
Robert Riefling	Valois & MHS	1960–1970?
Bernard Roberts	Nimbus	1981–1984
Peter Rösel	King Records	2012
Akiyoshi Sako	Camerata	2001 (live)
Fazil Say	Warner Classics	2018–2019
András Schiff	ECM Records	2004–2007 (live)
Artur Schnabel	EMI (Bechstein)++	1932–1935
Craig Sheppard	Romeo Records	2003–2004 (live)
Russell Sherman	GM Recordings	1993–1997
Kazune Shimizu	Sony (Japan)	1995–1997 (live)
Robert Silverman	Orpheum Masters	1999
Steven Herbert Smith	Soundwaves Recording	2009–2012
Takahiro Sonoda	Denon	1968–1969
Michael Steinberg	Elysium	1981–1988
Shoko Sugitani	IDC Classic	?—2007?
Peter Takács	Cambria	2011
Robert Taub	Vox	1995–1997

Igor Tchetuev	Caro Mitis	2019
Martino Tirimo	Hänssler Classic	2019
David Allan Wehr	Connoisseur Society	1998–2004
Gerard Willems	ABC	1997–2000
Llŷr Williams	Signum Classics	2015–2018 (live)
Yukio Yokoyama	Sony (Japan)	1997–2000?
Dieter Zechlin	Berlin Classic	2008
Mélodie Zhao	Claves	2014

* Arrau passed away before completing this recording, meaning that Op. 27 No. 1 and Op. 106 were taken from earlier Philips recordings.
** Op. 106 was recorded in 1952.
***Reissue Arcana, 2020.
+ Also on Brilliant Classics.
++ Also on the labels Naxos, Regis, Pearl, Musical Concepts.

Incomplete Cycles

Walter Gieseking: Thara, without Nos. 4, 5, 7, 20, 22.
Emil Gilels: DG, without Nos. 1, 9, 22, 24, 32. Died in 1985 before completing the cycle.
Glenn Gould: Sony, Nos. 1, 2, 3, 5, 6, 7, 8, 9, 10, 12, 13, 14, 15, 16, 17, 18, 23, 30, 31, 32.
Vladimir Horowitz: RCA, Nos. 7, 8, 14, 21; CBS, Nos. 8, 28; DG, No. 23; Sony, Nos. 14, 21, 23, 28.
Bruce Hungerford: Vanguard, 22 sonatas recorded; died in 1977 before completing the cycle.
Sviatoslav Richter: Decca, Nos. 1, 3, 4, 6, 7, 8, 9, 10, 11, 12, 17, 18, 19, 20, 22, 23, 27, 28, 29, 30, 31, 32.
Artur Rubinstein: RCA, Nos. 3, 8, 14, 18, 21, 23, 26.
Rudolf Serkin: Sony, Nos. 1, 6, 8, 11, 12, 13, 14, 16, 21, 23, 24, 26, 28, 29, 30, 31, 32.
Solomon: EMI, Nos. 1, 3, 7, 8, 13, 14, 17, 18, 21, 22, 26, 27, 28, 29, 30, 31, 32.

Cycles Still to Be Completed

Saleem Ashkar (Decca)
Boris Giltburg (Naxos; see: Beethoven32.com)
Andreas Haefliger (Avis)
Angela Hewitt (Hyperion)

Paul Komen (Globe)
Artur Pizarro (Linn Records)
Martin Roscoe (Deux-Elles)
Jeffrey Swann (Angora)

DVD Recordings

Pierre-Laurent Aimard: Op.110; Medici Arts, 2008
Claudio Arrau: Op. 2 No. 3, Op. 27 Nos. 1 and 2, Op. 53, Op. 57, Op. 81a, Op. 109, Op. 111; EuroArts 1970/1979
Claudio Arrau: Op. 57, Op. 111; BBC Television Studios 1959; ICA, 2012
Claudio Arrau: Op. 111; Vai, 1964
Claudio Arrau: Op. 111; EMI, 1970 (with bonus: Solomon, Op. 57, 1956)
Daniel Barenboim: 32 sonatas; EMI, 2005
Rudolf Buchbinder: 32 sonatas; Unitel, 2015
Alfred Brendel: Op. 106; EMI, 1970
Robert Casadesus: Op. 57, 3rd movement; Vai, 1964
Severin von Eckardstein: Op. 53; Vai, 2007
Ingrid Fliter: Op. 31 No. 3; Vai, 2006
Emil Gilels: Op. 26; Vai, 1978
Emil Gilels: Op. 53, Op. 101; DG, 1971
Nelson Goerner: Op. 81a; Verbier Festival DVD, 2009
Glenn Gould: Op. 31 No. 2 (1960), Op. 31 No. 2 (1967), Op. 109 (1964), Op. 110 (only Adagio ma non troppo and Fuga) (1963); Sony, 2011
Hélène Grimaud: Op. 110; Classicaltv Kultur (recorded 1987, released 2013)
Myra Hess: Op. 57, 1st movement; Beulah, 1945
Myra Hess: Op. 110; EMI, 1954
Michael Houstoun: Op. 109, Op. 110, Op. 111; Trust Records, 2007
Jenö Jandó: Op. 57; Armide, 2006
Wilhelm Kempff: Op. 106; VAI, 1964
Wilhelm Kempff: Op. 27 No. 2, Op. 31 No. 2, Op. 90; EMI, 1968/1970
Zoltan Kocsis: Op. 111; Silverline Classics, 2004

Lang Lang: Op. 2 No. 3, Op. 57; Sony, 2010
Yvonne Lefébure: Op. 110; Medici Arts, Classic Archive, 1963
Francesco Libetta: Op. 31 No. 3; Vai, 2002
Arturo Benedetti Michelangeli: Op. 2 No. 3, Op. 111; Opus Arte, 1962
Arturo Benedetti Michelangeli: Op. 22, Op. 26; Medici Arts, 1981
Arturo Benedetti Michelangeli: Op. 2 No. 3; Vai, 1970
Ivo Pogerelich: Op. 90, Op. 111; C Major, 1986
Ivo Pogerelich: Op. 22; DG, 2005
Menachem Pressler: Op. 110; Idéale Audience International, 2012
Jerome Rose: Op. 101, Op. 109, Op. 110, Op. 111; Medici Classics, 2008
Rudolf Serkin: Op. 109, Op. 110, Op. 111; DG, 2007
Grigory Sokolov: Op. 14 Nos. 1 and 2, Op. 28; Medici Arts, 2002; Op. 90, Op. 111; Deutsche Grammophon (recorded Turin 2017, released 2020)
Solomon: Op. 57; EMI, 1956 (as bonus with DVD by Claudio Arrau)
Alice Sommer-Herz: Op. 27 No. 2; Christopher Nupen Films, 2009
Stephan Vladar: Op. 2 No. 1; Naxos, 2000

YouTube (Film)

Claudio Arrau: Op. 2 No. 3, Op. 53, Op. 57, Op. 111
Bruno Leonardo Gelber: Op. 27 No. 2, 3rd movement
Emil Gilels: Op. 26
Glenn Gould: Op. 14 No. 2, Op. 109, Op. 110
Vladimir Horowitz: Op. 101
Louis Lortie: Op. 49 No. 2
Elly Ney: Op. 27 No. 2
Sviatoslav Richter: Op. 2 No. 1, Op. 31 No. 3, Op. 49 Nos. 1 and 2
Artur Rubinstein: Op. 57
Rudolf Serkin: Op. 27 No. 2, 3rd movement; Op. 53, 3rd movement; Op. 81a, Op. 109, Op. 111

Appendix: Keyboard Actions

Viennese (*Prellzungen*) Action

When the key (1) is depressed, the end of the key lever rises, whereby the damper stool (2) raises the damper (3) from the string (4), which can then vibrate freely. At the same time, the end of the hammer (5), known as the beak (6) due to its shape, is blocked by the pawl, or escapement tongue (7) (this is the *Prellzunge*), which means that the head of the hammer is catapulted against the string. The pressure of the beak against the pawl causes this to move backwards. The beak passes it and is "released." After the impact, the falling hammer hits the check (8). With the release of the key, the string is damped again, the spring (9) forces the pawl back to its original position, and the hammer returns to its departure point.

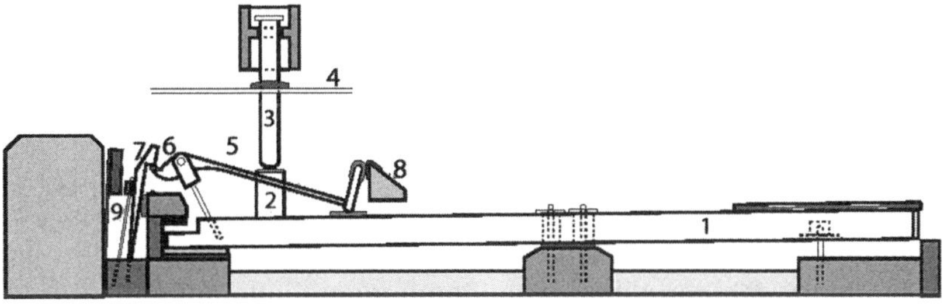

Viennese action

English Action

When the key (1) is depressed, the jack (2) attached to it is pushed against the hammer butt (3) and this moves the hammer (4) toward the string (5). With this motion, the jack is uncoupled from the hammer butt, so that the hammer makes the rest of its way to the string independently (the "release"). At the same time, the damper (6) is pushed up by the end of the key so that the string can vibrate freely. After the impact, the hammer falls back to some extent, but is interrupted by the backcheck (7) for as long as the key is depressed. When the key is released, the check releases the hammer, and through the force of the escapement spring (8) the jack returns to its departure point.

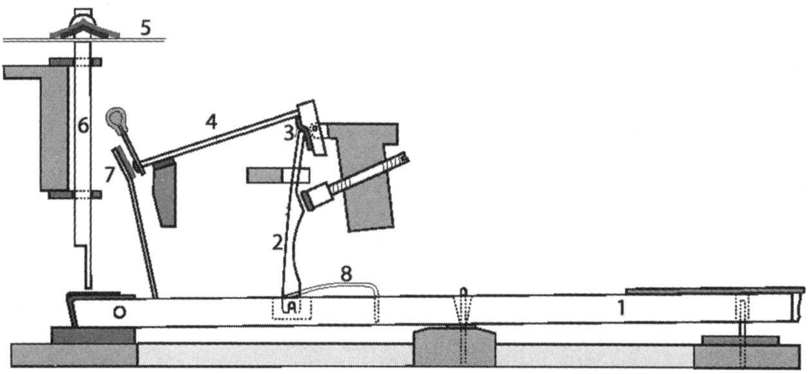

English action

Piano Action from Around 1870 to the Present Day

When the key (1) is depressed, the capstan (2), located at the end of the key, presses the wippen (3) upward. Pressing the key also lifts the damper (4) from the string (5). The jack (6) pushes the hammer knuckle (7) upward, moving the hammer shank (8) so that the hammer head (9) moves toward the string (5). Shortly before the hammer head touches the string, the jack makes contact with the let-off button (10) and as a result escapes from the hammer knuckle. Because the upward movement of the repetition lever (11) is stopped by the drop screw (12), the hammer moves toward the string in free flight for the last part of the stroke. (It is the functioning of the let-off button and the drop screw that gives this action its name "double-escapement action.")

After striking the string, the hammer head (9) rebounds and is caught halfway by the hammer backcheck (13). At the same time, it presses the repetition lever (11) down, tightening the repetition lever spring (14). As soon as the key is released, the repetition lever presses the hammer upward, the repetition spring is released, and the jack returns under the hammer knuckle, ready for the next stroke. When the key is released completely, the hammer is released from the backcheck (13), and falls back onto the hammer rest (15), and the entire repetition mechanism returns to its original position.

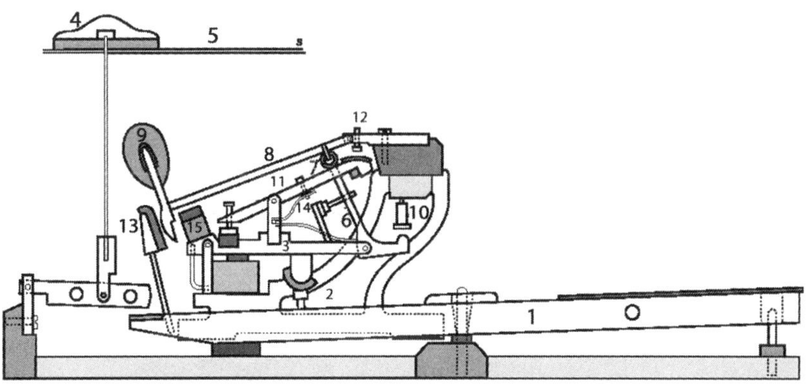

Piano action from around 1870

Notes

Preface

1. See Heinrich Schenker: *Die letzten fünf Sonaten van Beethoven. Kritische Ausgabe mit Einführung und Erlaüterung*, Opp. 109 (1913), 110 (1914), 111 (1915), and 101 (1920), Vienna: Universal Edition. (These "explanatory editions" remained limited to four sonatas. Due to the absence of Beethoven's manuscript, Schenker could not complete his work on Op. 106.) See the Bibliography for Tovey, Uhde, and Rosen.
2. The concept of "original printing" is used here to indicate the earliest publication of a Beethoven sonata, from a historical perspective, irrespective of whether this was authorized as an "original edition" by the composer himself. See Unverricht, p. 9, for this terminological problem.

Chapter One. The Sonatas

1. Beethoven here makes effective usage of the "Mannheim rocket," a permutation of the Mannheim school, a musical movement that included Johann Stamitz, František Xaver Richter, Christian Cannabich, and Carl Stamitz. The "rocket" comprises rapidly ascending broken chords of scale passages, often used at the opening of a fast movement. Such an opening can also be found in the first movement of Beethoven's Sonata Op. 10 No. 1.
2. The Adagio, K. 540, which Mozart entered on March 19, 1788, in his thematic catalog, has in the music literature often been associated with the death of his father on May 29, 1787. It is, however, more probable that it was composed for a remembrance service for the Freemasons, which Mozart had joined in Vienna in the "Zur Wohltätigkeit" (Beneficence) lodge in December 1784. The brevity of the Adagio would have made it highly suitable for such a service, and above all, the Coda evinces an optimistic

musical picture—the shift to B major in the final measures—a true Masonic idea, "the following of the path from darkness into light."

3. B minor is the key that Mozart used further only for the Adagio from the Flute Quartet K. 285. For Beethoven, this key was associated with intensely tragic emotions. For example, he uses it for the quartet "Er sterbe" in the third scene of Act II in his opera *Fidelio*, in which Don Pizarro wishes Florestan dead. It could be that Mozart's Adagio was even an inspiration for some of Beethoven's ideas in other sonatas. Compare, for example, the transfer of the hand and the distribution of *forte* and *piano* from m. 11 onward in the Adagio with the same construction and dynamic contrasts (mm. 17 ff.) in the last movement of this sonata, Op. 7, a sonata that was published in 1797, or in the first movement of his Sonata Op. 31 No. 2 (mm. 21 ff.). Also in a sonata he composed much later, the quick succession of modulations in the Development of the first movement of Op. 110 (mm. 44–56) may be inspired by an identical process of modulations (mm. 22 ff.) in Mozart's Adagio.
4. The tonality of this Sonata in F minor was also Beethoven's choice for his first piano sonata with an opus number (Op. 2 No. 1), composed over a decade later. Together with the three "Electoral" Sonatas (WoO 47), so called because Beethoven dedicated them to Elector Maximilian Friedrich (1708–1784), better known as the "Kurfürsten" Sonatas, the total of his piano sonatas comes to thirty-five.

   It is fortunate that publications of the complete sonatas for the ABRSM (Associated Board of the Royal Schools of Music) by Barry Cooper in 2007 and by Jonathan Del Mar for Bärenreiter in 2019 are bringing these sonatas more prominently to our attention. A separate edition of the three "Kurfürsten" Sonatas, edited by Jochen Reutter with fingerings by Nils Franke, was published by Wiener Urtext in 2020. (See also Chapter 4.)
5. Sonatas with an opening movement comprising a theme with variations are also to be found in works of, among others, Haydn. Mozart's well-known Sonata in A major, K. 331, is also a fine example.
6. See Czerny (II), p. 48.
7. Beethoven's advice for reading *The Tempest* came about after Schindler had told him that Czerny's playing of the Sonatas Op. 31 No. 2 and Op. 57 had made such a great impression on the audience. That led to confusion as to which sonata Beethoven meant, a subject that has been discussed over the centuries by many authors, including Schindler himself. Connections between Shakespeare's text and Beethoven's music, as discussed in Chapters 1, 4 (Pedaling), and 6, are clearly in favor of Op. 31 No. 2, but indeed, the last movement of Op. 57 is also a very "stormy" one. But what a difference there is between the two finales of these sonatas: Op. 31 No. 2, a *perpetuum mobile*, no goal, disappearing into nothing; and Op. 57, a *perpetuum mobile* as well, but striving toward a goal that indeed is found in a *fortissimo* Presto.

8. In the first English edition by Clementi & Co., this movement begins *forte*. Since this edition appeared shortly after the Viennese Nägeli edition and the Berlin Simrock edition, in which this movement begins *piano*, it is not inconceivable that this is a correction referring back to an unknown manuscript. For this, see Tyson (I), p. 45. A *forte* beginning would in any case reinforce the musical picture of "joy of a new era."
9. It is remarkable that Beethoven returns to the minuet in his *Diabelli Variations*, Op. 120. This work was composed between 1819 and 1823, while the minuet in the Sonata Op. 54 was composed in 1804. In Op. 120 it is the last variation, No. 33, with the inscription "Tempo di Menuetto moderato," indeed a kind of returning home to his youth.
10. With both of the sonatas for cello and piano, Op. 5, Beethoven had earlier composed sonatas comprising only two movements. Nevertheless, these, in contrast to Op. 49 and Op. 54, have long, slow introductions that could also be conceived as independent movements. Examples of two-movement sonatas can also be found in the works of Haydn and Mozart.
11. Beethoven took into account for the structure of the works that the minuets in his sonatas must not be too long. In an early sketchbook we read:

> "For the new sonatas very short minuets." [. . .]
> Not long after this he notes:
> "The minuets for the sonatas in future not longer than 16 to 24 measures."
>
> NOTTEBOHM, pp. 32 and 35

In Op. 54 the "minuet" theme in the first movement comprises twenty-four measures. Interrupted by a highly contrasting section in octaves, after this it returns twice, ever more varied. Here Beethoven employs a musical form that has some affinity to variation form and rondo form, a combination that is also called "French rondo" (see Badura-Skoda/Demus, p. 129). Edwin Fischer also observed some similarity to the sonata form if one regards mm. 39–70 as Development (see Fischer [II], p. 94).

12. The Andante assumed the name *Andante favori* because it was one of his most popular piano pieces and he loved playing it. See Czerny (II), p. 19.
13. Regarding the original length of the sonata, Ferdinand Ries noted that Beethoven's attention was drawn to this by a friend.

> A friend of Beethoven's suggested to him that the sonata was too long, whereupon he was taken to task most severely. Calmer deliberation, however, soon convinced my teacher that the remark had some truth to it. He then published the grand Andante in F major, in 3/8 time, on its own and later composed the interesting introduction to the rondo in its present form.

14. This French name ("L'Aurore": Dawn or Sunrise) can also be related specifically to the passage in the first movement, starting at m. 142, as the French pianist Yves Nat told his pupil Kenneth van Barthold, who published this idea in *International Piano* (July/August 2010), p. 5.
15. The right hand in Beethoven's manuscript has no *arpeggio* and must therefore be played *secco*. However, in many editions an *arpeggio* is indeed indicated, a mistake that already occurs in the first printing by the Bureau des Arts et d'Industrie. The Henle urtext and Wiener Urtext editions are correct.
16. The theme is taken from the *Deutscher Gesang*, marked *allegro molto*, the second part of this fifteen-minute-long ballet. Premiered on March 6, 1791, in Bonn, for a long time the work was attributed to Count Waldstein, who took credit for composing the ballet, until it became known that the twenty-year-old Beethoven had composed it. The theme returns in a slightly different form in the third movement of the Sonata for violin and piano in G major, K. 379, composed by Mozart in 1781.
17. The idea of including a fugue in a sonata was further used in his next opus, the Sonata for cello and piano, Op. 102 No. 2.
18. Liszt played Op. 106 at a very early age, as he wrote in a letter of October 26, 1876, to Carolyne zu Sayn-Wittgenstein:

    At the age of ten years I played it, without a doubt very badly but with passion—without anyone having taught me it.

    LA MARA, Vol. 4, p. 163

19. In the "grievous" key of F-sharp minor, one also finds the Adagio of Mozart's Piano Concerto in A major, K. 488, and the Andantino of Schubert's Sonata in A major, D. 959, among other works.
20. Johannes Brahms paid homage to Beethoven by using this theme from Op. 106 at the opening of his Piano Sonata Op. 1.
21. A musical motto such as this was not unusual for Beethoven, as is to be seen from a letter dated March 3, 1819, that he wrote to Rudolph to congratulate him on his birthday:

    [. . .] So I can only extend my congratulations about this honor to Y.I.H. along with the others. There is almost nothing that is good—without sacrifice, and this appears to apply directly to the nobler, superior man more than others, thereby his virtue becomes tested.

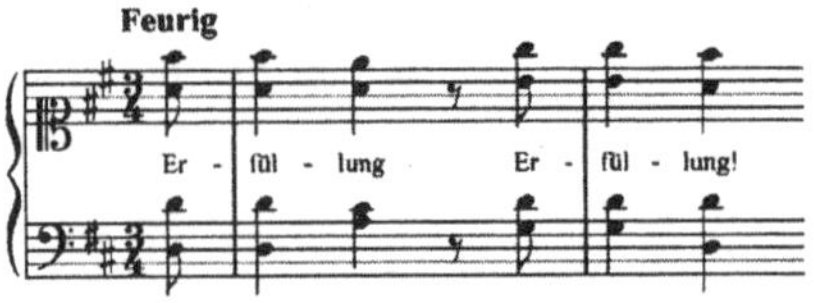

Ful—fill—ment
This I might sing out now from the bottom of my heart.
THAYER/FORBES, Vol. II, p. 719

22. Felix Mendelssohn-Bartholdy made the same quotation at the beginning of the main theme of the Presto of his String Octet Op. 20.
23. Beethoven's early knowledge of Handel's *Messiah* was mentioned by Carl Czerny. Czerny writes: "He did not know Graun's *Tod Jesu*. My father brought him the score. [. . .] Beethoven stated that the two fugues were tolerable, the rest ordinary. With the words, 'This is quite another fellow,' he then took Handel's *Messiah* and played through the most interesting numbers, pointing out several similarities to Haydn's *Creation*, etc. This happened in 1805" (Czerny [II] p. 13).
24. In 1794/1795 Beethoven received counterpoint lessons from Johann Georg Albrechtsberger, Kapellmeister of St. Stephen's Cathedral. From that period, thirty-eighty fugues of Beethoven are known that are based on themes by Albrechtsberger.
25. Beethoven writes "adagio espressivo" in small letters. "Adagio espressivo," with a capital "A," is printed in many editions. This presents a false picture: pianists could think that it means a new movement. The consequence is that the word *adagio* is taken so seriously that the music is performed at a much too slow tempo. The pulse of the Vivace, ma non troppo should just be continued in the "adagio espressivo." When one feels the four sixteenth notes of the upbeat from the beginning in one pulse, it is easy to feel its continuation in two sixteenth notes of the bass line in the "adagio espressivo." In this way, the unity between the two themes is retained.
26. Methodical music analysis can lead to different opinions and confusion, as is the case with the structure of the first movement of this sonata. Following Tovey, the movement is written in sonata form. It has an Exposition (mm. 1–15), Development (mm. 16–48), Recapitulation (mm. 49–66), and a long Coda (mm. 67–100). The difference from the usual sonata form is that the transition that normally leads from the first to the second theme is missing. Following this way of thinking, the "adagio espressivo" is the second theme. (See also the previous note.)
27. See also the discussion of pedaling and tempo in Chapter 4.
28. As a result of this structure, the musical center of gravity moves more toward the last movement in Beethoven's late sonatas.
29. It is of course possible that Beethoven completed this sonata precisely on this date, but in terms of musical content it is not all that credible. It is a pity that the date December 25 appears in no printing of any urtext whatsoever.
30. Thomas Mann describes the entry of the C sharp in an exceptionally graphic way in his novel *Doctor Faustus*, published in 1947 (see Chapter 6). It is probable that the idea was given to him by the German philosopher,

sociologist, and musicologist Theodor W. Adorno. Adorno worked for many years on a book about Beethoven's music in connection with philosophy. The plan, however, never came to fruition and progressed no further than a large number of notes and texts, including a note written in 1943:

> The C-sharp at the end of the variations [m. 170 f.] (a "human variation," a "humanized star").
>
> ADORNO, p. 53

At the time Mann was working on *Doctor Faustus*, both of these men were in exile in the United States, where they saw each other regularly and where Beethoven's Op. 111 was also a regular topic of conversation. One such occasion was an evening early in October 1943 at Adorno's home. In Thomas Mann's *Die Entstehung des Doktor Faustus*, the following can be read:

> At the beginning of October [1943] [. . .] we spent an evening with the Adornos. [. . .] I read three pages about the piano that I had recently inserted in my seriously hypertrophying chapter [Chapter 8 of *Doctor Faustus*], and our host shared a few things from his studies and aphorisms about Beethoven. [. . .] The ensuing conversation was about humanity as something refined and chthonic, about links between Beethoven and Goethe, about the humane as a romantic contradiction against society and convention (Rousseau), and as revolt (the prose scene in Goethe's *Faust*). Then Adorno played for me, while I was standing listening by the piano, the Sonata Op. 111 completely and in a highly instructive way. I had never been more attentive.
>
> MANN (II), p. 34

Chapter Two. Beethoven's Pianism

1. Fischer (II), p. 20.
2. Badura-Skoda/Demus, p. 63.
3. Matthews, p. 15.
4. The only possible way to give the impression of a *crescendo* anyway is to begin playing a note without the pedal and to introduce the pedal halfway, whereby the resonance increases.
5. Beethoven's advocacy of such a hand posture may also have resulted from the lessons he had from Neefe in Bonn and his appointment on July 1, 1784, as deputy organist at the court of Maximilian Franz, a post he shared with Neefe. Beethoven played the organ there for two years. A hand posture involving bent fingers was a usual habit, also because of the limited

length of the keys. There is even a compelling comparison with Johann Sebastian Bach's playing. A description of the playing of the cantor of St. Thomas's Church by Bach's first biographer, Johann Nikolaus Forkel (1749–1818), who was still corresponding with Bach's sons Carl Philipp Emanuel and Wilhelm Friedemann, reveals the similarities. Forkel writes:

> Bach placed his hand on the finger-board so that his fingers were bent and their extremities poised perpendicularly over the keys in a plane parallel to them. [. . .] Many advantages arise from holding the hand in Bach's position and from adopting his touch, on the Clavichord and Harpsichord, and on the Organ as well.
>
> FORKEL/TRANS. TERRY, pp. 50, 51

6. See Chapter 3.
7. Skowroneck counts eighteen examples of this technique with melody and trill in one hand in Beethoven's 1793 sketchbooks. See Skowroneck, p. 68.
8. Beethoven was at an early age already playing preludes and fugues from *The Well-Tempered Clavier* that he had studied with Neefe.
9. Thayer, Vol. 1, p. 568.
10. Johann Baptist Cramer (1771–1858), German composer and pianist working mainly in London. Among his many works were eighty-four Etudes. The first French edition was published by Érard in 1804, followed by a German edition published by Breitkopf & Härtel in Leipzig, the first book with forty-two etudes in 1805 and the second book with the other forty-two etudes in 1807–1808. Later editions followed by Steiner & Co., ca. 1822–1823, and Haslinger, probably 1826.

    The best-known edition of Cramer's Etudes is that of Hans von Bülow, published in 1869, which is for many still the only source of these works. It is a pity that von Bülow made all kinds of additions that he himself regarded as improvements. See Cramer (I) (Bibliography).
11. About the questionable authenticity of the annotations to Cramer's Etudes, see among others: William S. Newman (II), pp. 175–179; Sandra P. Rosenblum, pp. 94–101; Alan Tyson (IV), pp. 247–249.
12. The annotations made by Schindler are to be found in Cramer (II). Kann refers to the Haslinger edition as Beethoven's *Handexemplar*, a term normally understood to mean a copy that Beethoven himself owned and used. In Tyson's review (Tyson [IV]) about Kann's edition, it becomes clear that this proposition cannot be right. The Haslinger edition appeared most probably in 1826, one year before Beethoven's death, and could not have been used for Karl's piano lessons.
13. See Koebler's letter to Jähns, quoted in Chapter 3.
14. The first book of Clementi's *Gradus ad Parnasum* was published in 1817 by Clementi & Co. Almost ten years later Beethoven recommended

Clementi's method in a letter of September 1826 to Stephan von Breuning with the following words:

> Here is Clementi's *Klavierschule* which I promised to send you for *Gerhard.* If he uses it in the way I shall instruct him to do later on, it will certainly produce good results.
>
> ANDERSON, Vol. II, p. 1313

15. According to Schindler, Beethoven used Cramer's Etudes for his lessons with Karl. For this, he most probably used the Breitkopf & Härtel edition (see note 10 above).
16. The way music and prosody are connected with each other is described in many methods. Examples are those of Johann Adam Hiller (Hiller, pp. 954 ff.) and Anton Reicha (Reicha, p. 471).

    (a) Iamb: an unstressed syllable followed by a stressed one.
    (b) Trochee: a stressed syllable followed by an unstressed one.
    (c) Dactyl: a stressed syllable followed by two unstressed ones.
    (d) Spondee: two consecutive syllables with approximately the same stress.

17. This second accent in triple time is described by, among others, Johann Samuel Petri (Petri, pp. 160–164).
18. The album announced is mentioned in Brandenburg, Vol. V, p. 226. Beethoven did not collaborate on this album, but Ries wrote his Op. 99 for it. Other composers apparently found this genre attractive. The young Liszt, for example, composed "Deux Allegri di bravura" in 1824/1825, which were published by Érard in 1825; Moscheles, "3 Allegri di bravura" Op. 51; Tomášek, "Tre Allegri capricciosi di bravura" Op. 81; and the Danish composer Christopher Ernst Friedrich Weyse (1774–1842) "6 Allegri di bravura" Op. 1 and further "Allegri di bravura" Op. 16.

Chapter Three. The Piano in Beethoven's Time

1. Beethoven was appointed second organist to Neefe on July 1, 1784, at an annual salary of 150 Gulden (100 Thaler).
2. This song was published only in 1805 as the first of eight songs Op. 52 entitled *Urians Reise um die Welt.* The first line reads: "Wenn jemand eine Reise tut, so kann er was erzählen" (If someone goes on a trip, there can be something to recount).
3. Johann Ignaz Willmann (1739–1815) was a musician in the court orchestra in Bonn and the father of three child prodigies: the cellist Maximilian Willmann (1767–1813), the pianist Maximiliana Valentina Walburga (1769–1835), and her younger sister Johanna Willmann-Galvani

(1771–1801). They had made their debuts in Vienna on March 16, 1784. On March 7, 1787, all three gave a benefit concert for themselves at the I[imperial] R[oyal] Theater next to the Kärntnertor (the Kärntnertor Theater). Considering Beethoven's strong relation with the Willmann family, one may assume that he was present at this concert.

On this occasion, the elder daughter played a piano concerto by Mozart. It is usually suggested that this was K. 503, and that she gave the first performance of it, but there is no convincing evidence for this assertion, or even that she was a student of Mozart. (See Cliff Eisen, p. 48.)

Mozart had just finished this piano concerto, which he dated December 4 in his thematic catalogue.

The *Bayreuther Zeitung* of March 12, 1787 (Anhang, p. 112), reported a concert Mozart gave on February 28, 1787. "Yesterday Mr. Mozzart [sic] was permitted to give a musical academy for his benefit and had good receipts." It is possible that Mozart played on this occasion his new piano concerto, but there is no evidence for this either. In the Advent season of 1787 Mozart had planned, as he had in three successive years before, other concerts as well. His father, in a letter to his daughter dated December 8, 1786, mentions that Wolfgang planned to give a series of four subscription concerts in the "casino" of the Trattnerhof during Advent that year. This was another possibility for him to perform his new concerto. However, no proof can be found that these concerts took place. Because Beethoven was still in Vienna at the time, it would have been—besides Mozart's concert on February 28—the only other possibility for Beethoven to attend a public performance by Mozart. (See Haberl, pp. 215–255.)

4. For the new evidence regarding Beethoven's journey to Vienna in 1787, see the research by Dieter Haberl, which has determined that Beethoven's first journey to Vienna was far longer than previously assumed and that he did not leave the city at the news of his mother's illness, as also previously assumed.
5. That several of these instruments were available at the court is mentioned in a report in Cramer's *Magazin der Musik* of July 26, 1787 (Vol. II, p. 1386). In the same report, among the names of several amateur pianists, the young "Bethoven" (sic!) is also mentioned.
6. Franz Jacob Spath, in later literature also named Späth. See Skowroneck, p. 58.
7. In the principle of straight (or parallel) stringing, the strings run parallel to each other. The cross-stringing system, which was developed especially to be able to subject a frame to heavier stringing, was first used in vertical pianos by the French builder Pape, who obtained a patent for this in 1828. In 1858 a patent was granted to the brothers Carl (Charles) Steinway (1829–1865) and Wilhelm (William) Steinway (1835–1896) for its application in grand pianos.

8. The strings of the instruments were not yet spun to be able to produce sufficient volume for the low notes. A non-spun string must therefore be longer in order to produce the same pitch.
9. The supposition that Beethoven's lessons with Haydn were not a success was spread by Ferdinand Ries in his biographical notes. (See "Beethoven Remembered" in the biographical notes of Franz Wegeler and Ferdinand Ries, p. 75.) This has been convincingly corrected by Dr. Julia Ronge in her book *Beethovens Lehrzeit* (pp. 26–27). Beethoven studied for over a year with Haydn, longer than one year with Albrechtsberger, and another year with Salieri. During Haydn's life, Haydn and Beethoven stayed on good terms.
10. The confrontation between Mozart and Clementi took place on December 24, 1781, in the Hofburg in Vienna, with Emperor Joseph II in attendance.
11. What is remarkable is that the emotional impact of the music preceding these chords apparently reached such a pitch that Beethoven lost control over his playing of them. His pupil Ferdinand Ries described an amusing event during music-making at the home of Count Johann Georg von Browne-Camus (1767–1827):

> One evening at Count Browne's I was to play a Beethoven sonata (A minor, Opus 23), a work not often heard. Since Beethoven was present and I had never studied this sonata with him, I declared myself willing to play any other sonata, but not that one. Beethoven was then approached and finally said: "Well, you will surely not play it so badly that I cannot listen to it," and so I was obliged to play it. As usual, Beethoven turned pages for me. At a leap in the left hand, where one particular note must be brought out, I missed a note completely, and Beethoven tapped me on the head with one finger. Princess L. . . . . . . [Josephine von Liechtenstein?] who sat leaning against the piano facing me, noticed this with a smile. When I had finished, Beethoven said: "Very good. You did not need to study this sonata with me first. The finger-tap was just meant to prove that I was paying attention." Later that evening Beethoven was also obliged to play and chose the D-minor sonata (Opus 31), which had just been published. The Princess, who probably expected that Beethoven too would make a mistake somewhere, now stood behind his chair while I turned pages. In mm. 53 to 54 Beethoven missed the entry, and instead of descending two notes and then two more, he struck each quarter note in the descending passage with his whole hand (three or four notes at once). It sounded as if the piano was being cleaned. The Princess rapped him several times on the head, not at all delicately, saying: "If the pupil receives one tap of the finger for one missed note, then the Master must

be punished with a full hand for worse mistakes." Everyone laughed, Beethoven most of all. He started again and performed marvelously. The Adagio in particular was incomparably played.

WEGELER/RIES, pp. 81–82

12. This concert must have taken place between 1785 (Reicha's arrival in Bonn) and November 1792 (Beethoven's departure for Vienna). See Skowroneck, p. 54. The instrument that Beethoven used at this concert was most probably one by Stein from Augsburg.
13. The usual transition of the stringing in earlier fortepiano construction between brass and iron took place around a^1. For an optimal sound, the string must not only be thin but must also be stretched sufficiently—almost to breaking point. The material was, however, much softer than the steel wire that is used in present-day piano construction and therefore much more fragile. To make the stringing more reliable, in early forte-piano construction thicker strings were regularly being tried out. The thicker strings had, however, to be stretched even more tightly. For a string has the most harmonic overtones just under its breaking point. This had considerable consequences for the man-hours and the construction of the frame. The use of thicker strings also had consequences for the sound, which lost clarity and was not at all appreciated by everyone, especially in Vienna (and including Streicher).

    The use of steel wire became possible after William Brockedon (1787–1854), painter/author and son of a watchmaker, was granted a patent in 1819 for the drawing of a very strong steel wire of constant thickness. Steel wire can be stretched much more tightly than iron or brass to attain the same pitch. It was, however, only around 1835 that this began to be used in piano construction.

    From the inception of the pianoforte, several strings were used to produce one note via the hammer blow, the so-called multiple stringing. In early pianoforte construction double or triple stringing was typically used from the middle register up to and including the treble. This was also the subject of experiment. Beethoven's Érard was, for example, completely triple-strung; his Broadwood was triple-strung in the descant and double-strung in the bass, while his last grand from Conrad Graf was triple-strung in the bass and even quadruple-strung in the descant. The extra, fourth, string in Graf's instrument did not produce more sound but was probably introduced to spread the force of the hammer head over more strings, thus reducing the risk of strings snapping. See Mertin, p. 99.
14. Despite the great progress in piano construction, the snapping of strings remained a common feature even after several decades, a reason for Franz Liszt (1811–1887) in his early years as touring virtuoso to have several grands on the podium to cope with calamities. The critic Joseph Heinrich

Adami (1807–1865) reported in the *Allgemeine Theaterzeitung* of April 21, 1838, a concert that Liszt gave in Vienna for which there were three grand pianos on the podium, including an Érard and a Graf.
Adami writes:

> [. . .] Liszt played his three compositions on Graf instruments which can honorably hold their ground next to the Parisian Erard regarding tone and tuning. The instrument cannot be faulted for the tearing of strings with such a marked and energetic performance, the less so because the presence of three pianos already seemed to presuppose the strong likelihood for this to occur. Liszt was, incidentally, not in the least inconvenienced by this, he broke off the last piece at an appropriate point and began it again on a new instrument.
>
> LEGÁNY, p. 26

15. The number of forty piano builders in 1803 was mentioned by Joseph Rohrer in a letter of April 15, 1803. See Rohrer, pp. 280–296. Between 1815 and 1833, 387 organ and pianoforte builders were counted in Vienna. From the list it can be gathered that 200 of these were pianoforte builders. See Ottner.
16. Haydn bought his fortepiano from Schanz in October 1788, for which he paid thirty-one ducats—probably including one ducat extra for the transport of the instrument from Vienna to Esterháza. The prices went up around 1800. Referring to the 1796 *Jahrbuch der Tonkunst von Wien und Prag*, Schönfeld wrote (pp. 88–89): "The second master is Mr. Schanz who lives [. . . .] He began his own business after his brother's death five years ago and is now selling his instruments in the range of 40 to 100 ducats." In May 1810 Beethoven wrote a letter to Baron Ignaz von Gleichenstein, in which he asked if he could buy a fortepiano by Schanz for the wife of Beethoven's physician *M[alfatti]* for not over 500 florins, and in a letter to Joseph von Varena, of July 23, 1815, he mentioned a price of 400 florins or 450 florins if he wanted an instrument with decorations. For someone else the price would be 600 florins.
17. Concerning the currency: At the time the principal currency in Austria was the Gulden, abbreviated "fl." or "f." (florins). The words "Gulden" and "florins" are used interchangeably. Another term widely used was ducat (a silver or gold coin); 1 ducat = ca. 4½ florins (1 florin = 60 kreutzer). (See Robbins Landon, p. 6.)

    The price of 30 ducats means that Beethoven did not want to pay more than 135 florins for this instrument. Comparing this with other expenses he incurred, we have the following information from his memorandum book that he kept during this time: House rent = 14 florins; one pair of winter silk stockings = 1 florin + 40 kreutzers; a pair of boots = 6 florins; a fortepiano = 6 florins + 40 kreutzer.

From the amount of money he paid for the fortepiano it is clear that he did not buy it, but rather rented it. Financially, his start in Vienna in 1792 was rather difficult. In the same memorandum book we notice: "In Bonn I counted on receiving 100 ducats here, but in vain." (See Thayer/Forbes, p. 135.)

In May 1793 Elector Maximilian Franz at the Court in Bonn granted him an additional income of 300 florins to be paid in quarterly installments. (See Jan Swafford, p. 136.) Barry Cooper's *Beethoven Compendium*, p. 69, notes that the average income for a middle-class bachelor in Vienna around 1804 was 967 florins for basics, and with some luxuries around 1,200. Swafford (p. 968) assumes that Beethoven's income must at that time have been about 1,000 florins a year.

18. From various sources it can be deduced that during his lifetime Beethoven used instruments of at least the following builders:

Stein (1796)
Walter (1801)
Jakesch (1802)
Bohak (1802)
Moser (1803)
Érard (1803)
Streicher (from 1809)
Vogel (1812)
Schanz, Johann (1815)
Kirschbaum (1817)
Broadwood (1818)
Graf (1825)
Böhm (?)

19. In 2005 the sale was discovered in the Érard archives. See Maria Rose, "Beethoven and His French Piano: Proof of Purchase," *Musique, Images, Instruments* 7 (2005), pp. 110–122. See also Skowroneck, pp. 86 and 87.
20. The *mécanisme à échappement (simple)* is still far removed from Érard's most important invention, the *mécanisme à double échappement*, for which he obtained a patent in London in 1821 and in Paris in 1822. This mechanism forms the basis for current grand-piano construction.
21. While Walter's earliest pianos were still provided with hand registers, a system borrowed from harpsichord construction, Stein went over to using a knee lever for the release of damping. The great advantage was that this could be employed without the pianist having to take his hands from the keyboard. In late eighteenth-century English harpsichord construction, pedals were used to engage the registers, a system that was adopted in fortepiano construction. In the early part of the nineteenth century this still made it possible to engage various registers. While there are

sometimes as many as seven pedals on the Viennese grands, Érard limited himself to four different possibilities for Beethoven's grand piano.

22. See Rowland, p. 32.
23. Beethoven's compulsive musical expression, in which he often exceeded the limits of possibility, was aided by a mechanism that offered more resistance and did not play too lightly. In our times, too, examples are to be found of pianists wanting a grand that is set more heavily than usual. While the average setting for the play weight (or touch weight) of the modern grand is about 1.75 ounces (50 grams), Sviatoslav Richter (1915–1998) had his grand set to an average of 2.1 ounces (60 grams). In contrast, Vladimir Horowitz (1903–1989) preferred a very lightly set instrument. In his grand, the average play weight was 1.27 ounces (36 grams). To make this grand more generally playable after his death, the play weight was increased from 1.27 to 1.48 ounces (from 36 to 42 grams). See Schoones, pp. 34–40. In comparison, the average play weight of a Walter instrument is around 0.5 ounce (15 grams).
24. There are various opinions regarding the reconstruction of mechanisms. Josef Mertin, for example, believes that because the key's pivot was moved and the dip, even after the adaptation, was still twice that of a Walter instrument, more force was needed when playing the Walter instrument than is needed when playing Viennese grands. On the other hand, Tilman Skowroneck is of the opinion that by removing wood from underneath the rear end of the key and attaching lead on the front end, the balance is retained and the mechanism does not play more heavily. See Mertin, p. 99, and Skowroneck, pp. 92 and 93.
25. In 1825 he gave it to his brother Johann. After that, the grand ended up in the Oberösterreichische Landesmuseum in Linz, where Johann was living, where it is now again to be found after spending some years in the Kunsthistorisches Museum in Vienna.
26. Although it is these days usual to tune the a^1 to 440 hertz, there can also be heard examples of 443 hertz, especially in Germany, where an ever-higher tuning has been stimulated by, among other considerations, the opinions of the famous conductor Herbert von Karajan.
27. This instrument is now in the Smithsonian Institution in Washington, DC.
28. Thomas Broadwood (1786–1861) was a son of John Broadwood (1732–1812), who arrived in London in 1761 and there became the business partner of the harpsichord and fortepiano builder Burkat Shudi (1702–1773), who was of Swiss origin. After Shudi's death, John continued with the business, at first together with Shudi's son and from 1782 on his own.
29. This is a rather enthusiastic report, for the instrument of course reached only c^4.
30. In the "Les Adieux" Sonata, the f^4 is found in m. 59 of the third movement. Beethoven could also profit from the bass in the Broadwood lying

a third lower than in the Érard. That was pleasing because he most decidedly needed that range by 1816, two years before he had the Broadwood at his disposal, in his Sonata Op. 101.

In the autograph of the last movement, Allegro, he notates EE in mm. 223–225 in an exceptional way by not just writing the chords but, as a special note, also writing "Contra E" along with this. At the foot of the page he then writes this again in pencil with a note to the printer, "NB. Print these letters in the engraved version too." Beethoven, in these of all measures, wished to leave no misunderstanding about the need for the expression of such a low bass, and this is of course due to the resulting intensification of the return of the dominant in *fortissimo*—the sparkling return of the theme in A major a few measures further on. See also Chapter 5.

31. Beethoven applied the shifting by means of the *una corda* with his Érard in, among other instances, the middle part of the cadence of his Fourth Piano Concerto, composed in 1805–1806, where he writes *due e poi tre corde*. In the first movement of his Sonata Op. 101, composed in 1816, thus still at a time when he was in possession of his Érard, he also writes *mit einer Saite* (with one string), and later *Nach und nach mehrere Saiten* (ever more strings). When Beethoven had his Broadwood grand, he used this effect in the third movement of his Sonata Op. 106, where he writes *poco a poco due ed a llora tutte le corde* (little by little two and then all strings). On these grand pianos, this results in, along with a reduction or increase in volume, also—much more than with a modern grand—a different tone color.
32. We now know the "Kaiserhymne" as the German national anthem.
33. Internal disagreements in the business between the Streicher couple and Nanette's brother led to the brother setting up his own workshop in 1810.
34. After Beethoven's death, the Broadwood was included in an auction of Beethoven's effects. However, a purchaser for the Broadwood, which ten years earlier had represented the high point of piano building, could scarcely be found due to its terrible condition and what was perceived as its limited sonority. The eventual purchaser was the music publisher Carl Anton Spina (1827–1906), who bought it for 181 florins. Spina, who would play an important role as publisher of the works of the Johann Strauss family, gave the instrument to Franz Liszt in 1846, who had it standing in the music salon of the Altenburg in Weimar. Out of gratitude for the festivities accompanying his golden jubilee as an artist in 1873, he gave it to the National Museum in Budapest (letter dated 1874). It was, however, not until 1887, a year after his death, that it found its home there. The grand now stands on a loan basis in the Liszt Memorial Museum.
35. After Beethoven's death, the borrowed grand was returned to Graf and now stands in the Beethoven-Haus in Bonn.

Chapter Four. Performance Practice and Beethoven's Notation

1. It is remarkable that Beethoven did not recommend a method of his pupil Czerny. Half a year later, in a letter of January 21, 1826, he wrote to von Breuning: "Do not take Czerny's *Klavierschule;* these past days I have received information about another." Czerny's method, *Der Wiener Clavier-Lehrer*, was published in December 1825. See Brandenburg, Vol. VI, p. 207.
2. In 1801 the spiritual sound world of the Aeolian harp attracted Beethoven's attention. New research, also published by Norbert Gertsch and the American pianist Murray Perahia in the preface of their publication of the Sonata Op. 27 No. 2 by Henle in 2012, proved that in 1801, the year of the work's composition, Beethoven had an interest in purchasing such an instrument, to which Johann Friedrich Hugo von Dalberg (1760–1812) had just dedicated a prose text under the title *Die Aeolsharfe. Ein allegorischer Traum* (published by Beyer und Maring, Erfurt, 1801). Beethoven copied down the title of this essay when it was reviewed in the *Allgemeine musikalische Zeitung* (*AmZ*, April 1801, Vol. III, pp. 473 ff.), together with the information that such an instrument could be purchased from the instrument maker J. W. Bindernagel in Gotha for 2 Laubthaler, and made from better wood there for 1 louis d'or. In London, too, it was possible to purchase these instruments. Von Dalberg mentions the well-known piano manufacturers Longman & Broderip and Clementi (see also Chapter 6). The novel by von Dalberg can be found on the main website of Kite Musical Instruments/Literature (http://www.windmusik.com/html/litratur.htm#aeolian, Part B: "Literatur/Original Texte").
3. This edition originally appeared in 1804, but was revised with an added German translation in 1805.
4. Although Türk says that the notation of a wedge is associated by some with playing a note shorter than when indicated with a dot, this mark is not to be confused with the *staccatissimo* as sometimes seen in, and especially after, the Romantic era. For the Viennese Classical school, it had the meaning of an accentuation and is also seen on longer notes, such as half or quarter notes, where playing *staccatissimo* would make no sense whatsoever.
5. The "stroke" in the manuscript is often presented in print by a so-called *Keil*, a wedge.
6. The Wiener Urtext uses only the wedge as a sign for the detached touch (*Abstoßen*), which therefore applies to these measures too. The Henle edition uses only the dot for this.
7. According to L. M. Middleton, Playford printed "the new ty'd note" no earlier than 1658. See Playford, p. 22.

8. The importance of the beam for articulation in the Romantic period is addressed in, for example, Huizing, *Chopin*. Later on, some examples of this are still to be found in the piano works of Béla Bartók.
9. Although it might seem that the small filled-in circles in m. 216 indicate a kind of contrary accentuation, in fact Beethoven is correcting his original notated C into a D-flat. However, because the notes are still written too low down, he writes for the sake of clarity in his characteristic hand an open D on these places underneath, all played as D-flat due to the key of F minor.
10. While there is to my knowledge no discussion with regard to this pedal indication, the pedal indication for the first chords of the first movement is quite a different matter. All publishers and pianists agree that the release of the pedal after the last chord in m. 4 and at similar places in this movement must be taken literally and that there must really be silence. In the first Artaria edition the sign for the release of the pedal is even printed *before* the rests and the *fermate* and not, as in many editions, after them. This is, however, different when these chords return in m. 267. Here, the last chord should be able to sound through the rests, because in the first Artaria edition the sign for releasing the pedal is given only *after* the *fermate* and the rests. This is also the opinion of the Austrian pianist Rudolf Buchbinder, as written in his book *Mein Beethoven*. Upon closer examination of the Artaria edition, however, it is seen that m. 267 is printed at the end of the grand stave and that there is little room to print this sign before the *fermata*. It could therefore be a printing mistake, meaning that many publishers correct the position of the sign.

    An argument for Buchbinder's view, however, is that, in contrast to the B-flat-major chords in the opening, these are now transposed to B minor, the "black key," and the key that plays such an important role in the whole sonata. These *fortissimo* chords are now also embedded between *pianissimo* measures, a context very different from the spirited opening.
11. The freedom of movement is therefore not arbitrary, but must be motivated by keeping the meaning of each phrase or part thereof in line with the totality of the work. This form of *rubato*, not notated in a composition, is an important tool in stressing the structure of a work and is therefore sometimes called structural *rubato*.
12. It is probably this kind of *rubato* that Mozart describes in a letter to his father dated October 24, 1777:

    > What these people cannot grasp is that in tempo rubato in an Adagio, the left hand should go on playing in strict time. With them the left hand always follows suit.
    >
    > ANDERSON, Vol. I, p. 340

13. Not all that unusual, however, to those—only a few in Beethoven's time—who were familiar with the works of J. S. Bach, as was Beethoven himself,

who knew *The Well-Tempered Clavier* thoroughly. See, for instance: the Andante in the Italian Concerto, BWV 971; the twenty-fifth variation of the *Goldberg Variations*, BWV 988; or the Sarabande in the Sixth Partita, BWV 830.

14. The concept of "meter" was originally associated with the *tactus*, arising out of the mensural notation that replaced so-called modal meter around the middle of the thirteenth century. In mensural notation not only was the relative duration of the notes discernible from the written music, but also the more or less absolute duration. This somewhat absolute duration was called the *tactus*, corresponding to a resting pulse rate and indicated by moving the hand, baton, or roll of paper up and down. The *tactus* was always taken from an established note value, or duration, initially the *maxima*. Later (between ca. 1200 and 1350) this changed via the *longa* and the *brevis* into the *semibrevis*. This was continued through the Renaissance and the Baroque. This standard value, from which the other note durations were derived, was termed the *integer valor notarum*, in other words, the actual duration of the intact (i.e., undivided) notes. Because the *integer valor notarum* was identical to the *tactus* motion, a reasonably accurate tempo could be determined from the music as set down. From the fifteenth century it also became possible to influence this tempo by the use of the *signa proportionate*.

If, for example, ¢ was notated instead of c (*proportio dupla* instead of *integer valor* meter), then it was the intention that two notes—for example, two *whole notes* that were therefore equal in duration to one *brevis*—be played with the duration of (in this case) one *semibrevis*, thus halving the original duration. That was the reason for the use, as early as the sixteenth century, of the term *alla breve* and *alla semibreve*—mensural notation that was not intended to establish the movement in a metrical sense. The *tactus* concept is therefore a long way from our understanding of meter, even though both marks were adopted in the Baroque and Classical periods and thus continued to play a role as regards tempo. There was thus an association between the time signature c and the so-called *tempo ordinario*, a moderate tempo (*moderato*). Accordingly, 3/8 time, for example, counted as fast. Beethoven used these time signatures, and also time signatures that were commonplace in the Baroque but had descended into obscurity, in combination with the Italian tempo/character indications that had emerged during the Baroque. In this way he could alter the original character of a time signature by having it played more slowly or quickly, which in turn meant that he could notate larger or smaller durations to express a "lighter" or "heavier" character in the music, as was earlier discussed in connection with the 3/8 notation as applied in the Largo in the Third Piano Concerto.

15. This development meant that the heavy/light relationships no longer corresponds to the usual accentuation within a notated time, but are

grouped together over the measures. In the case of a *due battute*, the first measure feels heavy and the next one light; in *tre battute* the first measure is heavy and the next two light; and in *quattro battute* the first and third measures are heavy, the second and fourth light. In this way, in this hypermeasure each measure counts as a "beat" within the overall movement.

The usual Italian term for these combinations was notated only now and then by Beethoven, as in, for example, the Scherzo of his Ninth Symphony Op. 125 and the first movement of his String Quartet Op. 131, with the indications *ritmo di tre battute* and *ritmo di quattro battute*.

16. The movements with a hypermeasure, the last measure of which is notated as a rest, are: movement I, Op. 2 No. 2; movement I, Op. 7; movement I, Op. 10 No. 1; movements II and III, Op. 10 No. 2; movements I and III, Op. 10 No. 3; movement I, Op. 13; movement II, Op. 14 No. 1; movement III, Op. 14 No. 2; movements I and III, Op. 28; and movements I and III, Op. 31 No. 1.

17. Beethoven learnt Kirnberger's method at a young age from Tobias Friedrich Pfeiffer, a lodger at the Beethovens' house in Bonn who gave Ludwig piano lessons as well as lessons in music theory in 1779 and 1780 (see Ronge, p. 115).

18. If one wished (and was able) to play the trills in mm. 129 and 130 according to Mozart's notation and to follow the distribution of the ties in this respect, then the trill in m. 129 would have to begin with the main note, but that in m. 130 with the auxiliary—playing that, to my knowledge, has so far never been achieved by any (forte)pianist.

19. According to Schindler, Beethoven played the second movement of Op. 14 No. 1 once as an Allegro furioso instead of an Allegretto.

20. A direct influence on the sound as a result of the touch also takes place when playing the clavichord, where, like the fortepiano (where the hammer strikes the string), it is a small metal blade, called the "tangent," that makes the contact, whereby, depending on the speed of the key, graduated dynamics can be made. However, the sound of this instrument is distinctly softer than that of a fortepiano, and the dynamic variations are relatively limited. This instrument could easily be placed in a small household, because it was moderate in size and less expensive compared to a fortepiano or a harpsichord. Concerning the possibility that Beethoven played this instrument, Skowroneck (p. 29) writes: "There can be little doubt that a typical instrument for keyboard lessons of a talented child, in a German city around 1777 with teachers all born in the first half of the eighteenth century, would have been the clavichord."

It is recorded that Beethoven's father and Pfeiffer, coming home in the middle of the night from the tavern, would shake the boy awake and drag him to the keyboard, where he was forced to play into the early hours. (See note 17 above and Swafford, p. 32.)

Practicing fortepiano or harpsichord in the middle of the night in the house at Rheingasse 24, to which the family had moved around 1774, would certainly have disturbed the neighbors.

21. Maelzel had adopted the idea for such a chronometer from the instrument maker and inventor Dietrich Nikolaus Winkel, whom he visited in November 1814 in Amsterdam on his way to London to demonstrate his Panharmonicon and his automaton trumpeter.

22. Kolisch worked right up to his death in 1978 on the basic principles that he had published in 1943.

23. A completely different approach was discussed by, among others, Talsma and von Gleich (see Bibliography). They developed the idea that two ticks, to and fro, of the metronome represent one beat, in the way a conductor moves his arm upwards followed by a downward movement, to show the beat to the orchestra. It means that in their opinion, many of the fast tempi must be played at half the tempo indicated by the metronome.

However, any kind of historical written proof about this way of approaching the metronome is missing. The footnote written by Moscheles in 1841 in an English translation of Schindler's biography about the metronome indications of the Sonata Op. 106 shows that he was unaware of such a manner of metronomization (see note 26 below), which is very strange for this celebrated pianist and composer, who was a personal friend of Beethoven and Czerny. Moscheles came to Vienna in 1808. In 1810 he met his idol Beethoven, who entrusted him with the preparation of the piano score of his opera *Fidelio*. In the fall of 1816 Moscheles left Vienna, but returned in 1823, where on December 15 he used Beethoven's Broadwood for a concert at the Kärntnertor Theater (see Chapter 3).

24. The Beethoven sonatas with metronome indications by Czerny are published by:

Haslinger, Vienna, 1833?
Cocks and Co., London, 1835
Haslinger, Vienna, 1842
Simrock, Bonn, 1856–1868

The Beethoven sonatas with metronome indications by Moscheles are published by:

Cramer and Company, London, before 1840
Holle, Wolfensbüttel, ca. 1848
Hallberger, Stuttgart, 1858

See also Rosenblum, pp. 323–333.

25. A facsimile of this letter is reproduced in an article written by Ernesto Paolone. See Bibliography.

26. Anton F. Schindler, *Biographie von Ludwig van Beethoven*, Münster: Aschendorf, 1840.

Translated(?) and edited by Ignaz Moscheles as *The Life of Beethoven*, 2 vols., London: Henry Colburn, 1841. The footnote about this metronome mark by Moscheles can be found on p. 252 of Vol. II.

27. Tempi for the other movements are experienced as a little less problematic. Nevertheless, the third movement, Adagio sostenuto, where the metronome indication gives ♪ = 92, is often performed in a very slow tempo. However, these interpretations do not do justice to the 6/8 notation, where the heavy/light pulsation must be divided within the measure. In the case of too slow a tempo, one is hearing two 3/4 measures within the 6/8 notation.

28. The details of these metronomes are taken from Schindler (I), p. 249.

29. "I [Beethoven] cannot yet send you the Tempi because my metronome is broken; and I shall not have it back for a few days" (Anderson, Vol. III, p. 804).

30. See Brussee (Bibliography).

31. Beethoven published the metronome numbers for his Symphonies 1–8, his Septet Op. 20, some smaller works, and his first twelve string quartets in 1817 and 1819. His Broadwood grand piano arrived in the summer of 1818. For the Ninth symphony, completed at the beginning of 1824, his nephew Karl helped him to notate the metronome numbers.

Chapter Five. The Editions

1. Reprints of all original printings were published in 1989 by Tecla Editions, Preacher's Court, Charterhouse, London, under the editorship of Dr. Brian Jeffery.

2. It concerned here not only sloppiness, but also headstrong interference with Beethoven's text, such as the four measures that the publisher Nägeli added at the end of the first movement of Op. 31 No. 1. When Ferdinand Ries played it in this form for Beethoven, the latter flew into a temper, with the result that an *Edition très correcte* was published by Simrock in Berlin.

3. See Rosenblum, p. 330.

4. The sonatas mentioned in the 1830 article are: Op. 13, Op. 26, Op. 31 Nos. 1 and 2, and Op. 110. They are to be found in *Livraison* 1 and 2 of the M. Schlesinger edition. Fétis was not only the founder of the journal *Revue musicale*, but until 1831 also the sole editor. The loose issues have been bundled in collective editions of more than 600 pages. In the Bibliothèque nationale de France (BnF) in Paris this article is to be found in Part VI, pp. 211–213.

5. In the Schlesinger edition, only Sonatas Op. 10 and Op. 27 are provided with metronome indications, which correspond to those of Czerny from

the first Haslinger edition. Czerny's edition of these sonatas must have appeared very shortly before the Schlesinger edition, and Liszt must have become acquainted with them in that and have adopted them. Because both Czerny and Moscheles were involved in further editions later on, Liszt must have doubted their authenticity. (See Rosenblum, pp. 355–361.) This can be the reason for Liszt's decision with the Holle edition in 1856 not to give the sonatas metronome indications, with the exception of Op. 106.

6. *Erste vollständige Gesammtausgabe unter Revision von Franz Liszt*, Wolfenbüttel: L. Holle, 1858–1861. Facsimile edition edited by Janos Cegledy and Laszlo Simon, Tokyo: Zen-On Music Co., Ltd., 1995.
7. The Sonata Op. 106 is missing from Czerny's Haslinger edition, as are the Sonatas Op. 2 and Op. 7, because Artaria, who provided the original printings, did not give permission for these to be republished by Haslinger.
8. See Czerny (II), p. 111.
9. Liszt does not adopt all changes from *alla breve* to **c** from the Cramer edition. In the Cramer edition, for example, the original *alla breve* designation for the last movement of the Sonata Op. 14 No. 1 is changed to **c**, but Liszt retains Beethoven's original *alla breve* notation.
10. Facsimile edition of the "Moonlight" Sonata, Bonn: Verlag Beethoven-Haus, 2003. In the facsimile publication of Liszt's Holle edition (see note 6 above), the time signatures changed by Liszt are "corrected" again, so that this is in fact no longer a true facsimile. This change from the original publications is explained in the preface.
11. The Victor recording made by Bauer in 1926 has been reissued (among other works) on the Appion Publications & Recordings (APR) label, No. 7302 (*Harold Bauer: The Complete Recordings*). From this, it turns out that the recording time of 4'37 does not correspond to the actual length of the recording, which is 4'48. (In the accompanying CD booklet, 4'53 is mistakenly given.) Bauer's recording also exceeds the maximum of 4'40 mentioned in his book. Nevertheless, the performance is faster than the earlier interpretations he mentions in his book, which were based on a performance in common time and took just over five minutes.
12. Cotta's edition appeared in a twelve-part series with works of Bach, Beethoven, Chopin, Clementi, Dussek, Field, Haydn, Hummel, Mendelssohn, Mozart, Schubert, and Weber. As well as Sigismund Lebert and Hans von Bülow, Immanuel Faisst, Ignaz Lachner, and Franz Liszt worked on this series. In addition, Liszt collaborated on the editions with works of Schubert and Carl Maria von Weber. For the edition of Beethoven's sonatas, Lebert was responsible for editing Volumes I—III and Von Bülow for IV and V.
13. One of Clara's interventions in her husband's compositions concerned Schumann's metronome indications. Clara collaborated on two editions in which she altered these markings. In a *Gesamtausgabe* published in the

years 1879–1893 she collaborated with Johannes Brahms. It is noticeable that the differences are fewer in this edition than in her own "instructive" edition of the *Sämtliche Klavierwerke* of 1886. Apparently, Brahms kept her on the straight and narrow out of respect for Schumann. Clara's instructive edition with many extra suggestions is published in seven volumes and is still available from Breitkopf & Härtel. The edition on which she collaborated with Brahms is available as a reprint in three volumes from Dover Publications, New York.

14. The alteration to the notes in Op. 101 suggested by von Bülow is also mentioned as an alternative in a footnote in the d'Albert edition.
15. The octaves on Contra E are tied in mm. 224–226, as can be seen in Beethoven's autograph and in urtexts like Henle and Bärenreiter. Unfortunately, in the Wiener Urtext the tie from m. 225 to 226 is missing, so that the construction of the theme in the augmentation becomes unclear.
16. Fluctuation within a tempo was not unusual in Beethoven's time either, as can be read in a report of the playing of Beethoven's favorite pianist Dorothea von Ertmann. See the section concerning *rubato* in Chapter 4.
17. This edition was published undated by Bote & Bock in Berlin in three volumes: Vol. I, Opp. 2–26; Vol. II, Opp. 27–57; Vol. III, Opp. 78–111.

    An advertisement by Hofmeister in December 1886 mentioning this edition suggests that it had appeared a little earlier. Karl Klindworth, born in Hannover but living many years in London, is named as *Carl* Klindworth in this.
18. In the preface to this edition is written, "Complete critically reviewed edition, revised throughout with permission from the original publishers." This popular edition enjoyed an even wider distribution through its publication in the Lea Pocket Scores series. Currently it can be downloaded free of charge via the Petrucci Music Library, to be found at www.imslp.org.
19. Schnabel was the first pianist to record all the piano sonatas, which he did for His Master's Voice between 1931 and 1935.
20. This was pointed out to Schnabel by his theory and composition teacher Eusebius Mandyczewski (1857–1929), who was a friend of Johannes Brahms and himself also produced an edition of Beethoven's piano sonatas.
21. In a revised edition, published in 1949 by Editioni Curzi, Milan; this edition is now available from Alfred Edition.
22. Frederic Lamond's edition saw the light of day around 1918 by Ullstein in Berlin and was reprinted in 1923 by Breitkopf & Härtel, through which it is still available. A reprint was also published by Musytschna Ukraina in Kiev in 1969.
23. Sir Donald Tovey (1875–1940), English composer, pianist, and author, played together with Joachim, Casals, Julius Röntgen, and others. Associated with Edinburgh University from 1914 onward, he wrote program

notes for Reid Orchestra concerts, which were later compiled as *Essays in Musical Analysis*. His analyses of Beethoven's piano sonatas are still relevant in our times.

24. Heinrich Schenker, Austrian musicologist, studied under Chopin's pupil Karol Mikuli (1819–1897), among others. The German conductor Wilhelm Furtwängler (1886–1954) was a great admirer of Schenker's analytical method, as is the pianist Murray Perahia (b. 1947) in the present day.
25. The Erläuterungs-Ausgaben of the last sonatas were published by Universal Edition in Vienna: Op. 109 in 1913, Op. 110 in 1914, Op. 111 in 1915, Op. 101 in 1920. It was originally the intention to include Op. 106, the "Hammerklavier," in this series, but this was not realized because of the absence of the original manuscript. For his edition of all thirty-two sonatas, appearing between 1921 and 1923, Schenker used Beethoven's manuscripts of Opp. 26, 27 No. 2, 28, 53, 57, 78, 81a (first movement), 90, 101, 109, 110, and 111. Only Opp. 53, 79, and 90 were not at his disposal. All of Beethoven's manuscripts known to date are, with the exception of the first movement of Op. 81a, now available in facsimile.
26. The sonatas that have thus far appeared in this edition are Opp. 2, 7, 13, 14, 26, 27, 28, 31, 49, 53, 81a, 90, and 101.
27. German organ music is these days also often published in landscape format (Peters), but French organ music hardly ever.

Chapter Six. Style and Interpretation

1. An exception to such a total concept is the independent first movement of the Sonata Op. 27 No. 2.

   It is also uncertain with regard to Op. 106 whether Beethoven had a preconception of the complete sonata. Although there is considerable coherence between the movements, among other things because the descending third is so significant in all the movements and there are also thematic associations to be made, it appears from a letter written by Beethoven to Archduke Rudolph dated June 4, 1819, in which he congratulates him on his appointment as archbishop of Olmütz, that the first two movements had been written earlier and the other movements had been added later on.

   > To the 2 pieces written by my hand on the name day of Y.R.H. two more have come, whereof the last is a great *Fugato*, so that it amounts to a grand sonata which will soon be published.
   >
   > BRANDENBURG, Vol. IV, p. 246

   This could also be an explanation for Beethoven's writing on April 19, 1819, to Ferdinand Ries, who was preparing the English edition of Op. 106 in London, that he could do whatever he wished with the compilation of the movements of the work just as long as it was published. This might, however, also have had something to do with the financial straits that he was experiencing in those days.

> Should the sonata not be suitable for London, I could send another one; or you might also leave out the Largo and start straightaway with the fugue in the last section; or use the first section, then the Adagio, and for the third movement the Scherzo and the Largo and *Allegro risoluto*.—I leave all that to you; do as you think best.
>
> WEGELER/RIES, p. 131

Beethoven's asking Ries in a letter of April 16, 1819, to add a measure to the beginning of the Adagio can also serve as an indication that this sonata was not originally a preconceived whole (Brandenburg, Vol. IV, p. 278). It is, however, obvious that he made the connection of the thematic material for the other movements after composing the first two. Concerning the addition of the first measure of the Adagio, where the ascending thirds counterbalance the descending thirds in this movement, Ries later wrote:

> Artistically a most remarkable thing happened with one of the last solo sonatas (in B-flat major with the great fugue, Opus 106, which is forty-one pages in print). Beethoven had sent it to me in London to be sold, so that it would be published there at the same time as in Germany. The engraving was finished and I expected daily a letter specifying the day of publication. When the letter arrived, it included the surprising instruction: "Insert at the beginning of the Adagio (which is nine or ten pages long) these two notes as an opening measure."
>
> I must admit that involuntarily I began to wonder if my dear old teacher had really gone daft, a rumor which was going about at the time. To add two notes to such a great work, which had been thoroughly reworked and completed half a year ago!! And yet, I was amazed at the effect of these two notes. Never again could such effective, important notes be added to a completed work, not even if they had been intended from the very beginning.
>
> WEGELER/RIES, pp. 94–95

2. About the "Kunstvereinigung," see Zenck, pp. 97–98.
3. Schubert spoke to Beethoven personally for the first time just a few days before Beethoven's death when he visited Beethoven at the latter's deathbed in the Schwarzspanierhaus along with the brothers Josef and Anselm Hüttenbrenner and the painter Josef Teltscher. To the question as to who should first come to him, Beethoven had apparently emphatically asked for Schubert. This information comes from Josef Hüttenbrenner, who

was the younger brother of Anselm, in whose presence Beethoven died. See *Drei Begräbnisse und ein Todesfall. Beethovens Ende und die Erinnerungskultur seiner Zeit* (catalog for an exhibition in the Beethoven-Haus in 2002), especially p. 60.

4. See Reti, *Thematic Patterns in Sonatas of Beethoven.*
5. See Brendel, *Music Sounded Out.*
6. There are also examples of program (or narrative) music in the eighteenth century, such as Kuhnau's *Biblical Sonatas* (with accompanying printed Bible texts), the opening of Haydn's *Creation*, the many harpsichord works of Couperin, Forqueray, or Duphly and Vivaldi's *Four Seasons.*
7. A reaction to this trend was inevitable and was formulated by the well-known and feared critic Eduard Hanslick (1825–1904), who, in his 1854 book *Vom musikalische Schönen*, which went to sixteen printings and was translated into English, Russian, and Japanese, among other languages, refers to musical content purely as "Tönend bewegte Formen" (forms moved by sound).
8. Cortot was familiar with Wagner's ideas concerning a Gesamtkunstwerk, and this will have certainly been due to his early meetings with Wagner's widow. Together with fellow student Edouard Risler (1873–1929), he had had early contact with Cosima Wagner-Liszt (1837–1930), for whom he performed transcriptions of operas by Wagner on two pianos. In 1902 Cortot conducted the French première of *Götterdämmerung* in the Théâtre du Château d'Eau in Paris.
9. Bernard Gavoty (1908–1981), French organist (pupil of Louis Vierne), musicologist, author, and famous music critic of *Le Figaro* under the pseudonym Clarendonc.
10. Romain Rolland (1866–1944) studied history and literature in Paris and Rome and, with others, established the *Revue d'histoire et critique musicale.* From 1913 to 1939 he lived in Switzerland, where he concentrated on literature. Among other works, he wrote the ten-part novel *Jean Christophe* (1905–1912), with the idealized figure of Beethoven as the main character. Further works included *Vie de Beethoven* (1903), *Voyage musicale au pays du passé* (1919), *Goethe et Beethoven* (1932), and *Le chant de la résurrection* (1937).
11. In this American journal, the name Backhaus is written "Bachaus" (sic!), as it also appears on some early record labels.
12. Among the many stories is the one that is mentioned by Edwin Fischer in his book about the sonatas (Fischer [II], p. 69). A sketch by Beethoven that seems to bear some resemblance to the "Moonlight" can be compared with Act I of Mozart's opera *Don Giovanni*, directly after the Count has been mortally wounded by Don Giovanni: not only because of the accompaniment in triplets, but also because Mozart's music has been transposed in C-sharp minor, the music of the "Moonlight."'

However, research by the Beethoven-Haus in Bonn brought to light that this sketch could not have been an inspiration for this composition. The sonata was composed in 1801 and the sketch, now in the Beethoven-Haus, was according to the research without doubt not written before 1803/1804.

13. Beethoven copied down the title of the essay as reviewed in the *Allgemeine musikalische Zeitung*, together with the information regarding where this instrument could be purchased.

    See Hans-Werner Küthen, *Ein unbekanntes Notierungsblatt Beethovens aus der Entstehungszeit der "Mondscheinsonate" im Familienarchiv Chotek in Benešov, Tchechische Republik*, Prague: Edition Resonus, 1996. See also Chapter 4, note 2.

14. Thomas Mann's choice of the name Kretzschmar is clearly inspired by the German musicologist Hermann Kretzschmar (1848–1924), who formulated his theories of music in the doctrine of musical hermeneutics. Kretzschmar regarded music not as an autonomous phenomenon, but rather as a form of poetry, as a less exact and clear grammar than language, but with a more subtle associative capacity and a more intense effect.

15. Mann wrote *adagio molto, semplice et cantabile*, with the comma after *molto*. In Chapter 1 it has already been mentioned in the context of Op. 111 that the comma should have been placed after the word *adagio* and that the *molto* refers to *semplice*.

16. In Mozart's piano sonatas, *ff* (*fortissimo*) appears only in the first movement of his Sonata in A minor, K. 310.

Chapter 7. The Recordings

1. Recordings by Lamond of the Sonatas Opp. 13, 26, 27 No. 2, 31 No. 2, 53, 57, and 110 have been rereleased on the Biddulph label, LHW 042 and LHW 043.

    The recordings made by d'Albert in the years 1921/1922 of the Scherzo from Op. 31 No. 3 and the third movement of the "Waldstein" Sonata have been rereleased by Arbiter Records.

2. Schnabel played all the sonatas on four Sundays in Berlin during the Beethoven Year 1927 and repeated this a year later in London and in 1936 in Carnegie Hall in New York. With regard to his recordings it must be pointed out that "live" in concert hall can have a result very different from "live" in a studio.

    Many studio recordings made by pianists in those years depended on the maximum playing time of 78-rpm records, which was never longer than five minutes per side. Because of this, the tempi of movements were sometimes increased to reduce the number of records needed for a longer work.

3. Recordings by Hans Richter-Haaser have been rereleased on CD by Philips and EMI Classics. A number of CD recordings by Andor Foldes are to be found on the APR label. LP recordings of his were released on, among other labels, Heliodor and Deutsche Grammophon. Eduardo Del Pueyo's remastered recordings are on Decca "Eloquence."
4. Egon Petri's complete Columbia and Electrola solo and concerto recordings 1929–1951 are on the APR label. Murray Perahia's recording was released in 2018 on Deutsche Grammophon.
5. Glenn Gould's recordings of the Sonatas Opp. 2, 10, 13, 14, 26, 27, 28, 31, 57, 109, 110, and 111 were released with the five piano concertos on the Sony label.
6. The recording of Peter Serkin can be found on the Musical Concepts label. It was recorded in St. Mary's Chapel, St. Paul Seminary, St. Paul, MN. Unfortunately, many details of Serkin's playing are lost, due to the highly resonant acoustics of the chapel.

   Malcolm Bilson recorded the sonatas together with Tom Beghin, David Breitman, Ursula Dütschler, Zvi Meniker, Bart van Oort, and Andrew Willes on the Claves label.
7. Live recordings of Sidney Foster were published in 2018 by the American label Marston.

Bibliography

Adam, Louis: *Méthode de piano du Conservatoire*, 1804; facsimile, Geneva: Minkoff, 1974.

Adorno, Theodor W.: *Beethoven: The Philosophy of Music* (fragments and texts ed. Rolf Tiedemann; trans. Edmund Jephcott), Stanford: Stanford University Press, 1998.

Anderson, Emily (ed. and trans.): *The Letters of Beethoven*, 3 vols., New York: St. Martin's Press; London: Macmillan, 1961.

Bach, Carl Philipp Emanuel: *Essay on the True Art of Playing Keyboard Instruments* (trans. and ed. William J. Mitchell), New York: W. W. Norton, 1949.

Backhaus, Wilhelm: "Beethoven. Sonata Pathétique, Op. 13, Movement I" in: *Piano Lessons in the Grand Style: From the Golden Age of* The Etude *Music Magazine (1913–1940)* (ed. Jeffrey Johnson), New York: Dover Publications, 2003.

Badura-Skoda, Paul: *Edwin Fischer. Meisterkurs in Luzern 1954*, Düsseldorf: Staccato, 2011.

Badura-Skoda, Paul, and Jörg Demus: *Die Klaviersonaten von Ludwig van Beethoven*, Wiesbaden: F. A. Brockhaus, 1974.

Barthold, Kenneth van (I): *The Story of the Piano*, London: BBC Books, 1975.

Barthold, Kenneth van (II): *International Piano*, July/August 2010, London: Rhinegold.

Bauer, Harold: *His Book*, New York: W. W. Norton, 1948.

Beck, Hermann: "Studien über das Tempoproblem bei Beethoven," Ph.D. diss., Friedrich-Alexander Universität, 1954; summarized under the title "Bemerkungen zu Beethoven's Tempi," *Beethoven-Jahrbuch II* (1955–1956), pp. 24–54.

Beethoven Almanach 1970, Vienna: Lafite, 1970.

Beethoven Congress, Detroit, 1977, Detroit: Wayne State University Press, 1980.

Benz, Richard: *Goethe und Beethoven*, Stuttgart: Reclam, 1948.

Berlioz, Hector: *Critique musicale*, Vol. II (ed. Marie-Hélène Coudroy-Saghaï and Anne Bongrain), Paris: Buchet/Chastel, 1998.

Bettermann, Silke, et al.: *Drei Begräbnisse und ein Todesfall. Beethovens Ende und die Erinnerungskultur seiner Zeit*, Bonn: Beethoven-Haus / Kassel: Museum für Sepulkralkultur, 2002.

Bettermann, Silke (ed.): *Erinnerungen an Beethoven. Skizzen, Zeichnungen, Karikaturen*, Bonn: Beethoven-Haus, 1987.

Biss, Jonathan: *Beethoven's Shadow*, New York: Rosetta Books, 2011.

Blom, Eric: *Beethoven's Pianoforte Sonatas Discussed*, New York: Da Capo Press, 1968.

Brandenburg, Sieghard: *Ludwig van Beethoven. Briefwechsel, Gesamtausgabe*, 7 vols., Munich: Henle, 1996.

Brendel, Alfred: *Musical Thoughts and Afterthoughts*, London: Robson Books, 1976.

Breuning, Gerhard von: *Memories of Beethoven: From the House of the Black-Robed Spaniards* (ed. Maynard Solomon; trans. Henry Mins and Maynard Solomon), Cambridge: Cambridge University Press, 1992.

Brussee, Albert: "De tempo-problematiek," *Oktaaf* 2/3 (1989), rpt. in *Piano Bulletin*, no. 3, 2003.

Buchbinder, Rudolf: *Mein Beethoven*, St. Pölten, Salzburg, and Vienna: Residenz Verlag, 2014.

Caeyers, Jan: *Beethoven: A Life*, Berkeley: University of California Press, 2020.

Clementi, Muzio: *Introduction to the Art of Playing on the Piano Fort*e, 1801; facsimile, New York: Da Capo Press, 1974.

Cortot, Alfred: *Studies in Musical Interpretation* (trans. Robert Jaques), London: George Harrap, 1937.

Cooper, Barry: *The Beethoven Compendium: A Guide to Beethoven's Life and Music*, New York: Thames and Hudson, 1992.

Cramer, Johann Baptist (I): *60 Ausgewählte Klavier-Etüden* (ed. Hans von Bülow [1869]), rpt., J. V. Wöss, Vienna: Universal Edition No. 1304, 1926.

Cramer, Johann Baptist (II): *21 Etüden für Klavier nebst Fingerübungen von Beethoven, nach dem Handexemplar Ludwig van Beethoven*, Hans Kann, Vienna: Universal Edition No. 13353, 1974.

Czerny, Carl (I): *Erinnerungen aus meinem Leben*, ca. 1860; rpt., Strasbourg and Baden-Baden: Heitz, 1968.

Czerny, Carl (II): *On the Proper Performance of All Beethoven's Works for the Piano*, 1842; facsimile (ed. Paul Badura-Skoda), Vienna: Universal Edition, 1970.

Czerny, Carl (III): *Complete Theoretical and Practical Piano Forte School*, Op. 500, 3 vols. (trans. James A. Hamilton), London: Cocks, 1839.

Dalberg, Johann Friedrich Hugo von: *Die Aeolsharfe. Ein allegorischer Traum*, Erfurt: Beyer und Maring, 1801.

Demus, Jörg: *Abenteuer der Interpretation*, Wiesbaden: Brockhaus, 1970.

Diruta, Girolamo: *Il Transilvano*, Venice: Vincenti, 1593 (trans. Edward Soehnlen), Ann Arbor: University of Michigan Press, 1975.

Drake, Kenneth (I): *The Sonatas of Beethoven: As He Played and Taught Them* (ed. Frank Stillings), Cincinnati: Music Teachers National Association, 1972.

Drake, Kenneth (II): *The Beethoven Sonatas and the Creative Experience*, Bloomington: Indiana University Press, 1994/2000.

Eisen, Cliff: *New Mozart Documents: A Supplement to O. E. Deutsch's Documentary Biography*, London and Basingstoke: Macmillan, 1991.

Ferguson, Howard: *Keyboard Interpretation from the 14th to the 19th Century*, New York and London: Oxford University Press, 1975.

Fermor, Gotthard (ed.): *Spiritualität der Musik. Religion im Werk von Beethoven und Schumann*, Rheinbach: CMZ, 2006.

Fischer, Edwin (I): *Musikalische Betrachtungen*, Leipzig: Insel-Verlag, 1949.

Fischer, Edwin (II): *Ludwig van Beethovens Klaviersonaten*, Leipzig: Insel-Verlag, 1956.

Forkel, Johann Nikolaus: *Über Johann Sebastian Bach. Leben, Kunst und Kunstwerke*, Leipzig: Hoffmeister und Kühne, 1802; *Johann Sebastian Bach: His Life, Art, and Work* (translated, with notes and appendices, by Charles Sanford Terry), New York: Harcourt, Brace, and Howe, 1920.

Forner, Johannes: *Ludwig van Beethoven. Die Klaviersonaten. Betrachtungen zu Werk und Gestalt*, Altenburg: Kamprad, 2011.

Frescobaldi, Girolamo (I): *Orgel und Klavierwerke*, Vol. 4, Kassel: Bärenreiter, 2004.

Frescobaldi, Girolamo (II): *Toccate e partite: Libro primo*, Rome, 1637; facsimile, Florence: Archivum Musicum, Collana di testi rari No. 3, 1980.

Galston, Gottfried: *L. v. Beethoven*, Munich: Halbreiter, 1921.

Gavoty, Bernard: *Un grand maître français: Alfred Cortot* (text accompanying Alfred Cortot's Chopin LP recordings), EMI, 1977.

Geminiani, Francesco: *Rules for Playing in a True Taste on the Violin, German Flute, Violoncello, and Harpsichord*, Opera VIII, London, 1739 (ed. Peter Walls), Bologna: Ut Orpheus, 2012.

Glasenapp, Carl Friedrich: *Das Leben Richard Wagners*, Leipzig: Breitkopf & Härtel, 1911.

Gleich, Clemens-Christoph von: *Mozart. Takt und Tempo. Neue Anregungen zum Musizieren*, Munich and Salzburg: Katzbichler, 1993.

Goldschmidt, Harry: *Die Erscheinung Beethoven*, Leipzig: Deutscher Verlag für Musik, 1974.

Haberl, Dieter: "Beethoven's Erste Reise nach Wien: Die Datierung einer Schülerreise zu W. A. Mozart," *Neues musikwissenschaftliches Jahrbuch* Vol. 14 (2006), pp. 215–255.

Hanslick, Eduard: *Vom musikalische Schönen*, Leipzig: R. Weigel, 1854; *On the Musically Beautiful* (translated and with commentary by Geoffrey Payzant), Indianapolis: Hackett, 1986.

Hiller, Johann Adam: *Anweisung zum musikalische-zierlischen Gesange*, Leipzig: Johann Friedrich Junius, 1780, 1798.

Hinrichsen, Hans-Joachim (ed.): *Beethoven. Die Klaviersonaten*, Kassel: Bärenreiter, 2013.

Hoffmann, Ernst Theodor Amadeus: "Beethoven's Instrumental Music," *Musical Quarterly*, Vol. 3 No. 1 (Jan. 1917), trans. from E.T.A. Hoffmann's *Kreisleriana*, with an introductory note by Arthur Ware Locke.

Huizing, Jan Marisse: *Chopin: The Etudes: History, Performance Practice, Interpretation* (e-book SDP 124), Mainz: Schott, 2015.

Kaiser, Joachim: *Beethovens 32 Klaviersonaten und ihre Interpreten*, Frankfurt a. M.: Fischer, 1975.

Kerst, Friedrich (I): *Die Erinnerungen an Beethoven*, 2 vols., Stuttgart: Hoffmann, 1913.

Kerst, Friedrich (II): *Beethoven: The Man and the Artist, as Revealed in His Own Words* (translated and edited, with additional notes, by Henry Edward Krehbiel), New York: Dover Publications, 2016.

Kinderman, William: *Beethoven*, New York and London: Oxford University Press, 2009.

Kirnberger, Johann Philipp: *Die Kunst des reinen Satzes in der Musik*, 1776–1779; facsimile, Hildesheim: Olms, 1968.

Kolisch, Rudolf: "Tempo and Character in Beethoven's Music," *Musical Quarterly* (1977), Part I: pp. 90–131, Part II: pp. 268–342.

Kopitz, Klaus Martin, and Rainer Cadenbach: *Beethoven aus der Sicht seiner Zeitgenossen*, 2 vols., Munich: Henle, 2009.

Küthen, Hans-Werner: *Ein unbekanntes Notierungsblatt Beethovens aus der Entstehungszeit der "Mondscheinsonate" im Familienarchiv Chotek in Benešov, Tschechishe Republik*, Prague: Edition Resonus, 1996.

La Mara (Ida Marie Lipsius) (ed.): *Franz Liszt's Briefe*, Vol. 2, Leipzig: Breitkopf & Härtel, 1893.

Legány, Dezső: *Franz Liszt. Unbekannte Presse und Briefe aus Wien 1822–1886*, Vienna, Cologne, and Graz: Böhlau, 1984.

Lenz, Wilhelm von (I): *Beethoven et ses trois styles*, 2 vols., Paris: A. Lavinée, 1855; rpt., New York: Da Capo Press, 1980.

Lenz, Wilhelm von (II): *Beethoven. Eine Kunst-Studie*, 5 vols., Hamburg: Hoffmann & Campe, 1860.

Lenz, Wilhelm von (III): *Die grossen Pianoforte-Virtuosen unserer Zeit aus persönlicher Bekanntschaft*, 1872; rpt., Düsseldorf: Staccato, 2008.

Lenz, Wilhelm von (IV): *The Great Piano Virtuosos of Our Time* (translated and with an introduction by Philip Reder), London: Kahn & Averill, 1983.

Ley, Stephan: *Beethoven*, Berlin: Propyläen, 1939.

Liepsch, Evelyn, and Reiner Schlichting (eds.): *Beethovens Wort den Jüngern recht zu deuten. Liszt und Beethoven* (exhibition catalog), Stiftung Weimarer Klassik, Bonn: Beethoven-Haus; Budapest: Liszt-Ferenc-Gedenkmuseum, 2002.

Liszt, Franz: *Briefe an die Fürstin Carolyne Sayn-Wittgenstein* (published by La Mara), Leipzig: Breitkopf & Härtel, 1902.

Löhlein, Georg Simon: *Klavierschule oder Anweisung zum Klavier- und Fortepiano Spiel. Sechste Auflage, ganz umgearbeitet und sehr vermehrt von A. E. Müller*, Jena: Frommann, 1804.

Ludwig, Emil: *Beethoven: Life of a Conqueror* (trans. George Stewart McManus), New York: G. P. Putnam's Sons, 1943.

Lütge, Wilhelm: "Andreas und Nanette Streicher" in: *Der Bär, Jahrbuch von Breitkopf & Härtel*, Leipzig: Breitkopf & Härtel, 1927.

Mann, Thomas (I): *Doctor Faustus. The Life of the German Composer Adrian Leverkühn as Told by a Friend*, 1947 (trans. John E. Woods), New York: Knopf, 1997; rpt., New York: Vintage Books, 1999.

Mann, Thomas (II): *Die Entstehung des Doktor Faustus*, Frankfurt a. M.: Fischer Verlag, 1949, 1984.

Marek, George R.: *Beethoven: Biography of a Genius*, New York: Funk & Wagnalls, 1969.

Marpurg, Friedrich Wilhelm (I): *Anleitung zum Clavierspielen*, 1755; facsimile, New York: Broude, 1969.

Marpurg, Friedrich Wilhelm (II): *Die Kunst das Clavier zu spielen*, 1762; facsimile, Hildesheim: Olms, 1969.

Marx, Adolf Bernhard: *Anleitung zum Vortrag Beethovenscher Klavierwerke*, Berlin: Janke, 1863.

Matthews, Denis: *Beethoven Piano Sonatas*, London: BBC Publications, 1967.

Mauser, Siegfried: *Beethovens Klaviersonaten. Ein musikalischer Werkführer*, 2nd ed., Munich: Beck, 2008.

Mertin, Josef: "Über die Klaviere Beethovens," in: *Beethoven Almanach 1970*, Vienna: Lafite, 1970.

Mies, Paul: *Beethoven's Sketches*, 1929; rpt., New York: Dover Publications, 1974.

Milchmeyer, Johann Peter: *Die wahre Art das Pianoforte zu spielen*, Dresden: Meinhold, 1797.

Mozart, Leopold: *A Treatise on the Fundamental Principles of Violin Playing*, 1756 (trans. and ed. Editha Knocker), Oxford: Oxford University Press, 1985.

Mozart, Wolfgang Amadeus: *The Letters of Mozart and His Family* (chronologically arranged, translated, and edited with an introduction, notes, and indexes by Emily Anderson; 2nd ed. by Alexander Hyatt King and Monica Carolan), New York: St. Martin's Press, 1966.

Newman, William S. (I): "Liszt's Interpretation of Beethoven's Piano Sonatas," *Musical Quarterly*, Vol. 58 (1972), pp. 185–209.

Newman, William S. (II): *Beethoven on Beethoven: Playing His Piano Music His Way*, New York and London: W. W. Norton, 1988.

Nivers, Guillaume-Gabriel: *Premier livre d'orgue*, Paris: Author and S. Ballard, 1665.

Nottebohm, Gustav: *Zweite Beethoveniana. Nachgelasse Aufzätze*, Leipzig: Peters, 1887.

Ottner, Helmut: *Der Wiener Instrumentenbau 1815–1833*, *Wiener Veröffentlichungen zur Musikwissenschaft*, Vol. 9, Tutzing: Hans Schneider 1977.

Paolone, Ernesto: "L'originale autografo della lettera del 16 aprile 1819 di L. van Beethoven inviato a F. Ries, con le indicazioni metronomiche della 'Hammerklavier-Sonata' op. 106," *Nuova rivista musicale italiana*, Vol. 15 (1981).

Pembaur, Joseph: *Von der Poesie des Klavierspiels*, Munich: Wunderhorn, 1911, 1918 (4th ed.); new ed. (ed. Ludwig Striegel), Fernwald: Muth, 1998.

Petri, Johann Samuel: *Anleitung zur praktischen Musik*, Leipzig: Breitkopf, 1782; facsimile of 2nd ed., Wiesenfelden and Munich: Musikverlag E. Katzbichler, 1969.

Pfeiffer, Theodor: *The Piano Master Classes of Hans von Bülow: Annotated Translation of Theodor Pfeiffer's* "Studien bei Hans von Bülow" *and Its Supplement by Vianna da Motta*, 1896 (trans. and ed. Richard Louis Zimdars), Bloomington: Indiana University Press, 1993.

Playford, John: *An Introduction to the Skill of Musick*, 12th ed. (rev. Henry Purcell), London, 1694; rpt., New York: Da Capo Press, 1972.

Prod'homme, Jacques-Gabriel (I): *Les sonates pour piano de Beethoven*, Paris: Delagrave, 1937.

Prod'homme, Jacques-Gabriel (II): "From the Unpublished Autobiography of Antoine Reicha," *Musical Quarterly*, Vol. 22 No. 3 (1936), pp. 339–353.

Quantz, Johann Joachim: *On Playing the Flute*, 1752 (translated, with notes and introduction, by Edward R. Reilly), 2nd ed., London: Faber & Faber, 2001.

Reicha, Anton: *Compositionslehre*, Vienna: A. Diabelli, 1813.

Reichardt, Johann Friedrich: *Vertraute Briefe, geschrieben auf einer Reise nach Wien und den Oesterreichischen Staaten zu Ende des Jahres 1808 und zu Anfang 1809*, Munich: Georg Müller, 1915.

Reinecke, Carl: *Die Beethoven'schen Clavier-Sonaten: Briefe an eine Freundin*, 3rd printing, Leipzig: Gebr. Reinecke, 1917.

Reti, Rudolph: *Thematic Patterns in Sonatas of Beethoven*, London: Faber & Faber, 1967.

Riemann, Hugo: *Analyse von Beethovens Klaviersonatas. L van Beethovens sämtliche Klavier-Solosonaten. Ästhetische und formal-technische Analyse mit historischen Notizen*, 3 vols., Berlin: Max Hesse, 1919–1920.

Robbins Landon, H. C.: *1791: Mozart's Last Year*, London: Thames and Hudson, 1988.

Rohrer, Joseph: *Bemerkungen auf einer Reise von der Türkischen Gränze über die Bukowina durch Ost- und Westgalizien, Schlesien und Mähren nach Wien*, Vienna: Anton Pichler, 1804, rpt. Berlin: Scherer, 1989.

Rolland, Romain (I): *Beethoven : Les grandes époques créatrices* (édition définitive); rpt., Paris: Albin Michel, 1966.

Rolland, Romain (II): *Beethoven the Creator*, 1929 (trans. Ernest Newman); rpt., New York: Dover Publications, 1964.

Ronge, Julia: *Beethovens Lehrzeit, Kompositionsstudien bei Joseph Haydn, Johann Georg Albrechtsberger und Antonio Salieri:* Bonn: Verlag Beethoven-Haus Bonn/Carus, 2011.

Rosen, Charles (I): *Beethoven's Piano Sonatas: A Short Companion*, New Haven and London: Yale University Press, 2002.

Rosen, Charles (II): *The Classical Style: Haydn, Mozart, Beethoven*, London: Faber & Faber, 1971.

Rosenblum, Sandra: *Performance Practices in Classic Piano Music: Their Principles and Applications*, Bloomington: Indiana University Press, 1988.

Rothschild, Fritz: *Vergessene Traditionen in der Musik*, Zürich: Atlantis, 1964.

Rowland, David (ed.): *The Cambridge Companion to the Piano*, Cambridge: Cambridge University Press, 1998.

Schenker, Heinrich: *Beethoven. Die letzten Sonaten. Kritische Einführung und Erläuterung* (with Opp. 101, 109, 110, and 111), explanatory editio (rev. Oswald Jones), 4 vols., Vienna: Universal Edition, 1971–1972.

Schiff, András: *Beethovens Klaviersonaten und ihre Deutung. "Für jeden Ton die Sprache finden . . . . " András Schiff im Gespräch mit Martin Meyer*, Bonn: Beethoven-Haus, 2007.

Schindler, Anton Felix (I): *Beethoven as I Knew Him* (trans. Ignaz Moscheles), London: Henry Colburn, 1841.

Schindler, Anton Felix (II): *Beethoven as I Knew Him*, 1841 (trans. Ignaz Moscheles); rev. ed. (ed. Donald W. MacArdle; trans. Constance S. Jolly), New York: Dover Publications, 1996.

Schönfeld, Johann Ferdinand von: *Jahrbuch der Tonkunst von Wien und Prag*, Vienna and Prague: Im von Schönfeldischen Verlag, 1796.

Schoones, Eric: "Horowitz' vleugel in Nederland," *Piano Bulletin*, Vol. 31 (1994), pp. 36–40.

Scott, Marion M.: *Beethoven*, London: Dent, 1934.

Seyfried, Ignaz Ritter von (ed.): *Ludwig van Beethoven's Studien im Generalbasse, Contrapuncte und in der Compositions-Lehre*, Vienna: Haslinger, 1832.

Shedlock, John S.: *Beethoven's Pianoforte Sonatas*, London: Augener, 1918.

Skowroneck, Tilman: *Beethoven the Pianist*, Cambridge: Cambridge University Press, 2010.

Solomon, Maynard: *Beethoven*, New York: Schirmer Books, 1977.

Sonneck, Oscar G. (ed.): *Beethoven: Impressions by His Contemporaries*, New York: Dover Publications, 1967.

Stradal, August: *Erinnerungen an Franz Liszt*, Bern and Leipzig: Paul Haupt, 1929.

Streicher, Andreas: *Kurze Bemerkungen über das Spielen, Stimmen und Erhalten der Fortepiano*, Vienna, 1801; facsimile, The Hague: K. Lelieveld, 1979.

Sulzer, Johann Georg: *Allgemeine Theorie der Schönen Künste*, 1793; facsimile, Hildesheim: Olms, 1967.

Swafford, Jan: *Beethoven: Anguish and Triumph*, London: Faber & Faber, 2014.

Talsma, Willem Retze: *Wiedergeburt der Klassiker*, Innsbruck: Wort und Welt Verlag, 1980.

Taub, Robert: *Playing the Beethoven Sonatas*, Portland: Amadeus Press, 2002.

Thayer, Alexander Wheelock: *Thayer's Life of Beethoven* (rev. and ed. Eliot Forbes), 2 vols., Princeton: Princeton University Press 1967, 1973.

Thayer, Alexander Wheelock, Hermann Deiters, and Hugo Riemann: *Ludwig van Beethovens Leben*, 1910; rpt., Nicosia, Cyprus: T. P. Verone Publishing House, 2017.

Thomas-San-Galli, Wolfgang Alexander: *Ludwig van Beethoven*, Munich: Piper, 1913.

Tovey, Donald Francis: *A Companion to Beethoven's Pianoforte Sonatas*, London: Associated Board of the Royal Schools of Music, 1931.

Türk, Daniel Gottlob: *School of Clavier Playing*, 1789 (translated, with introduction and notes, by Raymond H. Haggh), Lincoln and London: University of Nebraska Press, 1982.

Tyson, Alan (I): *The Authentic English Editions of Beethoven*, London: Faber & Faber, 1963.

Tyson, Alan (ed.) (II): *Beethoven Studies*, 3 vols., Oxford and New York: Oxford University Press, 1977.

Tyson, Alan (ed.) (III): *Beethoven Studies 3*, Cambridge: Cambridge University Press, 1982.

Tyson, Alan (IV): review of Johann Baptist Cramer, *21 Etüden*, edited "from Beethoven's copy" by Hans Kann, with keyboard exercises by Beethoven, Vienna: Universal Edition, 1974; *Music and Letters*, Vol. 58 No. 2 (1977), pp. 247–249.

Uhde, Jürgen: *Beethovens Klaviermusik*, Stuttgart: Reclam, 1974.

Unverricht, Hubert: *Die Eigenschriften und die Originalausgaben von Werken Beethovens in ihrer Bedeutung für die moderne Textkritik*, Kassel: Bärenreiter, 1960.

Walther, Johann Gottfried: *Musicalisches Lexikon oder musikalische Bibliothek*, 1732; facsimile, Kassel: Bärenreiter, 1967.

Wegeler, Franz Gerhard, and Ferdinand Ries: *Beethoven Remembered: The Biographical Notes of Franz Wegeler and Ferdinand Ries* (trans. Frederick Noonan, with Foreword by Christopher Hogwood and Introduction by Eva Badura-Skoda), Arlington: Great Ocean Publishers, 1987.

Westerby, Herbert: *Beethoven and His Piano Works*, London: William Reeves, 1931.

Winter, Robert, and Bruce Carr, eds.: *Beethoven, Performers, and Critics: The International Beethoven Congress, Detroit 1977*, Detroit: Wayne State University Press, 1980.

Zenck, Martin: *Die Bach-Rezeption des späten Beethoven*, Wiesbaden and Stuttgart: Franz Steiner Verlag, 1986.

Autographs in Facsimile Editions

Op. 26	Friedrich Cohen, 1895
Op. 27 No. 2	Beethoven-Haus, Bonn, 2003
Op. 28	Beethoven-Haus, Bonn, 1996
Op. 53	Beethoven-Haus, Bonn, 1984
Op. 57	Edition Peters, Leipzig, 1970
Op. 78	Drei Masken Verlag, Munich, 1923
Op. 90	Beethoven-Haus, Bonn, 1993
Op. 101	Henle Verlag, Munich, 1998
Op. 109	Robert Owen Lehman Foundation, 1965
Op. 110	Ichthys Verlag, Stuttgart, 1967
Op. 111	Dover Publications, New York, 1968
Op. 111	Edition Peters, Leipzig, 1952
Bagatelles Op. 126	Edition Schott, ED 7420

In 2011 Laaber-Verlag also issued facsimile editions of Opp. 57, 109, 110, and 111.

Index of Sonatas

Index of Persons (Excluding Discography)

Illustration Credits

ii: Frontispiece: Klein, Bust of Beethoven, Beethoven-Haus, Bonn
22: The young Ludwig van Beethoven, contemporary master, Archives of the Strecker Foundation, Mainz
32: Ludwig van Beethoven, Piano Sonata in E-flat major, Op. 81a, Leipzig: Breitkopf & Härtel (First Edition)
35: Dorothea von Ertmann, Photo of an anonymous miniature, Beethoven-Haus, Bonn
58: Kloeber, Drawing, H. C. Bodmer Collection, Beethoven-Haus, Bonn
103: Kloeber, Drawing, H. C. Bodmer Collection, Beethoven-Haus, Bonn
122 (bottom two figures) and 123: Ludwig van Beethoven, Piano Sonata in F minor, Op. 57 ("Appassionata"), Facsimile of Autograph, Leipzig: Edition Peters, 1970
132 (top): Ludwig van Beethoven, Piano Sonata in A major, Op. 101, Facsimile of the Autograph in the Beethoven-Haus, Bonn, rpt. Sieghard Brandenburg, Munich: G. Henle Verlag, 1998
132 (middle): Ludwig van Beethoven, Piano Sonata in F minor, Op. 57 ("Appassionata"), Facsimile of Autograph, Leipzig: Edition Peters, 1970
137: Ludwig van Beethoven, Piano Sonata in A-flat major, Op. 26, Facsimile Edition, published by Erich Prieger, Bonn: Friedrich Cohen, 1895
138: Ludwig van Beethoven, Piano Sonata in C minor, Op. 111, Reproduction of the Autograph Manuscript (together with a Reprint of the Breitkopf & Härtel Complete Works Edition), rpt. Eric Simon, New York: Dover Publications, 1968
139: Ludwig van Beethoven, Piano Sonata in F minor, Op. 57 ("Appassionata"), Facsimile of Autograph, Leipzig: Edition Peters, 1970
158: Ludwig van Beethoven, Piano Sonata in A-flat major, Op. 110, Facsimile of the Autograph (Autograph Mus.ms.autogr. Beethoven, Artaria 196, in the possession of the Prussian Culture Estate Foundation [Stiftung des Preussischen Kulturbezitz], Tübingen Depot of the State Library), rpt. Karl Michael Komma, Stuttgart: Ichthys Verlag, 1967

159: Ludwig van Beethoven, Piano Sonata in E minor, Op. 90, Facsimile of the Autograph, Bonn: Beethoven-Haus Publications, 1993
160 (bottom): Ludwig van Beethoven, Piano Sonata in A major, Op. 101, Facsimile of the Autograph in the Beethoven-Haus, Bonn, rpt. Sieghard Brandenburg, Munich: G. Henle Verlag, 1998
163: Wolfgang Amadeus Mozart, String Quartet K. 458, Robert Haas, Laaber: Laaber-Verlag, 1980
222: Ludwig van Beethoven, Piano Sonata in A major, Op. 101, Facsimile of the Autograph in the Beethoven-Haus, Bonn, rpt. Sieghard Brandenburg, Munich: G. Henle Verlag, 1998
235: Ludwig van Beethoven, Piano Sonata in A-flat major, Op. 26, Facsimile Edition, published by Erich Prieger, Bonn: Friedrich Cohen, 1895
240: Klosson, Drawing, Beethoven-Haus, Bonn
271, 272, 273: Keyboard Actions, © Leen van den Berg